The Communion of Saints

Radical Puritan and Separatist Ecclesiology
1570–1625

STEPHEN BRACHLOW

OXFORD UNIVERSITY PRESS
1988

Oxford University Press, Walton Street, Oxford OX2 6DP
Oxford New York Toronto
Delhi Bombay Calcutta Madras Karachi
Petaling Jaya Singapore Hong Kong Tokyo
Nairobi Dar es Salaam Cape Town
Melbourne Auckland
and associated companies in
Berlin Ibadan

Oxford is a trade mark of Oxford University Press

Published in the United States
by Oxford University Press, New York

British Library Cataloguing in Publication Data
Brachlow, Stephen
The communion of saints: radical puritan
and separatist ecclesiology, 1570–1625.
1. England. Puritanism, 1570–1640.
I. Title II. Series
285'.9'0942
ISBN 0–19–826726–6

Library of Congress Cataloging in Publication Data
Brachlow, Stephen.
The communion of saints: radical puritan and separatist
ecclesiology. 1570–1625 / Stephen Brachlow.
(Oxford theological monographs)
Bibliography: p. Includes index.
1. Puritans—Doctrines—History—16th century.
2. Puritans—Doctrines—History—17th century.
3. Church—History of doctrines—16th century.
4. Church—History of doctrines—17th century.
I. Title. II. Series.
BX9322.B73 1988 262'.059—dc19 88–3647
ISBN 0–19–826726–6

Set by Hope Services, Abingdon, Oxon
Printed and bound in Great Britain by
Biddles Ltd, Guildford and King's Lynn

For Dixie

PREFACE

THIS is a particularized study of the ecclesiological ideals that found expression in the polemical literature of Elizabethan and Jacobean radical puritans and separatists. As it is a specialized study, I have assumed a readership already acquainted with the standard modern histories of early English dissent, and especially with Patrick Collinson's magisterial book, *The Elizabethan Puritan Movement*, 1967, and B. R. White's lucid treatment of the subject in *The English Separatist Tradition*, 1971.

I wish to express my deepest gratitude to Dr White, Principal of Regent's Park College, Oxford, for whatever scholarly validity the present study may possess. He initially guided the work through its formative stages as an Oxford D.Phil. thesis, and more recently offered additional counsel and encouragement in his always conscientious and gracious manner, while the study was revised during a sabbatical in Oxford. I would also like to thank Richard L. Greaves for his considerate friendship over the past ten years; although we have met only once, and then briefly, he has repeatedly encouraged my work through his correspondence on numerous occasions.

There are many others who should be mentioned, including Dr Marvin Anderson, who first introduced me to ecclesiastical history at Bethel Seminary, St Paul; Dr Arthur A. Rouner, minister of the Colonial Church of Edina, who awakened in me a vision of pilgrim faith and an appreciation for the congregational way; and friends and colleagues at North American Baptist Seminary, Sioux Falls, in particular Donna Fodness, for her work in typing the final revisions. In addition, I wish to express my gratitude to the National Endowment for the Humanities for the financial assistance of a grant in 1985, and, not least of all, to my parents, who very liberally came to the aid of our young and sometimes impoverished family during three years of graduate study in Oxford.

Finally, I want to thank my own family for their support of my efforts to complete this small contribution to the vast Anglo-American scholarly industry of puritan studies. To my wife, Dixie Walker Brachlow, I am especially grateful for sharing with me a love of academic endeavour and for her unflagging devotion to this project. She has been my most searching critic of both style and content, and it has been my greatest joy to have had her assistance and companionship while wrestling, often long into the night, with the manifold complexities of puritan ecclesiology.

S. B.

Sioux Falls, South Dakota.
17 August 1987

CONTENTS

NOTE

In quotations, spelling and capitalization are modernized, but punctuation follows the original. Titles retain the spelling of the original. Lower-case initial letters have been used for the terms 'presbyterian', 'congregational', and 'baptist' when discussing the ecclesial polity of radical puritans and separatists prior to the 1640s. During the pre-revolutionary period the use of capital initial letters would be anachronistic to the extent that they suggest a level of fixed denominationalism which was largely unknown in left-wing English protestantism.

INTRODUCTION

'THE ocean of facts is infinite,' Franklin Littell has written with reference to the problem of periodization in history. Every historian, in the process of doing history, reveals his or her presuppositions in several ways, but 'never more clearly than by selecting certain persons to feature, certain reports to highlight, certain events to emphasize in telling the story'.[1] This is, of course, no less true for studies in the complex socio-religious phenomenon of English puritanism. There are many legitimate approaches to puritanism.[2] But the initial decisions to examine one group to the exclusion of another, one facet of their thought or activities independent of others, or to address the evidence from one scholarly discipline rather than another inevitably affect the outcome.

While the present study has attempted to take into account the recent proliferation of books and articles on puritanism from various disciplines, limitations of scope have naturally determined the extent to which those studies have been utilized. The focus of this work is rather narrowly confined to radical puritan ideas, in particular those ideas related to the issue of church polity. The method of the book is primarily analytical rather than chronological; it is more specifically theological than sociological, and concentrates almost exclusively upon the printed sources of nationally recognized left-wing puritan and separatist propagandists. Its aim is to explore the ecclesiological ideals promulgated by radical puritan and separatist ideologues in Elizabethan and Jacobean England, and to underscore the shared ecclesiological vision of both parties.

The direction of this study was determined largely during the initial stages of the work by a historiographical tradition—

[1] Franklin Littell, 'The Periodization of History', in Timothy George and Francis Church (eds.), *Continuity and Discontinuity in Church History* (Leiden, 1979), 18.

[2] For a critical examination of recent trends in English puritan studies, see Richard L. Greaves, 'The Puritan–Nonconformist Tradition in England, 1560–1700: Historiographical Reflections', *Albion*, 17 (1987), 449–86.

highly denominational in orientation—that has narrated the history of early English dissent as manifested in the separatist impulse.[3] However, the conclusions of this study often take issue with that tradition and its continued influence on puritan scholarship.

Intially, the study began as an examination of the polity of two early Stuart dissenters who have figured prominently in the denominational hagiography of Congregationalism: Henry Jacob, who founded at Southwark in 1616 the semi-separatist church which became a principal breeding ground for the radical puritan sectaries of the capital in the decades preceding the Civil War;[4] and John Robinson, pastor of the English separatist church at Leiden and spiritual mentor of the much celebrated Pilgrim Fathers. As the work progressed, it became increasingly apparent that in order to make a more balanced appraisal of their ecclesiologies and the vexed historical question about their relationship to the separatist tradition, the boundaries of the study would have to be extended considerably to include the ideals of other left-wing puritans and separatists in Jacobean England, as well as the writings of their predecessors in the Elizabethan era. Consequently, the study has grown into something much broader than originally conceived; it not only covers a larger cast of radical puritan figures, but also relates their ecclesiological convictions to the wider theological issues of eschatology, soteriology, and Calvinist covenant theology. In short, it has developed into a study of the ecclesiological ideals that took shape within the puritan theological context, from Thomas Cartwright, at the outbreak of the admonition controversy in the early 1570s, to Henry Jacob and John Robinson, before the implementation of William Laud's ecclesiastical policy so deeply polarized the Carolingian church.[5]

[3] Christopher Hill, 'History and Denominational History', *Baptist Quarterly*, 21 (1968), 65–71; see also the critique by Patrick Collinson, 'Toward a Broader Understanding of the Early Dissenting Tradition', in C. Robert Cole and Michael E. Moody (eds.), *The Dissenting Tradition: Essays for Leland H. Carlson* (Athens, Ohio, 1975), 3–38.

[4] Murray Tolmie, *The Triumph of the Saints, The Separate Churches of London 1616–1649* (Cambridge, 1977), 4.

[5] For the decisive impact of the Laudian creed after 1625 in the church struggle among English protestants, see N. R. N. Tyacke, 'Puritanism, Arminianism and

Having started with ecclesial issues pertinent to Jacob and Robinson's ideals and then worked backwards, as it were, into the Elizabethan radical puritan environment, I have utilized that body of puritan and separatist literature to which Jacob and Robinson had themselves appealed for support of their respective views of a godly polity. While there are clearly the dangers in this method of viewing the Elizabethan material too narrowly through the interpretative glasses of two Jacobean radicals, it has not, I believe, resulted in a one-sided treatment of the sources. Both ends of that historical continuum, from 1570 to 1625, have influenced my perception of the literature and have opened possibilities for some fresh views on the subject. One of the more rewarding discoveries was to recognize more fully the 'congregational' drift apparent in the literature of Elizabethan left-wing puritan propagandists, much of which anticipates ecclesiastical developments among Elizabethan separatists, as well as later Jacobean semi-separatists and Independents. At the same time, this method also allowed for the discovery of what might be called the more traditional conservative inclinations within the polities of Jacob, Robinson, and other separatist figures, who very often are cast by historians in the role of ecclesial extremists brandishing a new, and radical, congregationally oriented polity. There are, however, significant indications that those who embraced some form of ecclesiastical separatism were usually careful to curb the otherwise democratic force of their more extreme doctrines. This they might accomplish by, for example, preserving the function of a ministerial élite within the local congregation or allowing a measure of synodical authority over the affairs of gathered churches. In this way, they often drew back from the radical implications of their ecclesiological convictions and attempted to remain faithful to the more respectable elements within the English radical Calvinist tradition.

While the ecclesiological obsession of radical puritans and separatists certainly does not define the nature of Elizabethan and early Stuart puritanism any more than, say, the doctrine of predestination would define the character of international

Counter-Revolution' in Conrad Russell (ed.), *The Origins of the English Civil War* (New York, 1973), 129.

Calvinism, ecclesiology unquestionably provided the focal point of the discontent among left-wing puritans with the established church. 'The greatest controversy that this day troubles the world', according to William Fulke's Hampton Court sermon in 1570, 'is where the true church of God should be.'[6] If ecclesiology proved to be the *cause célèbre* of those restive saints who comprised the ranks of left-wing puritanism and separatism, there has been a notable lack of enthusiasm among historians of puritanism in recent decades to examine specifically and critically their ecclesial ideas.

The most recent history of the separatists, *The English Separatist Tradition*, published in 1971, by B. R. White—to which the present study remains deeply indebted—tells the story of the developing separatist tradition from the London protestant underground during the reign of Queen Mary to the Jacobean separatist and se-baptists, John Smyth, concluding with only a very cursory discussion of Robinson and the ecclesiology of Jacob. While White often emphasized the ideological links between separatism and puritanism, he rarely ventured beyond the recognized canon of separatist literature to support this claim. In addition, Dr White determined that discernable differences could be found between the ecclesiology of radical puritans and separatists that distinguished the two traditions at crucial points, distinctions which the present study finds untenable.

The earlier classic in this historiographical tradition was Champlin Burrage's *The Early English Dissenters*, published in 1912. Burrage uncovered several important manuscripts related to English religious radicalism between 1550 and 1647, and helped revise and refine its historiography. But in the tradition of many nineteenth-century denominational historians, Burrage's study was severely limited by what Patrick Collinson has more recently described as 'the tunnel vision' of the genealogical approach. Burrage tended to identify the dissenting tradition almost solely with English separatism and, as a result, isolated English radical religion perhaps too much from the wider stream of advanced

[6] William Fulke, *A sermon preached at Hampton Court on Sunday being the 12. day of November, in the year of our Lord. 1570* (London, 1570), Sig. B1–2.

puritanism.[7] The present work is an attempt to rectify this rather too narrow treatment of Elizabethan and early Jacobean ecclesial radicalism by extending the limits to include a broader range of puritan ideologues and issues which together informed the ecclesiological continuum running between the disciplinarian puritanism of Cartwright and strict separatism in early Stuart England.

As every serious student of the subject knows, pre-revolutionary English puritanism was a highly complex, often amorphous social, political, and religious entity, which seems to defy a comprehensive, yet meaningful definition. No attempt is made here to add yet another definition of puritanism to a debate that has a tangled and often inconclusive history of its own.[8] For the purpose of this study, however, it is necessary to comment briefly on the use of the terms 'radical puritan' and 'separatist' churchmen.[9] Radical puritans were the highly critical, often defiant members within the church of England who wanted to alter fundamentally the organization of the established church. Their ecclesial ideas stood in basic conflict with the institutionalized policies

[7] Collinson, 'Toward a Broader Understanding', 3–5.

[8] For discussions of the problems involved in defining puritanism, see Basil Hall, 'Puritanism: The Problem of Definition', in G. J. Cuming (ed.), *Studies in Church History*, ii (London, 1965), 283–96; Christopher Hill, *Society and Puritanism in Pre-Revolutionary England* (London, 1969), 15–30; Patrick McGrath, *Papists and Puritans under Elizabeth I* (London, 1967), 32–46; C. H. George, 'Puritanism as History and Historiography', *Past and Present*, 41 (1968), 77–104; William Lamont, 'Puritanism as History and Historiography: Some Further Thoughts', *Past and Present*, 44 (1969), 133–46; David Little, *Religion, Order, and Law* (Oxford, 1970) 250–9; Michael G. Finlayson, 'Puritanism and Puritans: Labels or Libels?', *Canadian Journal of History*, 8 (1973), 201–33; Thomas H. Clancy, 'Papist–Protestant–Puritan: English Religious Taxonomy 1565–1665', *Recusant History*, 13 (1976), 227–53; Paul Christianson, 'Reformers and the Church of England under Elizabeth I and the early Stuarts', *Journal of Ecclesiastical History*, 31 (1980), 463–82; and Patrick Collinson, 'A Comment Concerning the Name Puritan', *Journal of Ecclesiastical History*, 31 (1980), 483–8.

[9] 'Radical puritanism', as used here, should not be confused with 'popular religion', which refers more to the hopes and grievances of those outside the ruling groups in English society as expressed, for example, in aspirations of Henry Hart or, perhaps, in what Collinson has called 'rustic Pelagianism'. As we shall see, there were many conservative social and religious forces within radical puritanism and separatist ideology that supported a ruling élite in church and society. See the distinction between radical and popular religion in J. F. McGregor and B. Reay (eds.), *Radical Religion in the English Revolution* (Oxford, 1984), p.v. For Henry Hart see J. W. Martin, 'English Protestant Separatism at its Beginnings: Henry Hart and the Free-Will Men', *Sixteenth Century Journal*, 7 (1976), 55–74; and also Patrick Collinson, *The Elizabethan Puritan Movement* (London, 1967), 37.

of the church hierarchy 'by striking at the very root of contemporary assumptions and institutions'.[10] They were not simply seeking to improve the ecclesiastical system, but were intent upon replacing the status quo with a substantially different structure. While the radicals were not all in full agreement about the details or extent of their aims in this campaign,[11] they ardently opposed episcopacy and sought to move the English church into conformity with the more narrowly biblical design of a Calvinist, Genevan-styled ecclesiology. But in spite of the militancy of their platform and, very often, even of their practice, they always stopped short of a formal separation from the national church and vehemently disowned those who crossed into that forbidden world of ecclesial schism.

By contrast, the separatists were, as Dr White has aptly described them, 'hasty puritans', radical protestants who became impatient with the evident failure of the puritan campaign for reform. They may be distinguished from radical puritans by their blatant, public rejection of communion with the established church and their deliberate practice of setting up alternative congregations distinct from the existing parish system; it was this dramatic step that earned them the opprobium of their co-religionists in left-wing puritan circles.[12]

In terms of church polity, however, a more coherent centre of thought appears to have existed between the two parties than is commonly recognized by historians. Therefore, the breach between separatists and non-separating radical puritans is not to be explained as a difference of ecclesiology but as a difference of strategy, timing, and the extent to which each was willing (or unwilling) to disavow their allegiance to the church as constituted by English law.

While the compatibility of separatist churchmanship with left-wing puritan ecclesiology has sometimes been acknowledged,[13] the greater tendency among puritan historians has all

[10] Richard L. Greaves and Robert Zaller, *A Biographical Dictionary of British Radicals* (London, 1982), vol. i, p. viii. See also Richard L. Greaves, *Deliver Us From Evil: The Radical Underground in Britain, 1660–1663* (Oxford, 1986), 4–8.

[11] M. M. Knappen, *Tudor Puritanism: A Chapter in the History of Idealism* (Chicago, 1939), 289.

[12] B. R. White, *The English Separatist Tradition* (Oxford, 1971), xiv.

[13] Champlin Burrage, *The Early English Dissenters* (Cambridge, 1912), i. 28; G. F.

too often been to refract the picture of pre-revolutionary dissent into separate categories of puritan and separatist, each with their own peculiar and quite distinct ecclesiological and theological predilections, to the extent that, as David Zaret has recently averred, they are believed to have held 'diametrically opposed priorities on organization'.[14] Patrick Collinson is equally convinced that, for example, the 'difference between separatism and semi-separatism . . . ought not to be minimized.'[15] The separatists found no place in Collinson's magisterial work on the history of Elizabethan puritanism because he assumed that, by contrast with the puritans, separatists advocated a 'totally alien, select Christian society' like the Continental anabaptists.[16]

The most obvious way that separatism is continually distinguished ecclesiologically from radical puritanism has been by the commonplace dichotomy historians have drawn between the presbyterianism of Elizabethan puritan militants and the congregationalism of the separatists. Although it is occasionally noted that radical puritan ecclesiology gravitated toward 'congregationalism',[17] the impression remains firmly embedded in most studies of English puritanism that the more advanced puritans during the Elizabethan era were of a decidedly presbyterian persuasion while every separatist was, *ipso facto*, an advocate of 'the congregational way'. Apparently for this reason, S. J. Knox, for example, defined the church-

Nuttall, *The Holy Spirit in Puritan Faith and Experience* (Oxford, 1946), 9; White, *English Separatist Tradition*, xii, 33; Knappen, *Tudor Puritanism*, 1; and William Haller, *The Rise of Puritanism* (1st Penn. pbk. edn.; Philadelphia, 1972), 174–6, 390.

14 David Zaret, *Heavenly Contract: Ideology and Organization in Pre-Revolutionary Puritanism* (Chicago, 1985), 106.

15 Patrick Collinson, *The Religion of Protestants: The Church in English Society 1559–1625* (Oxford, 1982), 274.

16 Patrick Collinson, *Elizabethan Puritan Movement*, 12. More recently he has characterized the distinction between puritan and separatist conventicles as 'a very thin line to cross, a tiny ditch, but a Rubicon nevertheless': Patrick Collinson, 'The English Conventicle', in W. J. Sheils and Diana Wood (eds.), *Voluntary Religion* (Oxford, 1986), 244.

17 e.g. David Hall, *The Faithful Shepherd: A History of the New England Ministry in the Seventeenth Century* (rev. edn.; New York, 1974), 24–47; Paul S. Seaver, *The Puritan Lectureships: The Politics of Religious Dissent 1560–1662* (Stanford, 1970), 46–7; George Yule, 'Some Problems in the History of English Presbyterians in the Seventeenth Century', *Journal of the Presbyterian Historical Society of England*, 13 (1965), 4; C. Gordon Bolam *et al.* (eds.), *The English Presbyterians* (Boston, 1968), 32; and Patrick Collinson, 'Towards a Broader Understanding', 16.

manship of Walter Travers—that paragon of Elizabethan puritanism—as being 'entirely presbyterian',[18] while Collinson, who is not unaware of the congregational inclinations of radical puritanism, presumed that Henry Jacob sought a 'patently presbyterian formula' when, in 1603, he requested that the established church be reorganized according to the model of the Continental reformed churches.[19]

This bifurcated image of left-wing puritan and separatist thought has influenced the way historians perceive most other dimensions of their ecclesiology as well. The controlling assumption appears to be that the more dramatic course of action taken by the unyielding separatists produced a more radical form of polity. In just such a way, David Hall's study of puritan notions regarding ministerial function and power within the gathered congregation discerned that the separatists held more democratic views of the ministry than their more aristocratically minded Calvinist counterparts within non-separating radical puritan circles.[20] Apparently for this same reason, Peter Lake assumed in his recent study, *Moderate puritans*, that English separatism, in contrast with disciplinarian puritanism, represented a 'populist revolt against any sort of ministerial élite'.[21] With respect to the protestant understanding of the place of discipline as a note of the true church, Perry Miller and others have distinguished the ecclesiology of Elizabethan puritans from that of the separatists by taking for granted that only the separatists consistently insisted on the three-mark doctrine of Word, sacrament, and

[18] S. J. Knox, *Walter Travers: Paragon of Elizabethan Puritanism* (London, 1962), 46.

[19] Collinson, *Elizabethan Puritan Movement*, 454. The dichotomy also haunts Paul Christianson's attempt at clarifying the taxonomy of the Elizabethan and early Stuart religious spectrum, in 'Reformers and the Church of England', 463–82. This is also true of the survey of Elizabethan and Stuart dissent by Michael R. Watts, who, although arguing that initially the differences between separatists and puritans were not clearly defined, allowed the presbyterian / congregational dichotomy to colour his discussion of the two movements: *The Dissenters* (Oxford, 1978), esp. 25, 28–9, 56–9.

[20] David Hall, *Faithful Shepherd*, 35–47. I use the term 'aristocratic' here and in the discussion on ministerial authority in ch. 4, as it was employed by protestant theologians of the sixteenth and seventeenth centuries to describe the way in which the execution of the church's government was understood to rest in the hands of a spiritual, ministerial élite. This should not be confused with the term as it was sometimes also used to designate the class distinction of the nobility, who, by birth or fortune, were ranked above the rest of society.

[21] Peter Lake, *Moderate puritans and the Elizabethan church* (Cambridge, 1982), 89.

discipline, instead of the traditional two. Furthermore, some historians have suggested that the separatists alone desired visible purity within the gathered church, in contrast to the policy of the radical puritans who would have permitted indiscriminate church membership.[22]

Along more theological lines of inquiry, two recent studies, which considered the role that covenant thought played in puritan and separatist literature, have claimed that the separatists substantially departed from mainstream, radical puritan theology when they linked ecclesiology with a 'mutualist' or conditional interpretation of the covenant. Radical puritans, on the other hand, were portrayed as placing ecclesiology solely within an unconditional covenant framework.[23] Finally, it has been widely assumed that the separatists deserve a category all their own because of their more advanced proposals regarding the role of magistracy in ecclesial matters and their repudiation of not only the English national church but even the *concept* of an established church. Although radical puritans insisted on a policy of state-enforced religious uniformity, it is often axiomatically accepted that, by contrast, the more progressive separatists advocated voluntarism and religious toleration, thereby rejecting the coercive powers which puritans granted the prince in ecclesiastical causes.[24]

Each of these ecclesiological distinctions that recent historians have drawn—and there are others, as this study will point out—have perpetuated a historiographical bias that, if sometimes questioned, has often been too comfortably assumed in most analyses of Elizabethan and Jacobean puritan history and thought. In addition, and in a much more substantial

[22] Perry Miller, *Orthodoxy in Massachusetts 1630–1650*, Harper Torchbook edn. (New York, 1970), 55–7; similar statements may be found in Seavers, *Puritan Lectureships*, 26–7, and Leland H. Carlson in Robert Browne, *The Writings of Robert Harrison and Robert Browne*, eds. Albert Peel and Leland H. Carlson, (London, 1953), 22; and Paul D. L. Avis, *The Church in the Theology of the Reformers* (London, 1981), 46–7, 61–3.

[23] White, *English Separatist Tradition*, 55; Zaret, *Heavenly Contract*, 140–1.

[24] A. F. Scott Pearson *Thomas Cartwright and Elizabethan Puritanism 1535–1603* (Cambridge, 1925), 307–10; and also *Church and State: Political Aspects of Sixteenth Century Puritanism* (Cambridge, 1928), 112; W. K. Jordan, *The Development of Religious Toleration in England* (London, 1932), i, 263–75; White, *English Separatist Tradition*, 58–60; Timothy George, *John Robinson and the Separatist Tradition* (Macon, Ga., 1982), 43–4.

way, this great divide between puritan and separatist polity has been granted considerable scholarly credibility in the widely used essay by Professor Basil Hall, 'Puritanism: The Problem of Definition'.[25] basing his premiss largely on a passage attributed to John Robinson, which is cited in the *Oxford English Dictionary* under the entry 'Puritan', Basil Hall assumed that prior to 1640 all puritans were presbyterians standing in opposition to the congregationalism of the separatists, as much as they were opposed to the episcopacy of the bishops. As the Robinson passage, which first appeared in his *Justification of separation*, 1610, reads in both the *Oxford English Dictionary* and Professor Hall's article, the separatist is quoted as having said: 'The papists plant the ruling power of Christ in the Pope, the Protestants in the bishop, the Puritans in the Presbytery, we in the body of the congregation of the multitude called the Church.'[26]

In this way, words ascribed to the Leiden separatist have been pressed into the service of a historiographical perspective in which the Elizabethan and Jacobean ecclesial spectrum is viewed through the lens of subsequent denominational divisions. But an examination of the passage as it appeared in its original context reveals that this is a serious misunderstanding and distortion of it. Aside from the fact that the passage was inaccurately dated (given as 1625) in both the dictionary and Hall's article, neither authority recognized that those words were indeed *not* Robinson's but words of the puritan conformist, Richard Bernard, whom the separatist was quoting. And far from agreeing with Bernard's taxonomy of the contemporary religious situation, Robinson discounted it at the very point where Bernard made an ecclesiological distinction between puritans and separatists. To quote the passage in full from Robinson's *Justification of separation*:

> The difference you [Bernard] lay down in the next place . . . is corruptly related, and specially in the particular concerning us, that where the papists plant the ruling power of Christ in the Pope; the Protestants in the bishops; the Puritans as you term the reformed churches and those of their mind in the Presbytery; we (whom you name Brownists) put it in the body of the congregation, the multitude

[25] Hall, 'Puritanism', 283–96.
[26] Ibid. 292.

called the church, odiously insinuating against us that we do exclude the elders, in case of government, where, on the contrary, we profess the bishops or elders to be the only ordinary governors in the church, as in all other actions of the church's communion, so also in the censures.[27]

The point made by Robinson highlights one of the many false assumptions about separatist ecclesiology in his own day that, with the passage of time, has had the cumulative effect of driving a historiographical wedge between the ecclesiological ideals of the two major expressions of English radical protestantism in left-wing puritanism and separatism at the turn of the seventeenth century.[28]

The present study attempts to clarify the common ecclesial vision shared by these two parties through a careful examination of the theoretical literature on both sides of the radical puritan and separatist divide. The argument is not only that Elizabethan and Jacobean separatists more than likely derived their ideals from left-wing puritan writings and associations, but that, more importantly, the ecclesiological lines between advanced puritans and separatists were never very precise. Certainly they were not as categorically tidy as historians tend to define them; while recognizing that there were presbyterian as well as congregational tendencies within the two movements, these were by no means always clear nor denominationally fixed. Puritans, even in the Elizabethan period, were not always inclined to one and separatists to the other; rather, the ecclesiological distinctions between left-wing puritanism and separatism were fluid and often entirely blurred to the extent that in Elizabethan and early Stuart England, ecclesial classifications of episcopalian, presbyterian, and congregational polities do not submit themselves easily to, as Trinterud has put it, 'those infallibly stable definitions and connotations which function as controlling assumptions in many historical studies'.[29]

[27] John Robinson, *A justification of separation from the church of England* (Amsterdam, 1610), 8–9.

[28] A very similar misreading of a passage in William Ames's preface to Bradshaw's *English puritanisme*, as rendered by Miller in *Orthodoxy in Massachusetts*, 78, has also been uncritically accepted by modern authorities: e.g. Watts, *Dissenters*, 53–4. For a critique of Miller's use of this passage, see below, ch. 6, n. 23.

[29] See Leonard J. Trinterud, *Elizabethan Puritanism* (New York, 1971), 14.

In terms of later denominational divisions, left-wing puritan ecclesiology of this period had not yet hardened into a firm structure. It was, relatively speaking, an ecclesiology still in its infancy, largely untested by the moulding experience of long-standing, unhindered practice, and bearing within itself the possibilities of development in more than one ecclesial direction. For this reason, radical puritan ecclesiology would prove to be a rich and many-layered source that, by the middle of the seventeenth century—when denominationalism began perforce—provided an ideology both Independents and Presbyterians could manipulate for historical support of their respective polities.[30]

But this also means that the ecclesial ideals of Elizabethan and Jacobean radical puritans and separatists were open to exploitation by themselves, as well as by their opponents. Thus, as we shall see, left-wing puritans and separatists would often emphasize, to their own benefit, certain dimensions of their ecclesiology while passing by others, depending upon the demands of a given situation. At the same time, the multi-dimensional nature of their views made their ecclesiological model vulnerable to distortion and misrepresentation by the episcopal opposition, a practice to which puritans and separatists were no less inclined when they clashed in controversy with each other.

In this respect, the present study reveals that these highly-principled members of the protestant 'left' in English religion were as often driven by very human concerns as they were by their penchant for ideological purity. Indeed, this comprises one important feature of the common ground shared by separatists and radical puritans. In much the same way that Peter Lake has noted the ambiguity in the aims of militant puritans like Thomas Cartwright and William Bradshaw,[31] the present study underscores the fact that English separatists were never consistently hard-line ideologues either. There were inevitably points at which even the separatists drew back

[30] Philip J. Anderson, 'Presbyterianism and the Gathered Churches in Old and New England 1640–1662: the Struggle for Church Government in Theory and Practice' (Oxford University D.Phil. thesis, 1979), 117, 127; see also George Yule, Continental Patterns and the Reformation in England and Scotland', *Scottish Journal of Theology*, 22 (1969), 318.

[31] Lake, *Moderate puritans*, *passim*.

from the radical force of their principles and, in the process, rediscovered dimensions of moderation and accommodation that generated the anomalies of what Dr Lake calls 'moderate extremism'. Invariably, these very inconsistencies provided polemical 'hay' for their opponents, who ridiculed their halting part of the way along the leftward pilgrimage of radical Calvinism. Common as such criticisms were, it must still have been painful to hear their own radical convictions used against themselves whenever they retreated from the logic of their views, views which, if followed consistently, threatened to drive them entirely outside the protective walls of the international Calvinist community.

The inconsistencies and fluctuations in their writings should also serve as an important reminder that the dry and often technically subtle ecclesiological debates of left-wing puritans and separatists were waged by people of flesh and blood, not heartless ideologues. Their principles could take them only so far from the protestant mainstream before the claims of the human community—the need for friendship and acceptance, as well as their very real fears of social anarchy in the uncertain times of pre-revolutionary England—worked to turn them back from the brink of that complete isolation which the individualism of a radical mentality so often breeds. Very few, it seems, whether puritan or separatist, were willing to follow unrelentingly the logic of their views, a logic leading to exile and complete disenfranchisement from the official church and the larger society in which they lived. Those who did, like John Smyth, the se-baptist, found themselves at the end of an often transient passage through various stages of radical religion, pushed beyond even the margins of English dissent into the demonstrably 'foreign' world of Dutch anabaptism. Yet even there, as we shall observe, the ideological lines of continuity with left-wing protestant and separatist thought remained remarkably visible and intact.

Smyth's move to believer's baptism, however consistent with certain principles and forces inherent to radical puritan ecclesiology, was a significant, but all the more unrepresentative event. It was certainly a harbinger of things to come in the following decades. Yet for most radical puritans and separatists in Jacobean England a strong disposition toward order and the desire to remain within the larger community of English Calvinism, despite their many criticisms of the puritan establishment, tempered their radical proclivities at one point or another. Thus, just as Patrick Collinson has observed about the puritan mainstream,[32] there were centripetal as well as centrifugal forces at work across the broad spectrum of radical dissent also. The present study reveals that separatist ideals developed in an atmosphere of ideological ferment and not ossification. The very same conflicting dynamics that informed moderate puritan thinking were equally at work within separatist thought. They served to produce the rich mixture of ideas that comprised separatist ecclesiology and helped generate the dynamic and often fluid character of left-wing puritan and separatist convictions.

While this study focuses on the ecclesiological and theological continuity between radical elements in English dissent, it should be apparent by now that, in so doing, there is no intent to disregard or mask the mutual recriminations that often flared between left-wing puritans and separatists, or even to deny that among themselves puritans and separatists sometimes perceived an ideological rift between their respective positions. It is only too evident from the volatile character of left-wing puritan and separatist polemics that, as Keith Sprunger commented, 'the search for perfection of church government powerfully motivated Puritans in their controversies against the hierarchical Church of England, and then created deep divisions within the movement itself'.[33] These divisions led them to distinguish their respective ecclesial positions, but often at the cost of mutual misrepresentation. In most instances, of course, it was puritan radicals who sought to distance their ecclesiology from the infamy of separatism, while the separatists were more than eager to prove their agreement with the writings of the more acceptable puritans. As John Robinson was to insist in 1610, the ecclesiological underpinnings of separatist practice had all been anticipated in the literature of Elizabethan left-wing

[32] Patrick Collinson, *Religion of Protestants*, 141–88, esp. 182.

[33] Keith Sprunger, *Dutch Puritanism: A History of English and Scottish Churches of the Netherlands in the Sixteenth and Seventeenth Centuries* (Leiden, 1982), 459.

puritanism, a point which Richard Bancroft had been only too pleased to underscore some fifteen years earlier.[34]

Indeed, the 'staple puritan fare' which made up a large percentage of the holdings in separatist libraries and which issued from their printing presses bears this out. John F. Wilson seems almost to have stumbled onto the implications of this when he noted the vast number of puritan publications coming from the separatist press of John Canne, in Holland: 'If this be so, a common interest of sorts may have been shared by at least some of those exiles—"Separatists", "Congregationalists", and perhaps even "Presbyterians"—usually thought to have been exclusively engaged in irreconcilable controversy.'[35] It was this abundant literary evidence of an ecclesiological continuity between puritans and separatists that formed the basis upon which Canne developed the compelling thesis of his 1630 publication, *A necessitie of separation.*

This is not to argue that Canne was correct in his fundamental hypothesis that the writings of puritan radicals proved the necessity of separation, but only to point up the surplus of evidence available to Canne and others showing that separatist ecclesiology was firmly rooted in puritan literature. At the same time, the grass-roots manuscript evidence of what is sometimes called the *de facto* separatism that flourished in puritan parishes and conventicles is too strong to accept Canne's basic argument that separatism was the *inevitable* consequence of accepting the principles of the puritan disciplinarians.[36] His thesis was, no doubt, convincing

[34] John Robinson, *Justification*, 76; Albert Peel (ed.), *Tracts Ascribed to Richard Bancroft* (Cambridge, 1953), 18–19. The point is well made by Peter Lake, 'The Dilemma of the Establishment Puritan: the Cambridge Heads and the Case of Francis Johnson and Cuthbert Bainbrigg', *Journal of Ecclesiastical History*, 29 (1978), 34, who observed 'a natural progression' in Francis Johnson's move from puritanism to separatism.

[35] John F. Wilson, 'Another Look at John Canne', *Church History*, 33 (1964), 39. For further evidence of the extensive puritan holdings in separatist libraries, see Rendel Harris and Stephen K. Jones, *The Pilgrim Press* (Cambridge, 1922), 31–3; Lawrence D. Geller and Peter J. Gomes, *The Books of the Pilgrims* (New York and London, 1975), 6.

[36] See e.g. Christopher Hill, *Society and Puritanism*, 87; Rosemary O'Day, 'The Reformation of the Ministry 1558–1642', in Rosemary O'Day and F. M. Heal (eds.), *Continuity and Change* (Leicester, 1976), 65; and Larzer Ziff, *Puritanism in America: New Culture in a New World* (Oxford, 1973), 34.

to a few, but, as Patrick Collinson has observed, the private religious conventicles of the godly cut both ways, sometimes contributing to the impulse toward separatism in puritan society, but more often acting as an inhibition to the centrifugal force of religious radicalism.[37]

The perception that the ecclesial ideals of left-wing puritanism were entirely compatible with those of the separatists also provides a solution to questions that have surrounded the appearance of the so-called 'non-separating congregationalists' in early Stuart England. The rise of this coterie of Jacobean radicals, which included William Ames, Robert Parker, Paul Baynes, and William Bradshaw, along with Henry Jacob, has been problematic for historians because it has been taken for granted that their congregationalism signalled a dramatic departure from the assumed presbyterianism of Elizabethan radical puritans. This, in turn, has provoked historical questions about the source of the novel polity advocated by non-separating congregationalists. The most obvious answer, first suggested by Daniel Neal and still accepted by most historians who have explored the issue, was that they had been influenced by the congregational polity of the separatists.[38] However, several other historians, including Champlin Burrage and Perry Miller, found this explanation unsatisfactory because, as they said, Jacob and the other non-separating congregationalists—although sharing a similar view of the church with the separatists—forswore the necessity of separation and roundly repudiated those who did. While the genesis of their non-separating congregational convictions

[37] Collinson, *Religion of Protestants*, 276. The point is also made in Collinson, 'The English Conventicle', 223–59; and Claire Cross, 'The Genesis of a Godly Community: Two York Parishes', in Sheils and Wood (eds.), *Voluntary Religion*, 209–22.

[38] Daniel Neal, *The History of the Puritans* (London, 1794), ii, 47. Much of the attention to this issue has been centred on the supposed influence of separatist polity on Jacob, either through his encounter with Francis Johnson in 1599, or through his acquaintance with John Robinson in 1610. See Robert S. Paul, 'Henry Jacob and Seventeenth-century Puritanism', *Hartford Quarterly*, 7 (1967), 112; White, *English Separatist Tradition*, 91, 165–71; Slayden A. Yarbrough, 'The Ecclesiastical Development in Theory and Practice of John Robinson and Henry Jacob', *Perspectives in Religious Studies*, 5 (1978), 183–97; Watts, *Dissenters*, 51–2, 55 (though elsewhere (53) he admits that the origins of what he calls 'Jacobite' ecclesiology are unknown); Tolmie, *Triumph of the Saints*, 7–12.

remained a mystery to Burrage and Miller, they did not think the separatists were, therefore, responsible.[39]

But if, as the present study argues, there was a continuity of ecclesiological aims between Jacobean radicals (like Henry Jacob) and Elizabethan left-wing puritans, then the source of Jacobean non-separating congregationalism is surely to be discovered in the puritan, not the separatist, tradition. The Jacobean radicals were, in their congregational polity, simply clarifying a sometimes vague but, none the less, developing strain of independency that already existed within the literature of earlier left-wing puritanism. That appears to be the case when one simply considers the esteem in which the Jacobean non-separating congregationalists held the ideals of the previous generation of puritan militants, as well as the numerous references they made in their own treatises to such Elizabethan puritan notables as Thomas Cartwright, Dudley Fenner, Walter Travers, John Udall, Thomas Wilcox, and John Field. All the evidence suggests that there would have been no need for them to look elsewhere for their polity since they could readily find it in the writings of their left-wing puritan predecessors.[40]

This study has been organized around six ecclesiological themes in left-wing puritan and separatist thought. The first three chapters deal with the puritan and separatist rationale for a reformed ecclesiology. Chapter 1 looks at the soteriological value they accorded the practice of a biblical

[39] Champlin Burrage, *Early English Dissenters*, i, 281, 92; Perry Miller, *Errand into the Wilderness* (New York, 1964), 17; Miller, *Orthodoxy in Massachusetts*, 75; Douglas Horton, *Congregationalism: A Study in Church Polity* (London, 1952), 570; John von Rohr, 'The Congregationalism of Henry Jacob', *Transactions of the Congregational Historical Society*, 19 (1962), 107, though in a later article, '*Extra Ecclesiam Nulla Salus*: An early Congregational Version', *Church History*, 36 (1967), 117–19, von Rohr indicates that he now believed Jacob 'had moved a long way toward . . . Separatist views' after his controversy with Francis Johnson in 1599; and W. R. Goehring, 'Henry Jacob (1563–1624) and the Separatists' New York University Ph.D. dissertation, 1975.

[40] This was, in fact, the way they perceived themselves. As William Ames explained in his preface to Bradshaw's *English puritanisme*, he was convinced Bradshaw walked in 'the same way and steps' as 'Cartwright, Fenner, Fulke, Whitaker, Reynolds and Perkins': William Bradshaw, *English puritanisme, containing the main opinions of the rigidest sort of those that are called puritans* (n.p., 1604), preface, not paginated. See also, Stephen Brachlow, 'The Elizabethan Roots of Henry Jacob's Churchmanship: Refocusing the Historiographical Lens', *Journal of Ecclesiastical History*, 34 (1985), 228–54.

ecclesiology, especially within the context of English Calvinist covenant theology. Chapter 2 considers the eschatological dimensions of their ecclesial convictions, while Chapter 3 explores the compatibility of the radical puritan and separatist emphasis on visible saints in church membership and the importance of congregational participation with prevailing Calvinist notions about saving faith and assurance.

Chapter 4 investigates the continuity between the radical puritan and separatist emphasis on visible churchmanship and the ecclesiology of the first English baptists who evolved out of the exiled separatist congregations in Amsterdam. The last three chapters focus on organizational issues. Chapter 5 analyses the distribution of power between officers and people within the gathered congregation, a discussion which is followed by a chapter on the historiographically crucial issue of synodical authority and its relationship to the autonomy of particular churches. The final chapter assesses radical puritan and separatist views of magisterial functions in ecclesial affairs, along with their concern to protect the voluntary nature of the faith.

Each chapter—with the exception of the one on English baptist ecclesiology—will pursue the argument of this study by examining the views of radical puritans and separatists in the Elizabethan and early Stuart periods, allowing separate sections for the ecclesiological thought of Henry Jacob and John Robinson. The writings of these two men receive special attention because, while holding prominent places in the prehistory of Old and New England Congregationalism, their location on the ecclesiastical landscape that ran between puritanism and separatism has been one of continued debate.[41] In this respect, the confusion over their relationship

[41] See Stephen Brachlow, 'More Light on John Robinson and the Separatist Tradition', *Fides et Historia*, 12 (1980), 6–22; Stephen Brachlow, 'John Robinson and the Lure of Separatism in Pre-Revolutionary England', *Church History*, 50 (1981), 288–301; and, Stephen Brachlow, 'Puritan Theology and Radical Churchman in Pre-Revolutionary England' (Oxford University D.Phil. thesis 1979), 245–55. In addition to the studies already cited in the notes above, see Slaydon A. Yarbrough, 'Henry Jacob, A Moderate Separatist, and His Influence on Early English Congregationalism' (Baylor University Ph.D. dissertation 1972). John Robinson has also received the attention of several biographies, including Robert Bartlett, *The Pilgrim Way* (Philadelphia, 1971). Announced as a 'scholarly treatise' on the 'religious concepts' of the Pilgrim pastor (see the 'Forward', xi), the book is an often fanciful

to the puritan and separatist streams of English Calvinist dissent underlines the historiographical difficulties created by the distinctions that historians have assumed between the churchmanship of puritans and separatists.

While it will become evident that the ecclesiology of the radical puritans and separatists in many respects reflected the legalistic spirit of the new and more narrowly dogmatic English Calvinists who came to the fore in the 1570s, it is important to keep well in mind G. F. Nuttall's sagacious remark that 'underlying the seemingly disproportionate concern with forms of government, there was, nevertheless, a passionate desire to recover the inner life of New Testament Christianity'.[42] Left-wing puritan and separatist ideologues in late sixteenth- and early seventeenth-century England were by no means devoid of a sense of the living presence of God in their experience of faith and fellowship in the gathered church. Despite their penchant for the letter of the biblical law, they nevertheless possessed a vision of the church as being 'the body of Christ', a living, spiritual organism.[43] Indeed, most puritan theological thinking radiated outward, to use the words of Dewey D. Wallace, jun., 'from an inner and deeply existential core of Puritan piety', so that the 'Puritan concern with discipline and church polity was a way of realizing in community the consequences of a gracious election and the joys and demands of holiness'.[44] This vital experience of ecclesial fellowship infused the whole enterprise with a sense of spiritual life and preserved their ecclesiology from decaying into a moribund legalism.[45] As Henry Ainsworth

portrait of a denominational hero who anticipated 'the liberal Congregationalism of the nineteenth and twentieth centuries': ibid., 336. The most recent book-length analysis of Robinson's thought is George, *John Robinson*, an eloquent and critically executed study. Much less satisfactory is Stephen M. Johnson, 'The Soteriology of John Robinson, Pilgrim Pastor and Advocate of the Reformed Faith', *Westminster Theological Journal*, 44 (1982), 31–57.

[42] G. F. Nuttall, *Visible Saints 1640–1660* (Oxford, 1957), 3.

[43] John S. Coolidge, *The Pauline Renaissance in England* (Oxford, 1970), 23–54; see also the discerning discussion of Robinson's use of this motif in George, *John Robinson*, 105–10.

[44] Dewey W. Wallace, jun., *Puritans and Predestination: Grace in English Protestant Theology, 1525–1695* (Chapel Hill, NC, 1982), xi.

[45] G. F. Nuttall, *The Puritan Spirit: Essays and Addresses* (London, 1967), 95–103. See also, Richard L. Greaves, 'The Nature of the Puritan Tradition', in R. Buick Knox

described with spiritually emotive language the experience of godly life in a reformed congregation:

[The Lord's people] taste in this world of the powers of the world to come, and do walk in the light of his face and feel his holy presence with them. Which presence, although it be with every one of his saints in all places where they become, yet it is most lively seen in their assembly . . . For this cause did his people love the habitation of his house.[46]

(ed.), *Reformation Conformity and Dissent: Essays in Honour of Geoffrey Nuttall* (London, 1977), 255–73.

[46] Henry Ainsworth, *The communion of saints* (Amsterdam, 1607), 144.

1

ECCLESIOLOGY AND SOTERIOLOGY

Elizabethan Radical Puritans

IN 1588, the year that marked the beginning of a definite decline in the fortunes of the puritan movement,[1] the puritan preacher and pamphleteer of Kingston upon Thames, John Udall, published a manifesto for radical reform entitled *A demonstration of the trueth of that discipline which Christe hath prescribed in his worde for the gouernment of his Church*. The work was an impressive compilation of radical puritan arguments that had been devised during almost two decades of agitation in Parliament for ecclesiastical reform, beginning with the admonition controversy in 1572.[2] Udall opened his treatise in words that by then had become part of the well-worn rhetoric of the puritan campaign: 'the controversy is not about goat's wool . . . neither light and trifling matters, which may safely be followed or rejected . . . but about no less matter than this, whether Jesus Christ shall be a King or no.'[3]

Ever since 1570, when Thomas Cartwright first unveiled plans for a godly church government in his celebrated Cambridge lectures and a small group of London puritans in the parish of Holy Trinity, Minories, were already exercising the right to choose their own curates and preachers, the more advanced Elizabethan puritans had raised the stakes in their controversy with the prelates. The controversy had progressed from the single-issue crusade against clerical vestments that dominated puritan polemics of the 1560s to what the erudite

[1] Collinson, *The Elizabethan Puritan Movement*(London, 1967), 385.

[2] As Udall put it: 'The most of the things that are here expressed, I acknowledge to be gathered out of the books that have been published, and are extant (purposely) concerning this argument.' John Udall, *A demonstration of the trueth of that discipline which Christe hath prescribed in his worde for the gouernement of his Church* (n.p., 1588), 'To the Reader', not paginated.

[3] Ibid.

puritan theologian, Dudley Fenner, now declared was 'the great and weighty cause . . . of the whole discipline of the church of Christ'.[4] The failure of the English church to be constituted according to the holy discipline prescribed in the Word of God was, as radicals like Udall and Fenner perceived it, not only a serious error that, for the sake of the church's well-being (*bene esse*), needed to be redressed; they also believed it had the intolerable effect of depriving Christ's ruling, 'kingly' function within the established church, thus making a cruel mockery of his presence in that institution. 'For if none is said to be a king, but he that rules by the sceptre of his laws,' Udall explained, 'then the turning out of these orders which Christ has prescribed in his Word, for the ruling of the church, is to give him the title and deny him the authority belonging to the same, and so (in truth) to make him an idol, making him to carry a show of that which he is not.'[5]

This harsh criticism conveyed, in part, Udall's assessment of the *adiaphora* defence of episcopacy constructed by the guardians of the ecclesial hierarchy in the face of the unrelenting puritan assaults during the 1570s and 1580s. John Whitgift, whom Archbishop Matthew Parker had drawn into the fray to vindicate the prelates, answered the admonitioners along the Christian humanist lines of the moderate Calvinist episcopal tradition by defending the right of human discretion in matters which were not explicitly treated in the scriptures. Since he could find no evidence in the New Testament that Christ had delineated an organizational structure for the church with the precision and clarity Christ had employed in other doctrinal matters, Whitgift reasoned that ecclesiology must therefore be an *adiaphora* issue, an indifferent matter, secondary to the more substantive doctrinal teachings of the gospel. Even where scripture seemed to offer an apparently clear directive, Whitgift insisted that this did not mean Christ intended to shackle his church with 'that precise form that is

[4] Dudley Fenner, 'To the Christian Reader', in *A counter-poyson, modestly written for the time* (London, 1584), not paginated. For the beginnings of puritan radicalism, see Patrick Collinson, 'The Elizabethan Puritans and the Foreign Reformed Churches in London', in *Godly People: Essays on English Protestantism and Puritanism* (London, 1983), 259–60.

[5] Udall, *Demonstration*, 'To the Reader', not paginated.

there set down'. On the contrary, Whitgift argued that the form of ceremonies, orders, and discipline in the church depended largely upon historical conditions. Therefore, Christ intended that ecclesial matters should be left to the authority of the bishops, aided by the civil magistrate, who together could determine an appropriate polity for the church not according to biblical prescription, but by their good judgement.[6]

In opposition to Whitgift's *adiaphora* justification of episcopacy, the precisionist party within the Elizabethan church maintained that in the New Testament Christ had clearly prescribed a single pattern for the church which amounted to a 'perpetual and immutable' law for all succeeding generations living under the gospel.[7] Far from being a matter of indifference, the discipline of the church formed a fixed and indispensable component of Christ's message, the practice of which was as crucial to the preservation of the gospel as was adherence to orthodox doctrine in other matters. Walter Travers—who had recently been expelled from his Cambridge college by Whitgift for his hard-line puritanism[8]—argued in 1574 that discipline and doctrine were like 'two sisters who are twins', or 'two pillars . . . so twisted together that the one cannot stand without the other'.[9]

[6] Fenner, *Counter-poyson*, 2; Donald J. McGinn, *The Admonition Controversy* (New Brunswick, 1949), 56. The *adiaphora* defence of episcopacy remained the mainstay of the bishops' apology for the established order throughout most of the Elizabethan era until *jure divino* claims were formulated, originally by Richard Bancroft in a 1589 sermon given at Paul's Cross. Miller Maclure, *The Paul's Cross Sermons 1534–1642* (Toronto, 1958), 216; see also Patrick Collinson, 'Episcopacy and Reform in England in the Later Sixteenth Century', in *Godly People*, 158. Late in his career, Whitgift himself adopted a 'divine right' defence of episcopacy. See John S. Marshall, *Hooker and the Anglican Tradition* (London, 1963), 32. There are, however, earlier hints of the doctrine in his reply to the *Admonition*. See according to W. D. J. Cargill Thompson, *Studies in the Reformation: Luther to Hooker* (London, 1980), 100–1. By the 1630s and 1640s, *jure divino* claims formed the entire basis for the Laudian polemic against the reformists. See J. F. Woodhouse, *The Doctrine of the Church in Anglican Theology 1547–1603* (London, 1954), 107–23; William Lamont, *Godly Rule: Politics and Religion, 1603–60* (London, 1969), 56–9.

[7] Laurence Chaderton, *A fruitfull sermon, upon the 3. 4.5.6.7. & 8. verses of the 12 chapters of . . . Romanes* (London, 1584), 32; W. H. Frere and C. E. Douglas (eds.), *Puritan Manifestoes* (reprint edn., London, 1954), 95.

[8] H. C. Porter, *Reformation and Reaction in Tudor Cambridge* (Hamden, Conn. 1972), 173.

[9] Walter Travers, *A full and plaine declaration of ecclesiastical discipline* (n.p., 1574), 14;

Puritans like Travers believed from their reading of Matthew 28: 20 that Christ had revealed this design for the gospel church during the interim between the resurrection and ascension, when 'for the space of forty days together did he talk with his disciples touching his kingdom'.[10] During those days of instruction, so the radicals claimed, Christ outlined in considerable detail an explicit and 'most perfect regimen for the good and due ordering' of his church.[11] In this way, he fulfilled his Christological role as a Mosaic 'lawgiver' for the new covenant by prescribing an 'exact pattern of discipline'.[12] Consequently, the more precise Elizabethan protestants reasoned that subordinating ecclesiastical matters to other doctrinal issues, as the prelates did in their *adiaphora* apology, would have the tragic effect of undermining the confidence of people in Christ's ministry to the church by making 'God less careful of his Church under the gospel' and 'the ministry of Moses more excellent than that of Christ'.[13]

However narrow and unyielding this rhetoric of confrontation appeared to the more cultivated humanist tastes of Whitgift and other Elizabethan traditionalists, it is perhaps doing left-wing puritans a disservice to saddle them with Perry Miller's simple assertion that they believed 'even the minutiae of ecclesiastical practice' had been prescribed in scripture.[14] While, as we shall see, in certain circumstances radical puritans became more flexible on this matter—to the point of taking up the very same *adiaphora* defence of the English church used by their episcopal opponents[15]—most radicals, even in their most intransigent moments of opposition to the English hierarchy, willingly conceded that *some* ceremonies and rites could indeed be considered *adiaphora*.[16]

At the same time, this admission should not be taken to imply, as John S. Coolidge does, that radical puritans

A parte of a register countayning sundrie memorable matters, for the reformation of our church (n.p., 1593), 280.

[10] Travers, *Ecclesiastical discipline*, 4.

[11] *Parte of a register*, 102–3.

[12] Ibid., 122; Travers, *Ecclesiastical discipline*, 6–9; Udall, *Demonstration*, 3; Frere and Douglas (eds.), *Puritan Manifestoes*, 147.

[13] Fenner, *Counter-poyson*, 9.

[14] Perry Miller, *Orthodoxy in Massachusetts 1630–1650*, Harper Torchbook edn. (New York, 1970), 73.

[15] See below, nn. 59, 87–96 and Peter Lake's perceptive discussion of this in *Moderate puritans and the Elizabethan church* (Cambridge, 1982), *passim.*

[16] Fenner, *Counter-poyson*, 1–0

possessed a dynamic view of scripture which effectively divested their anti-episcopal rhetoric of its concern for the details of biblical prescriptions. To demonstrate his point, Coolidge cites Cartwright's concession to Whitgift that clerical apparel was circumstantial.[17] This does not, however, take into account the context of Cartwright's famous admission; it was made in one of his polemics against the church of Rome where he was defending his continued allegiance to the corrupt English church against the attacks of the papists, the demands of which, as Peter Lake has argued, drove him into an *adiaphora* posture.[18]

But in their confrontations with the English hierarchy over the issue of reform, radical puritans invariably took a hard line: it was there that they stressed the prescribed nature of ecclesiology. Even though a few things, such as the 'time and place for prayers' and so on, could be considered 'variable according to circumstance . . . yet are they by certain general rules so limited and prescribed, that no church can use them at their pleasure, but ought to frame them within the bounds set unto them of God'.[19]

The point that needs to be emphasized here is that the context of left-wing puritan pronouncements is often crucial for understanding what otherwise often appear to be inconsistent, mutually exclusive positions taken on given issues. Furthermore, the extremists did not always agree among themselves over these ideological fluctuations and they could become exceedingly sensitive about using them. Cartwright's admission to Whitgift that vestments could be considered circumstantial is a case in point. The London radical puritan organizers, John Field and Thomas Wilcox, believed it was an unwarranted departure from established puritan doctrine. Near the end of his life, even Cartwright seems to have had second thoughts about having moderated his stand on this matter and, according to later puritan claims, he came to regret the concession he had made to Whitgift.[20]

[17] John S. Coolidge, *The Pauline Renaissance in England* (Oxford, 1970), 6.

[18] Lake, *Moderate puritans*, 66.

[19] Fenner, *Counter-poyson*, 4–9.

[20] Albert Peel (ed.), *The Seconde Parte of a Register* (Cambridge, 1915), i. 138–9; William Ames, *A reply to Dr. Mortons generall defence of three nocent ceremonies* (n.p. 1622), 86.

As a general rule, then, it appears that radical puritans would adopt an *adiaphora* defence in order to prove their loyalty to the established church against both papists and separatists. But when taking up the cudgels against the English episcopate, they were driven, by the confrontational nature of that undertaking, to jettison that rather flexible approach in favour of a more rigidly doctrinaire form of argumentation. In this case, they tended to appeal to scripture as a book of immutable rules which contained a detailed and perspicacious polity for the church that had been established by Christ for all succeeding generations.

While admitting that the situation in the primitive church of the New Testament may have been somewhat more flexible when, according to Walter Travers, the Holy Spirit blessed that first generation of believers with extraordinary 'heavenly gifts' and a greater freedom from formal structures, such flexibility was now no longer applicable. With the passing of the charismatic age following the death of the apostles, a 'certain firm and stable order was set to govern the church by forever'.[21] Thus, for rigid puritans, the Bible became what Ernst Troeltsch has characterized as 'the Law-book of revelation',[22] while biblical ecclesiology became increasingly focused upon the legal rectitude of ecclesiastical structures built according to stable and set rules given in scripture. Furthermore, because they were convinced that lawful discipline was of equal value with orthodox belief, radical puritans asserted that ecclesiology should be as rigorously observed as any other theological doctrine.

In fact, they took this last argument one significant step further by drawing a direct link between ecclesiology and salvation, maintaining that issues of church polity comprised such an indispensable part of the gospel message that failure to exercise the biblical pattern for the church brought one's eternal salvation into jeopardy. As Udall put it in 1588, the bishops had 'mortgaged' the salvation of their own souls, and those of countless others, by ignoring the ecclesiological

[21] Travers, *Ecclesiastical discipline*, 74.

[22] *The Social Teachings of the Christian Church*, i, 347, as quoted in P. D. L. Avis, 'Moses and the Magistrate: A Study in the Rise of Protestant Legalism', *Journal of Ecclesiastical History*, 26 (1975), 163.

mandates of scripture.[23] Fifteen years earlier, in *A Second Admonition*, Job Throkmorton considered the perilous nature of the issues at hand and declared that 'there is no parish so small but if it have need of Christ, and to be saved, then it have need of Christ's orders'. A few pages later, he urged Parliament to reform the English church according to the scriptures in order that 'we may keep him our loving God and Father, and be kept by him to be his obedient servants and sons, here to serve him and after to inherit with him that crown purchased and promised unto us'.[24]

It was in the following year, 1574, that Thomas Cartwright, then living in exile as a consequence of his extreme views, gave the most emphatic and, for later generations of radicals, classic expression of this conviction in his ongoing controversy with Whitgift. Whereas Whitgift had argued that ecclesiology was an indifferent matter and, hence, of no soteriological value, Cartwright now claimed, without reservation, that 'matters of ceremonies, orders, discipline and government . . . are . . . of faith and of salvation'.[25]

At first glance, Cartwright's response to Whitgift appears to be a striking departure from the ecclesiology of John Calvin, who maintained in the *Institutes* that matters of church organization 'are not to be considered necessary for salvation'.[26] For this reason, several recent scholars have concluded that Whitgift emerged from the debate sounding like the better Calvinist,[27] a judgement shared by Whitgift himself, who reprimanded Cartwright for dodging the implications of Calvin's more moderate teaching on this critical matter:

If Mr. Calvin were alive and understood the state of our church and controversy truly, I verily believe that he would utterly condemn

[23] Udall, 'To the Bishops', in *Demonstration*, not paginated.

[24] Frere and Douglas (eds.), *Puritan Manifestoes*, 131, 133. For arguments supporting Throkmorton's authorship of the *Second Admonition*, see Leland H. Carlson, *Martin Marprelate, Gentlemen: Master Job Throkmorton Laid Open in His Colors* (San Marino, Calif., 1981), 324–8.

[25] Thomas Cartwright, *A reply to an answere made of M. Doctor Whitgifte* (n.p., 1574), 14.

[26] John Calvin, *Institutes of the Christian Religion*, ed. J. T. McNeill, trans. F. L. Battles (London, 1960), bk. 4, ch. 10, s. 27.

[27] David Hall, *The Faithful Shepherd: A History of the New England Ministry in the Seventeenth Century* (rev. edn., New York, 1974), 27.

your doings; . . . your passing over so lightly of quotations from Calvin does argue your lack of ability to answer them. Indeed they flatly determine this controversy and in effect overthrow your whole book.[28]

The burden of Calvin's doctrine about the *adiaphora* nature of ecclesiology was, of course, a convincing justification of Whitgift's assertion, especially when considered from Calvin's overriding concern about the alarming menace of sectarianism. However, this should not cloud other salient features of Calvin's thinking about the visible church which emerged following his experience with Martin Bucer in Strasburg,[29] features that, while always carefully guarded by the Genevan reformer, would eventually come to fruition in the more dogmatic ecclesiology of later Calvinists. At several points in later editions of the *Institutes*, Calvin appears to lean in the direction of something much closer to Cartwright's own doctrinaire convictions. While admitting that matters of 'outward discipline and ceremonies' were circumstantial, Calvin nevertheless asserted that 'the Lord has in his sacred oracles faithfully embraced and clearly expressed both the whole sum of true righteousness, and all aspects of the worship of his majesty . . . therefore in these the Master alone is to be heard'.[30] And although Calvin was willing to approve of what he called 'human constitutions', so long as they did not impair the purity of evangelical doctrine, he was, at the same time, concerned that the constitution of the visible church be 'founded upon God's authority, drawn from Scripture'.[31] As later radical puritans were so inclined to do, Calvin also portrayed Christ as the new Moses, 'the sole lawgiver' of the church's discipline and constitution, who revealed God's wishes concerning the church with even greater clarity than had the Old Testament lawmaker.[32]

[28] *Whitgift's Works* (Parker Society), i, 250, as quoted by Basil Hall, 'Calvin Against the Calvinists', in G. E. Duffield (ed.), *John Calvin* (Appleford, 1966), 36.

[29] See especially Harro Hopfl's suggestion that Calvin's thought and practice were 'moving, perhaps independently, in the same direction as Bucer's and Capito's on the subject of ecclesiastical discipline'. Harro Hopfl, *The Christian Polity of John Calvin* (Cambridge, 1982), 89. See also R. N. Caswell, 'Calvin's View of Ecclesiastical Discipline', in G. E. Duffield (ed.), *John Calvin*, 212, 221.

[30] Calvin, *Institutes*, bk. 4, ch. 10, s. 30.

[31] Ibid.

[32] Ibid., s. 17.

There were, then, these rigorist features in Calvin's thinking about the church that could easily have been taken up and woven into the more narrowly dogmatic ecclesiology of puritan extremists in England like Cartwright: faced with the apostasy and corruption of the Roman church, Calvin appears almost as radically minded as the most uncompromising puritan Calvinist. While this is very likely the case, there is, nevertheless, a growing consensus in recent scholarship that a fundamental (if not irreconcilable) divide separates Calvin from his 'Calvinist' heirs in puritan England on several substantial issues, including ecclesiology.[33] This distinction between Calvin and left-wing puritan Calvinists is particularly clear in at least two ways: first, in their divergent attitudes concerning Christ as the new Mosaic lawgiver in matters of church organization; second, with respect to their dissimilar views about the soteriological value of obedience to those ecclesial laws.

Concerning the first issue, Calvin emphasized the simplicity and, therefore, clarity of Christ's ecclesiastical teachings over against the complex, often obscure intricacies in the Old Testament Mosaic law.[34] By contrast, English radical puritans stressed the close correspondence of Christ's precision and thoroughness of detail in his teachings about church polity with what they perceived to be a similar attention to detail in the law of Moses. Christ offered, as the more aggressive puritans repeatedly emphasized, an 'exact pattern' in which, according to Travers, he did 'not leave a loop of a curtain unmade, or make a button or clasp more or less' than did Moses.[35] Although Calvin was also unquestionably devoted to a biblically orientated ecclesiology as opposed to what he considered to be the humanly devised traditions of Rome, he never employed scripture in the legalistic fashion of the

[33] See e.g. Hall, 'Calvin Against the Calvinists', 19–37; R. T. Kendall, *Calvin and English Calvinism to 1649* (Oxford, 1979), 13–47; John Patrick Donnelly, 'Italian Influences on the Development of Calvinist Scholasticism', *Sixteenth Century Journal*, 7 (1976), 81–101; Avis, *The Church in the Theology of the Reformers* (London, 1981), *passim*.

[34] See Calvin, *Institutes*, bk. 4, ch. 10, s. 17, where Calvin explained that the teachings of Moses about the church were 'obscure, so to speak, because of its very many wrappings', while Christ brought a 'clearer doctrine'.

[35] Travers, *Ecclesiastical discipline*, 6; *Parte of a register*, 15.

English disciplinarians as a source-book of precise, immutable rules for church organization.[36]

With respect to the issue of ecclesiology and soteriology, Calvin, along with others in the reformed tradition, assumed the old patristic notion, *nulla salus extra ecclesiam* (there is no salvation outside the church), and so confessed that membership in a true visible church was ordinarily 'necessary . . . to our salvation'. At the same time, however, he studiously avoided drawing a correlation between the practice of a single form of discipline and its value for soteriological assurance, as his English successors in left-wing puritanism invariably did when pressing their case for reform.[37]

This inclination of radical puritan Calvinists to claim that ecclesial practice was an instrument of assurance is a curious modification of Calvin's convictions. It very likely stemmed from their peculiar understanding of the nature of saving faith and assurance, an understanding that flowered within the context of theological developments in late sixteenth-century reformed circles. Puritan theology was ostensibly rooted in the predestinarian system of Calvin; but there is evidence that Calvinism, especially as it was mediated to the protestant world of the 1570s through Theodore Beza, had undergone a serious though subtle transformation under the impact of the rationalizing process of protestant scholasticism. This was to have, as R. T. Kendall has recently argued, dramatic repercussions in puritan notions about saving faith and covenant theology, especially with respect to the pressing epistemological and pastoral question of Calvinist soteriology: 'How do I know that I am one of the elect?'[38]

[36] Calvin, *Institutes*, bk. 4, ch. 10, s. 30: Christ did not 'in outward discipline and ceremonies . . . prescribe in detail what we ought to do (because he foresaw that this depended upon the state of the times, and he did not deem one form suitable for all ages)'; cf. also Benjamin Milner, *Calvin's Doctrine of the Church* (Leiden, 1970), 174.

[37] Calvin, *Institutes*, bk. 4, ch. 1, s. 8; cf. also ibid. s. 4.

[38] Kendall, *Calvin and English Calvinism*, 29–76. It is outside the scope of this study to trace the rise of protestant scholasticism and the influence it may have had on the evolution of reformed theology. Kendall emphasizes the role of Beza in the formation of puritan rationalism, but it is worth noting, as Collinson has recently remarked, that 'the Aristotelian rot, if that is what it was, seems to have begun not with Beza but with the Italians Peter Martyr and Girolamo Zanchi'. Patrick Collinson, 'England and International Calvinism, 1558–1640', in Menna Prestwich (ed.), *International Calvinism 1541–1715* (Oxford, 1985), 217.

Calvin himself described saving faith as something passively received through the grace of God. He was inclined to advise doubting souls to look to Christ rather than the effects of sanctification in themselves for their assurance of salvation.[39] Reformed theologians after Calvin, however, tended to emphasize the importance of obedience to the moral law of scripture for assurance of true faith. From Beza to the Heidelberg theologians, the basis for assurance thus gradually shifted from Calvin's Christological centre to evidences of faith within the individual; particular stress was given by English puritans to the advice found in 2 Peter 1: 10, the *locus classicus* for puritan discussions of assurance, where believers are advised to make their election more sure through perseverance in good works.[40]

This voluntaristic emphasis was all the more encouraged by concurrent developments within reformed covenant, or 'federal' theology, a topic which has received considerable attention from historians of English Calvinist theology, especially since Perry Miller first discussed the issue of the covenant of grace in puritan thought.[41] Miller has subsequently been roundly criticized for distorting the puritan interpretation of the covenant relationship with God, making it into something like a covenant of 'works righteousness' and divesting it almost completely of anything even remotely related to Calvin's theology of grace. Nevertheless many of those who have explored the issue more recently suggest that there is between Calvin and his successors a difference in emphasis—if not entirely in substance—regarding covenant theology. Whereas Calvin emphasized the objective and gracious aspects of the covenant, succeeding English Calvinists, possibly under the influence of Tyndale and Zwingli, stressed the ethical implications of the covenant bond.

The result of this shift in the focus of Calvinist covenant thought was that the relationship between God and humanity increasingly came to be described by second-generation

[39] François Wendel, *Calvin: The Origin and Development of his Thought* (London, 1976), 274–7.

[40] Kendall, *Calvin and English Calvinism*, 9–41; see also Donnelly, 'Italian Influences', 93–9.

[41] See Perry Miller, *The New England Mind* (New York, 1939), 365–97.

Calvinists in terms of a biblical pact, or treaty, that depended as much upon human obedience to the laws of God as it did upon the faithfulness of God in keeping the promises of the covenant. This does not mean, strictly speaking, that the emerging covenant theologians believed that human fulfilment of the covenant demands in any way contributed to salvation. They all affirmed that salvation occurred in the first instance by grace alone, without human means or merit. Yet the direction which reformed 'federal' covenant theology was to take in the latter half of the sixteenth century tended, all the same, to stress the ethical obligations of the human side in this mutual contract.[42]

While Calvin's covenant theology was not entirely without the contractual features of later puritan formulations, he nevertheless emphasized more consistently the unconditional nature of the covenant bond. For Calvin, the covenant represented God's gracious and unmerited promise of salvation that obligated God for its fulfilment, an obligation which God had met in Christ. However, in the federalist covenant theory, which became a hallmark of the Rhineland reformers, the covenant relationship was defined more often in terms of a conditional promise on God's part in which the burden of fulfilment rested upon the faithful adherence of the elect to the demands of the law before God's reciprocal obligation would be brought fully into force.

In Elizabethan England this conditional covenant motif—derived perhaps as much from the earlier Tudor protestantism of William Tyndale and others as it was through the force-

[42] See Leonard J. Trinterud, 'The Origins of Puritanism', *Church History*, 20 (1951), 37–57; Everett H. Emerson, 'Calvin and Covenant Theology', *Church History*, 25 (1956), 136–44; Jens. G. Møller, 'The Beginnings of Puritan Covenant Theology', *Journal of Ecclesiastical History*, 14 (1963), 46–67; John von Rohr, 'Covenant and Assurance in Early English Puritanism', *Church History*, 34 (1965), 195–203; Richard L. Greaves, 'The Origins and Early Development of English Covenant Thought', *The Historian* 31 (1968), 21–55; George M. Marsden, 'Perry Miller's Rehabilitation of the Puritans: A Critique', *Church History*, 39 (1970), 91–105; Mark R. Shaw, 'Drama in the Theology of William Perkins', *Westminster Theological Journal*, 45 (1983), 41–72; Michael McGiffert, 'Grace and Works: The Rise and Division of Covenant Divinity in Elizabethan Puritanism', *Harvard Theological Review*, 75 (1982), 463–502; Richard A. Muller, *Christ and the Decree: Christology and Predestination in Reformed Theology from Calvin to Perkins* (Durham, NC, 1986), esp. 41, 176; and Charles Lloyd Cohen, *God's Caress: The Psychology of Puritan Religious Experience* (Oxford, 1986), 47–72.

ful influence of the Rhineland theologians—came to full expression in the systematic works of puritan theologians such as Dudley Fenner and William Perkins. As the latter expounded the covenant relationship:

God's covenant is his contract with man concerning the obtaining of life eternal, upon a certain condition. This covenant consists of two parts: God's promise to man, man's promise to God. God's to man is that whereby he bindeth himself to man to be his God, if he perform the condition. Man's promise to God is that whereby he voweth his allegiance unto his Lord, and to perform the condition between them.[43]

Turning from Perkins to the more ecclesiologically militant puritans of the 1570s and 1580s, there was a similar theological predilection for what George Yule has called the 'new legalism' of second-generation Calvinism.[44] They defined the covenant bond largely in terms of a contractual relationship. Individuals were encouraged to seek their assurance through the empirical means of a visible obedience to the doctrines and moral laws of scripture. As the two London activists, Field and Wilcox, explained in a letter of pastoral advice to one troubled puritan soul, even though 'we hold ourselves freed from the law and the ceremonial keeping of the same, yet we keep the doctrine thereof, as well for the better framing of our lives as also for the more confirming of us in the promises of the gospel'. A scrupulous and visible obedience to the laws of God enabled them to be assured 'thereby of salvation'.[45]

Whether the covenant thought of this English 'experimental predestinarian' school is an aberration of Calvin's theology or not, is an exceedingly complex and subtle issue over which there is not complete agreement and sometimes widely divergent interpretations by historians, as several critiques of R. T. Kendall's work on this subject underscore.[46] While this

[43] William Perkins, *A Golden Chaine* (Cambridge, 1591), 31–2, as quoted in Richard A. Muller, 'Perkins' *A Golden Chaine*: Predestinarian System or Schematized Ordo Salutis?', *Sixteenth Century Journal*, 9 (1979), 78.

[44] George Yule, 'Continental Patterns and the Reformation in England and Scotland', *Scottish Journal of Theology*, 22 (1969), 309–17.

[45] *Parte of a register*, 535–7.

[46] See, for example, the comments of Collinson, 'England and International Calvinism', 216–17; and the essay by Shaw, 'Drama in the Meeting House', 41–72.

is hardly the place to resolve such a complex issue, a brief comment is appropriate for the purposes of this study.

The problem with several modern assessments of puritan covenant thought is the tendency to cast the discussion in either / or, wholly dichotomous terms in such a way that the rich texture of puritan covenant theology is often reduced to a one-dimensional ideology. This happens, it seems, when historians attempt to iron out the inherent logical contradictions between the two poles of a conditional and an unconditional understanding of the covenant relationship. Certainly, the puritans themselves did not recognize the two as being antithetical. It is more likely that the presence of these two poles in their writings merely reflects their fidelity to the same tensions and ambiguities that, according to modern biblical scholars, exist between Mosaic and Abrahamic covenant themes in scripture.[47] Sixteenth-century puritans rarely acknowledged, or perhaps even noticed, this distinction in the biblical text;[48] but the presence of these two covenant models in scripture would certainly account for the use of both kinds in puritan literature.

Because of this ambiguity, puritan covenant thought was always open to a degree of manipulation, though puritans would never have viewed it as such. Whether they employed a mutualist or unconditional interpretation depended, as we shall see below, upon the context or perspective from which they wrote. From the vantage point of the objective realm of doctrinal truth, for example, they would emphasize the gracious and unmerited character of the covenant bond; but in relation to the subjective realm of puritan practical divinity there was often a subtle shift of emphasis to the conditional and ethical nature of the covenant through their use of voluntarist rhetoric. The effect of this change was, as Dr Porter has observed about William Perkins, that 'however Calvinist in the study, the preacher must be Arminian in the pulpit'.[49] For this reason, the conditional covenant language of

[47] For the use of the covenant motif in scripture, see Klaus Baltzer, *The Covenant Formulary in Old Testament, Jewish, and Early Christian Writings* (Philadelphia, 1971).

[48] Cohen, *God's Caress*, 51.

[49] Porter, *Reformation and Reaction*, 310; and Irvonwy Morgan, *The Godly Preachers of the Elizabethan Church* (London, 1965), 120–3. But see also Lake, *Moderate puritans*,

radical puritan churchmen should perhaps be understood more as a product of the practical demands of their cause than as the primary statement of their covenant theory. This is very evident in the way they set their ecclesiology within the conditional covenant framework and insisted upon the soteriological value of ecclesial practice.

The link between soteriology and ecclesiology has gone largely unrecognized in modern studies of Elizabethan puritanism, although it was one of the most salient themes in radical puritan propaganda. Indeed, it was the union of these two theological motifs in left-wing puritan thought that appears to have provided the *theological* imperative for their militant activity. This crucial connection came to pass when radical Calvinists brought together the 'experimental predestinarian' emphasis on obedience to the laws of God for assurance with the concomitant conviction of the disciplinarians that ecclesiological matters were not *adiaphora* but prescribed by Christ. Because they were convinced that the breach of even the least of Christ's commandments 'deserves death',[50] puritans who also professed that the practice of a biblical discipline was as necessary for salvation as a confession of doctrinal orthodoxy were, in their sincere concern for soteriological assurance, obliged by the demands of the covenant pact to adopt the combative, doctrinaire posture in their struggle for reform.

The conviction of the radicals about the soteriological significance of ecclesiology found its biblical source in their perception of the import of the second commandment in the Decalogue and its value for maintaining the covenant bond with God.[51] As puritanism's earliest systematic theologian, Dudley Fenner, explained in *A brief treatise upon the first table of the lawe*, the second commandment was directed specifically to the subject of ecclesiology: it prohibited all humanly devised worship—forms of worship not found in scripture, either

116–68, who underscores a Christological focus for assurance in puritan practical divinity.

[50] *Parte of a register*, 81.

[51] For the puritan emphasis on the first table of the Decalogue in contrast to the *Anglican* concern for the duties of the second table, see J. Sears McGee, *The Godly Man in Stuart England, Anglicans, Puritans and the Two Tables, 1620–1670* (New Haven and London, 1976), 2–5, 68–113.

expressly or by implication—and commanded the saints 'to acknowledge, love, desire, delight in, and outwardly practice all those parts of [Christ's] worship, which he in his Word has commanded'.[52] Having established the place of ecclesiology in the Decalogue, Fenner then fashioned a linkage between matters of church polity and Calvinist soteriology when he explained that a breach of the second commandment, as with any of the other nine, dissolved the covenant relationship between God and his children, while faithful obedience brought them 'into a covenant of life and blessedness, yea and that eternal'.[53]

During Cartwright's confrontation with Whitgift, the federalist covenant theology of second-generation Calvinism undoubtedly provided, in a similar way, the theological backdrop for his insistence that issues of church government were 'matters necessary . . . to our salvation'. Because assurance of true faith within this tradition depended so heavily upon visible fidelity to every commandment of Christ, the more advanced puritans like Cartwright were convinced—at least, in the matter of the urgency of their opposition to episcopacy—that failure to obey the biblical mandates regarding church polity would lead to eternal damnation. But by so doing, disciplinarian puritans made a deeply significant departure from the more moderate ecclesiological inclinations of Calvin, and, in this respect, followed the more doctrinaire path first trod by Calvin's successor in Geneva, Theodore Beza. It was the latter who initially hardened the boundaries of reformed ecclesiology in a decisive fashion and began to make the kind of exclusive claims for presbyterianism in Geneva that were to ring so stridently throughout the polemical writings of the 'forward' puritans in Elizabethan England.[54]

As Thomas Wood, an early Elizabethan activist with Genevan experience, explained in a letter to the Earl of

[52] Dudley Fenner, *A brief treatise upon the first table of the lawe* (Middleburg, 1587), Sig. C1–2.

[53] Ibid., Sig. D1.

[54] For Beza's claims about the divine right of presbyterianism see Tadataka Maruyama, *The Ecclesiology of Theodore Beza* (Geneva, 1978), esp. 209–16. On the influence of Beza in England see also Gordon Donaldson, *The Scottish Reformation* (London, 1960), 183–202; N. F. Sykes, *New Priest, Old Presbyter* (Cambridge, 1956), 42–4.

Leicester, the church in England could never be considered truly reformed without a true discipline 'which that godly learned Beza affirms to be one part of the Word of God and the ordinance of Christ, without the which it is not possible but the whole building shall fall down'.[55] Even before Cartwright's famous Cambridge lectures in 1570, London radicals were already citing Beza's dogmatic claims in defence of their argument for the necessity of discipline as a mark of the true church.[56] Significantly, when the *Admonition* came off its secret press in June 1572, Field and Wilcox (who were also to see two other ecclesiastical tracts by Beza into print) appended to the puritan manifesto a letter written by Beza to Archbishop Grindall about the matter of reform in England: the Genevan disciplinarian revealed his wish therein that the English church would abolish episcopacy along with the Prayer Book in favour of a more strictly biblical polity.[57]

Thus it was that in the last decade of Elizabeth's reign, the Bishop of London, Richard Bancroft, side-stepped Beza and turned to the works of Calvin (much as Whitgift had before him) for some weighty Continental support of his anti-puritan polemic of 1593, *A survey of the pretended holy discipline*. Rather than seeing them as the rightful heirs of Calvin's more temperate ecclesiology, Bancroft perceived that, in their righteous radicalism, those puritans who advocated fundamental reforms in the English church were more appropriately the descendents of Beza's extremism:

And that you may perceive what great difference there is betwixt our men's spirits and Master Calvin's; their outrage and his modesty: their pride and his humility: their rashness, ignorance and giddiness, and his sobriety, learning and judgment . . . But it may peradventure be said that, howsoever Calvin did carry himself in this cause, yet Beza is of another opinion. Indeed he is so, but it turns more and

[55] Patrick Collinson, 'Letters of Thomas Wood, Puritan, 1566–1577', in *Godly People*, 103.

[56] Patrick Collinson, 'The Elizabethan Puritans and the Foreign Reformed Churches in London', in *Godly People*, 259.

[57] Frere and Douglas (eds.), *Puritan Manifestoes*, 43–55. John Field also secured a letter of Beza written to the reformed Scottish nobility, which Field had published in London in 1580 under the title, *The judgement of a most reverend and learned man from beyond the seas, concerning a threefold order of bishops*. Two years later a certain 'T. W.', presumably Thomas Wilcox, wrote the Epistle Dedicatory to Beza's *A discourse, of the true and visible markes of the catholique churche* (London, 1582).

more daily to his own discredit. He succeeded Master Calvin in place, but neither in his learning nor in all his virtues.[58]

At the time Bancroft launched his literary effort against Elizabethan nonconformists, puritanism as an organized movement had already been effectively silenced. Five years earlier, in 1588, the party had lost its most aggressive leader together with its most valuable political support through the deaths of John Field and Robert Dudley, the 'puritan earl' of Leicester. Meanwhile, the traditionalists had recruited, along with Bancroft, the formidable services of episcopal apologists such as Richard Cosin, Matthew Sutcliffe, Richard Lewyn, and others, who together mounted an impressive anti-puritan literary campaign now waged on a new foundation of the *jure divino* prerogatives of episcopacy.

The effect of all of this, combined with Elizabeth's determined efforts to root out radical dissent following the end of the Spanish threat in 1588, was that puritanism as a quasi-political movement completely collapsed. Faced with defeat, a handful of the more assertive radical puritans crossed the English ecclesiastical Rubicon into separatism. But the majority moderated their ecclesiological principles in light of the new political realities by adopting an *adiaphora* attitude toward reform and quietly diverting their religious fervour into the cultivation of personal piety. And so, within the space of a few years, the tables had turned: the bishops now claimed divine authorization for episcopacy and the puritans conceded the whole issue was, after all, an indifferent matter.[59]

Although in this way the revolutionary spirit of puritan churchmanship had been sapped as the end of Elizabeth's reign drew near, puritan theology received at the same time the systematic attention of William Perkins, the famous practical theologian and lecturer at Great St Andrews, Cambridge. Within his works, Perkins offered few indications of his ecclesiastical predilections; yet the theological seed for the kind of radical activism that so characterized puritan

[58] Richard Bancroft, *A survay of the pretended holy discipline* (London, 1593), 127.

[59] Collinson, *Elizabethan Puritan Movement*, 383–8, 433. See also William Haller, *The Rise of Puritanism* (Philadelphia, 1972), 116–27, for a survey of puritan literature on the cultivation of individual godliness. For the *jure divino* claims of episcopacy, see above, n. 6.

extremists of the 1570s and 1580s remained alive, buried deep within the fertile ground of Perkins's rich doctrine of assurance.

Identified as the fountainhead of the 'experimental predestinarian tradition', Perkins developed and popularized more effectively than any of his puritan predecessors the idea that soteriological assurance could be derived through careful obedience to the moral law.[60] 'Knowledge of God's will joined with obedience', Perkins had said, was 'an infallible mark of one that is in communion.'[61] Thus, orthodox belief and godly conduct comprised the two signs of true faith. At the same time, Perkins also reasserted the old claim of militant puritanism that the practice of a biblical church order was equally as critical for attaining assurance as the possession of an orthodox creed. Put the other way around, the Cambridge preacher warned that 'they which abide not in the doctrine of the prophets and apostles, but set up some other form of worshipping God, abide not in the Son and the Father'.[62] Like Dudley Fenner during the heyday of puritan radicalism, Perkins now argued in the 1590s that adherence to a biblical polity was demanded by the Decalogue under the second commandment; disobedience in this matter alone, Perkins indicated, was enough to break the heavenly contract with humankind. He also insisted that although inward worship was the principal means of obedience to this commandment, visible obedience should not be neglected: 'For this cause, not only soul, but also body, must stand in subjection to Christ.'[63]

For this reason, R. T. Kendall's claim that Perkins should never be classified as a puritan because he 'never published a word calling for modifications in Church government'[64] is entirely too categorical and it completely misses the potentially volatile ecclesiological import of Perkins's exposition of the second commandment. Moreover, the conviction expressed by Perkins that excommunication 'must be done in the face of

[60] Kendall, *Calvin and English Calvinism*, 51–78.

[61] William Perkins, *The works of that famous and worthie minister of Christ . . . M. W. Perkins* (London, 1605), 374.

[62] Ibid. 814.

[63] Ibid. 31, 855; see also, 33. Perkins' exposition on the second commandment was almost identical to Fenner's interpretation in *A briefe treatise*, Sigs. C1–2, D1.

[64] Kendall, *Calvin and English Calvinism*, 5.

the Church, by the consent of the whole Church'[65] was itself shot through with left-wing puritan sentiment. The reason for his relative silence on the subject of ecclesiology in the 1590s, when Perkins was going to the press, probably had as much to do with the repressive political environment under Whitgift's and Bancroft's policies as it did with any purely ecclesial preference on the part of Perkins. When assessing puritans during the last decade of Elizabeth's reign on the basis of their expressed (or unexpressed) ecclesiological convictions, as Kendall does, one should keep in mind that even outspoken militants like Walter Travers chose to cool their reforming passions in those 'silent' years between 1588 and the renewal of radical puritan activism in 1604.[66]

While the majority of puritans during the 1590s (including Perkins) thus avoided the radical ecclesiastical implications of their understanding of the second commandment through their pursuit of individual godliness, there were a few who, during that decade, did not. They acted on the conviction that the second commandment demanded visible obedience to what they believed to be the ecclesiastical polity of scripture and willingly followed their radical proclivities into open separation from the established church. Behind the radicalism of separatism lay, as we shall see, the theological legalism of puritan notions concerning soteriological assurance. Significantly, however, when the separatists confronted puritans with the radical ecclesiological implications of the puritan doctrine of assurance, they found that even the more extreme puritans would suspend their convictions about the conditional nature of the covenant when faced with the spectre of separatism. Thrown on the defensive, Elizabethan puritans turned to a theology of unmerited grace and invoked the mystery of inward faith in order to justify their continued presence in an institution they had previously so incessantly maligned.

Before exploring the theology and churchmanship of English separatism and the response of radical puritans to the threat posed therein, it will be useful to first take a brief look at

[65] Perkins, *Works*, 143.

[66] S. T. Knox, *Walter Travers: Paragon of Elizabethan Puritanism* (London, 1962), 138–9.

the resurgence of the *jure divino* defence of puritan radicalism that developed in Jacobean left-wing puritanism in the decade immediately following the Hampton Court conference of 1604.

Jacobean Radical Puritanism

In the by then well-defined tradition of Elizabethan puritan radicalism, left-wing puritans under the reign of James I rallied round the old militant claim that ecclesial issues had a prescribed status: all true worship 'both for matter and manner', explained the Derbyshire puritan preacher, William Bradshaw, in 1604, 'ought to be according to the prescript rule of God's Word only. Neither has any mortal man authority to frame according to his own conceit any form or fashion of God's service and worship.'[67] Bradshaw's treatise was one of several tendentious pamphlets issued by a new generation of hard-core puritan radicals—Perry Miller's 'non-separating congregationalists'[68]—who surfaced in the years immediately following the breakdown of the puritan initiatives at the Hampton Court conference in 1604. Dismayed by the utter failure of the four moderates who represented the puritan cause directly to confront the prelates with the 'unlawfulness' of episcopacy, the post-Hampton Court radicals contended that it was precisely over the *adiaphora* issue that the moderate puritan spokesmen had foundered; they had neglected to press the bishops at the conference with the puritan *jure divino* claim, a claim that had always provided the foundation of puritan demands for reform.[69]

[67] William Bradshaw, *Several treatises of worship and ceremonies by the reverend Mr. William Bradshaw* (London, 1660), 10.

[68] Miller, *Orthodoxy in Massachusetts*, chap. 4.

[69] Stuart Barton Babbage, *Puritanism and Richard Bancroft* (London, 1962), 71. M. H. Curtis claimed that the Hampton Court conference itself was a puritan success in which James I made significant concessions to them. In the long run, however, Curtis believed the puritans lost out because the king failed to get the Hampton decisions implemented by a hierarchy that was antagonistic to the puritan aims. See M. H. Curtis, 'The Hampton Court Conference and its Aftermath', *History*, 46 (1961). For a reappraisal of this thesis, see James Shriver, 'Hampton Court Re-visited: James I and the Puritans', *Journal of Ecclesiastical History*, 33 (1982), 48–71, which argues that the king had a fundamental distrust of the puritans at the

Feeling betrayed and embittered, the new militants took the campaign into their own hands with a renewed commitment to the Elizabethan radical defence of reform. Making explicit the ideological link with the radical puritan tradition of the 1570s and 1580s, Robert Parker, the Jacobean extremist exiled in Holland, affirmed the opinion of Walter Travers that the Bible held a single, certain, and unchangeable format, 'exactly prescribed', for the discipline of the church.[70] The Jacobean radicals believed that Christ had settled his ecclesiastical estate before his ascension by leaving his followers 'as exact a church government' as Moses had done under the law.[71]

This did not mean that Jacobean radicals, any more than their Elizabethan counterparts, believed all the particulars of church order had been meticulously defined; there were those few indifferent matters that could be framed by the church and magistrate according to the circumstances of the age. But the number of these ceremonials was, all the same, sharply limited. In this respect, William Ames noted how 'little liberty is left unto men' in the Bible for indifferent things.[72] Bradshaw gave an example of just how far-reaching and exacting Christ had been when, during his earthly ministry of teaching the apostles, he had established in considerable detail the legal framework for the church. Even the posture of a communicant at the Lord's Supper, a matter many would think inconsequential, had been, Bradshaw insisted, the subject of divine prescription, not through a specific teaching, but by Christ's own example: 'our master Christ, who came not to break but fulfill the law . . . did eat the Passover sitting . . . seeing sitting was used by Christ and the signification thereof is found in scripture . . . For after the Passover he rose, washed his disciples' feet, and sat down again.'[73]

The Jacobean radicals acknowledged that since the advent

conference and granted them at most a few innocuous favours and some gracious words, but not much success.

[70] From a seventeenth-century MS translation of Parker's *De politeia ecclesiastica*, 1616, MS Eng. Misc., th. e. 158, Bodleian Library, Oxford (hereafter cited as Parker MS), i. 7.

[71] Ibid. ii, 40. See also Ames, *Reply to Dr Mortons generall defence*, 9–10.

[72] Ames, *Reply to Dr. Mortons generall defence*, 13.

[73] Bradshaw, *Several treatises*, 95

of the gospel, Mosaic ceremonial laws had been set aside as useless relics of an earlier dispensation. But when they elaborated their position on this sensitive issue, they appear to have thought that the ceremonials had been not so much *erased* by Christ as *replaced* with a more sophisticated, precise regimen for the church in the present age: 'the [Mosaic] law and the ceremonies thereof gave place as being less perfect, a childish pedagogy and beggarly rudiments . . . in respect of the more perfect Word of Christ'.[74] Like the Elizabethans before them, Jacobean left-wing puritans also argued that the ecclesiastical ordinances of Christ were given the force of biblical law by their inclusion in the second commandment of the Decalogue, 'wherein under one kind of idolatry all sorts are forbidden'.[75] As William Ames explained, this commandment was given for a specific 'direction, that in worshipping God we have a precise regard of God's own holy ordinances in the ministry of the Word, sacraments, and discipline: on the other part, that we despise all human devices'.[76]

The coupling of ecclesiology with soteriological assurance, so prominent in the writings of Elizabethan precisionists, became a hallmark of the early Stuart radical platform as well. Parker, for example, agreed with the views of Cartwright and Travers (against Whitgift) that church polity was a matter of faith. Those conformists who believed ecclesiology to be circumstantial, Parker reasoned, were risking their own salvation, along with the salvation of countless innocent souls who in blind ignorance participated in the popish practices of the parish churches.[77] Ames was convinced that those who had the opportunity to join 'the church of God instituted', but neglected to do so, could 'scarce be accounted for believers truly seeking the kingdom of God', no matter how orthodox their profession of faith.[78] Elsewhere in his catechism, Ames sounded a more sober warning to those who had disregarded the practice of a truly biblical polity: 'it is to be feared that

74 Ibid., Sig. A3.

75 Ibid. 79; see also William Ames, *Reply to Dr Mortons particular defence*, (n.p., 1623), 14–17.

76 William Ames, *The svbstance of Christian religion* (London, 1659), 219.

77 Parker MS, i., 10, 11, 37.

78 William Ames, *The marrow of sacred divinity*, in *the workes of the reverend and faithfull minister of Christ William Ames* (London, 1643), 142–3.

such Gallios have not part nor portion in this kingdom [of God]'.[79]

This link between ecclesiology and soteriological assurance was a by-product of the empirical approach to assurance that, as noted above, dominated the 'experimental predestinarian' theology of Elizabethan puritanism. In order to be sure of God's electing love, William Ames advised his readers, as the 'worthy Master Perkins' had done earlier, 'to forsake all unlawful things actually . . . else we cannot obtain the grace of God'.[80] Paul Baynes, Perkins's silenced successor at Cambridge, argued that because even 'the least swerving from or breach of God's law' deserved eternal damnation, believers should 'take heed' of the 'little things' for the assurance of their salvation.

Among the ecclesiologically minded militants, this concern for scrupulous obedience to biblical law extended beyond the sphere of the private practice of godliness, which was the focus of moderate puritan piety, to include public worship and discipline. Reflecting the language of 2 Peter 1: 10, Baynes explained that making one's 'calling and election sure' required not only the 'diligent use' of 'private' means, but also the 'public' means offered by Christ for salvation: 'If a physician bid one take three several things, he will not think it well to take one: no more when God prescribes . . . if we use some one, neglecting others.'[81] For that reason, Baynes urged his readers to obey the second commandment by observing all the prescribed ordinances of Christ's church 'so we may be approved and allowed of him'.[82]

It was from within these theological convictions that William Stoughton, the civil lawyer and MP who had introduced puritan petitions to Parliament in 1584, renewed his campaign for reform under James I. Rather than endangering themselves by reforming the established church according to the apostolic pattern, Stoughton was certain that the English people would actually 'seal up unto their own

[79] Ames, *Substance*, 284. Gallio was the careless Roman proconsul of Achaia mentioned in Acts 18: 12–17.

[80] William Ames, *Conscience with the power and cases thereof*, ii, 11, in *The workes of the reverend and faithfull minister of Christ William Ames* (London, 1643).

[81] Paul Baynes, *A helpe to trve happinesse* (London, 1618), 28–9, 205–6.

[82] Paul Baynes, *Briefe directions unto a godly life* (London, 1618), 144–6.

souls infallible testimonies of good and sincere consciences'.[83]

In an age when, as Carl Bridenbaugh has observed, people often seemed plagued by a gnawing sense of sin that spawned an intense, sometimes relentless search for personal religious security,[84] the argument of radical puritans like William Stoughton was likely to appeal to those who did their profoundest thinking from within a puritan theological framework. If the puritan segment of society was indeed convinced that, in the words of Ames, 'obedience does preserve and maintain peace of conscience', because it offers the most immediate sign of an effectual calling,[85] then the case for active nonconformity on the basis of the second commandment would have been a compelling one for many of the more serious-minded among them.

With the hardening of divisions within the English church in the decades leading up to the Civil War, this soteriological motive for reform became a legacy that would be taken up by the next generation of puritan radicals. As Larzer Ziff has noted, it provided a kind of theological mainspring for congregational preachers like John Cotton, John Davenport, and Thomas Goodwin, all of whom adopted an uncompromisingly militant ecclesiological posture in their confrontation with the repressive anti-puritan measures of Archbishop Laud.[86] But this same theological rationale was first to have a profound impact on another small, but significant, group of English dissenters early in the Elizabethan era who stood outside the puritan fold. This occurred when the left-wing penchant for tying soteriological assurance to ecclesial practice passed into the ideological arsenal of those erstwhile puritan radicals who, under the compunction of this doctrine, made their way into the religious underworld of ecclesiastical separatism.

[83] William Stoughton, *An assertion for true and christian church-policie* (Middelburg, 1604), 22–3.

[84] Carl Bridenbaugh, *Vexed and Troubled Englishmen 1590–1642*, rev. edn. (Oxford, 1976), 276.

[85] Ames, *Conscience*, iii, 61, in *Workes*.

[86] Larzer Ziff, *The Career of John Cotton: Puritanism and the American Experience* (Princeton, 1962), 68.

Elizabethan and Jacobean Separatism

In the 1573 crisis created by the admonition controversy, Edward Dering—a puritan preacher who had recently written to his friend, Lord Burghley, in support of Thomas Cartwright—abruptly found himself brought before Star Chamber to give his opinion of Cartwright's troublesome views. As the interrogation proceeded, Dering was asked 'whether there be any right ministry or ecclesiastical government at this time in the church of England, or no?' As a puritan who openly supported the cause of the admonitioners, he could hardly have been expected warmly to affirm the current ecclesiastical administration and ministry in the established church. Yet Dering was put in a rather awkward position by the question, for he also had to avoid the implication of separatism to which he would be subject if he rejected the ministry of the English church outright. Caught between this rock and a hard place, Dering replied by drawing a slender but none the less substantial distinction:

> If you mean right, having such a calling as the Word of God requires . . . I am sure you will confess it is not right. If you mean a right ministration, as concerning sacraments and doctrine, I humbly confess and think that no man ought to separate himself from the church which God has given us in this land.[87]

While not entirely abandoning the negative puritan critique of episcopacy, Dering managed in this highly nuanced repartee to justify his commitment to the national church and step round the pitfalls of separatism by appealing to the very same *adiaphora* defence of the church that had been used by episcopalian Calvinists like Whitgift against the admonitioners. In effect, Dering delicately negotiated his way between what Star Chamber no doubt saw as the infinitely narrow space separating conformity from schism by forsaking the very basis of the admonitioners' radicalism. However, by his admission that only the Word truly preached and the sacraments rightly administered (and not a godly discipline) were necessary to the essence of a true church, Dering had

[87] *Parte of a register*, 75.

also moved away from radical puritan ideology into the ambiguities of moderate puritanism.

In much the same way, the radicalism of Cartwright was demonstrably softened when he confronted the separatism of one of his former disciples at Cambridge, Robert Browne, and Browne's colleague, Richard Harrison. While on the offensive with Whitgift, Cartwright had professed that the practice of biblical discipline was a matter of salvation;[88] but in his letter to Harrison, he conveniently failed to mention the soteriological significance of ecclesiology and no longer identified discipline as a mark of a true church, saying only that discipline was 'necessary to the comely and stable being and not simply to tbe being of the church'.[89] In order to defend the parish churches in the face of Harrison's separatism, Cartwright directed the misguided schismatic to consider the unconditional nature of God's covenant relationship: 'the Lord is in covenant; this he does to our assembly in England, therefore they are the Lord's confederates'.[90] Significantly, the contractual features so characteristic of puritan covenant theology, with their emphasis on obligation and obedience,[91] are nowhere to be found in Cartwright's reply to Harrison.

As Cartwright grew older, he became increasingly dismayed by the outbreak of separatism among some of his most ardent devotees; it was clear that he was reaping a harvest he had never intended to sow, as he painfully discovered when his sister-in-law, Anne Stubbe, followed the logic of his militant principles into separatism. In correspondence with her, Cartwright dismissed—as he had with Harrison—the soteriological significance of a godly discipline.[92] It was commonplace for radical puritans in their exposition of the second commandment to warn that God would break his covenant for disobedience over the ecclesial laws of scripture, just as a man would divorce his wife for unfaithfulness.[93] However, Cartwright fundamentally reinterpreted this analogy for his separatist sister-in-law. He reminded her that even though a

[88] See above, n. 25.

[89] Albert Peel and Leland H. Carlson (eds.), *Cartwrightiana* (London, 1951), 53.

[90] Ibid. 51.

[91] See above, nn. 41–54.

[92] Peel and Carlson (eds.), *Cartwrightiana*, 64–5.

[93] e.g. Fenner, *A briefe treatise*, Sig. D1.

wife's duty to her husband was primarily that of obedience, 'yet it follows not that because she obeys not, therefore she is no wife'. Even if she committed adultery, Cartwright reasoned, she would not be

> forthwith out of account of a wife until she being convicted thereof, or for that cause divorced from her husband: so the church, notwithstanding her spiritual adultery, is not unchurched, neither ceases to be reputed a church, until such time as the Lord, taking away the ministry of the Word from her and the administration of the sacraments, has, at it were by bill of divorcement, disabled her.[94]

Obviously, this letter represents a significant shift of emphasis from the polemic Cartwright employed while embattled against the forces of the Antichrist within episcopacy. Confronted with separatism, he set aside the puritan requirement of unqualified obedience in all things and the necessity of practising a biblical discipline for soteriological assurance.[95] But while Cartwright tempered his radicalism in this way, lest his principles push him into the ecclesiastical nether regions of separatism, it was his separatist sister-in-law who, noting the Cambridge theologian's equivocation, remained faithful to the mentality of puritan radicalism: 'Truly, I think an indifferent judge will think you take shifts,' she chided her brother-in-law. 'You rehearse the place of Timothy, i.e. a crown of glory is laid up for all those that love his coming. I said . . . the Word of God is plain. He that obeys not the Son shall not see life, but the wrath of God abides on him.'[96]

[94] Peel and Carlson (eds.), *Cartwrightiana*, 64–5. The tendency among radical puritans to shift from conditional covenant theology when confronting traditionalists to unconditional covenant theology when opposing separatism is reminiscent of Calvin's strategy with Roman Catholics and anabaptists. Against the papists Calvin argued, 'the Lord nowhere recognizes any temple as his save where his Word is heard and scrupulously observed', and 'God . . . is ready to keep the covenant, but that when they do not reciprocate, they deserve to be repudiated', Calvin, *Institutes*, bk. 4, ch. 2, s. 3; but in response to the anabaptists he explained, 'the Lord's covenant remains, and shall remain forever inviolable, which he solemnly ratified with Christ, the true Solomon, and his members in these words: "If his children forsake my law and walk not in my judgments . . . I will visit their transgressions with the rod, their iniquities with stripes. But my mercy will I not utterly take from him."' Ibid., bk. 4, ch. 1, s. 27.

[95] Peel and Carlson (eds.), *Cartwrightiana*, 61.

[96] Ibid. 61. Contemporaries such as Richard Bancroft were aware that Cartwright was often inconsistent concerning the necessity of discipline when he shifted his polemic from conformists to separatists. A. F. Scott Pearson rejected Bancroft's

Thus it was that the theological underpinnings of Elizabethan and Jacobean puritan radicalism passed over into the thought and rhetoric of the more venturesome and—so long as they were on the offensive themselves—ideologically more consistent separatists.

In what must have been Richard Harrison's earliest writing as an apologist for separatism, the Norwich preacher pointed an accusing finger at certain puritan-minded members of the church in England who 'bow and bend the commandment of government of the church [into] a little commandment' in order thereby to avoid what he perceived to be the necessity of separatism. Whether he had Cartwright in mind or not, Harrison thought this impoverished view about the significance of ecclesiology to be a rather risky dogmatic position given the perspective of the puritan passion for eternal security. It was clear to him, at least, that the 'Lord has spoken of such' when he said in the Sermon on the Mount: 'yet they shall be little in the kingdom of God'.[97] Like most puritans, the separatist believed that ecclesial matters comprised the sum and substance of the second commandment, wherein 'we are forbidden . . . to worship God . . . under any outward likeness, or in any other manner or fashion, than [God] has appointed'. Those who fail in this biblical mandate quite obviously 'sin against this commandment'.[98]

In this way, Richard Harrison, along with Robert Browne, coupled the separatist practice of a biblical church polity with soteriology in the early 1580s. Like their contemporaries in left-wing puritan circles, they were convinced that those who wilfully worshipped outside the divinely prescribed boundaries were in 'grievous bondage' that could cause 'endless hurt' to their immortal souls by dissolving the covenant bond. Only membership in the true church, they said, echoing

charges, however, saying Cartwright 'could consistently defend the English Church no matter how imperfect against Separatists, while he claimed that the adoption of Presbyterianism was necessary to the Church's perfection': ibid. 370–1. While it is true that Cartwright consistently claimed that the established church of England was a true church, he was patently less consistent concerning the value of discipline for assurance and its place in the *notae ecclesiae*.

[97] Robert Browne, *The Writings of Robert Harrison and Robert Browne*, ed. Albert Peel and Leland H. Carlson (London, 1953), 49.

[98] Ibid. 128–9.

Cartwright's own sentiments, 'has assurance of salvation in Christ' and 'the promise of blessing and life for evermore'.[99]

The salience of the covenant motif in English separatist propaganda has been a point of special interest in two recent studies, both of which emphasize what they perceive to be the distinctive way in which separatist churchmen employed covenant terminology to justify their ecclesiological radicalism. In both instances the claim is made that the separatist treatment of covenantal theology stood in sharp contrast to its usage among contemporary disciplinarian puritans. B. R. White was the first to point out the importance of the covenant theme in separatist ecclesiology. In his book, *The English Separatist Tradition*, he maintained that the significant contribution which Robert Browne made was to place ecclesiology within a 'mutualist' or 'conditional covenant' framework, thus making the practice of the one true biblical polity a matter that affected the preservation of the covenant pact with God. Exactly how Browne came to this understanding is one element of the separatist story that eluded Dr White's lucid history of that tradition. As he explained:

> It is not easy to assert with any real certainty the source of Browne's rather unusual interpretation of the covenant relationship. While it would certainly be possible for him to derive it directly from scripture, the fact remains that the 'mutualist' interpretation was by no means characteristic of contemporary Puritan thinking, since this was primarily dominated by Calvinist emphases. This meant that, while stress upon the sovereignty of God did not exclude the implication that obedience was required, God's will, rather than the obedience or disobedience of man, was determinative for the stability of the covenant relationship.[100]

More recently, David Zaret, in *Heavenly Contract: Ideology and Organization in Pre-Revolutionary Puritanism*, an often highly perceptive sociological study of puritan covenant thought and popular religion, appears to have understood the matter in a way similar to Dr White. Zaret has argued that before 1590, 'the idea of the covenant in English Calvinism was limited to polemical writings directed against heresy and separatism'. Puritan polemicists used what he terms a 'unilateral' (or

[99] Browne, *Writings of Robert Harrison and Robert Browne*, 85, 87, 97, 255.
[100] B. R. White, *The English Separatist Tradition* (Oxford, 1971), 55.

unconditional) interpretation of the covenant to counter what they perceived to be the 'bilateral' (or 'mutualist') covenant concept of separatist apologists. It was only after the last decade of the sixteenth century, according to Zaret, that puritan divines made use of the bilateral covenant idea, though not ecclesiologically like the separatists, 'but in a new context, a pastoral context in which Puritan clerics described both the interior dimensions of faith and the external evidences of it that could provide certitude of salvation'.[101] Zaret does, however, get 'beneath' the top layers of the puritan conflict regarding the implications of the covenant for churchmanship to the extent that he accepted the denials of separatists who claimed their covenant theology did not ultimately imply a synergistic interpretation of salvation. Nevertheless, Zaret nowhere acknowledges the 'bilateral' use of the covenant theme among puritans for ecclesiological purposes and, thus, appears to make that a feature peculiar to the separatists alone.

The judgements of White and Zaret would be perfectly understandable, of course, if one reads only the debates waged between puritans and separatists, since it was there, as we have seen, that puritans opted for the gracious, 'unilateral' character of the covenant in order to defend their continued presence in a corruptly constituted church. But this would reveal only half the picture, for the fact remains, as we have also seen, that radical puritans had already applied a 'bilateral' interpretation to the covenant and placed the matter of ecclesiological reform within a 'mutualist' framework as early as the admonition controversy, a decade *before* Browne flourished as a separatist. Thus, rather than contributing something new in his utilization of the covenant, Browne seems more likely to have inherited his mutualist ecclesiology

[101] David Zaret, *Heavenly Contract: Ideology and Organization in Pre-Revolutionary Puritanism* (Chicago, 1985), 140–1. Zaret does get beneath the top layers of puritan and separatist debates to the extent that he accepts the separatist denials that their covenant theology (as the puritans claimed) upheld works righteousness, arguing that the real difference between the two parties was not their covenant interpretation but 'obstinancy', or wilful disobedience, a point which the present study also emphasizes. See below, n. 165. Nevertheless, Zaret nowhere acknowledges the 'bilateral' use of the covenant theme among puritans for ecclesiological purposes and, thus appears to make that a feature peculiar to the separatists alone.

from the theology that his puritan predecessors had already pressed into service in the cause of reform.[102]

During the second great wave of separatist activity in the early 1590s, practising biblical churchmanship was an equally urgent concern for the London separatist, Henry Barrow. In his controversy with the puritan vicar of Maldon, George Gifford, Barrow noted the puritan's use of the unconditional covenant to defend the 'mixed' congregations in the national church. Gifford had cited Exodus 20: 'I will be their God and the God of thy seed', to show that God accepted the people of Israel 'though many of them were wicked, idolatrous, reprobates'. What Gifford 'wittingly' suppressed from the passage, complained Barrow, was that the covenant promise made to Moses was originally a conditional one. Those who now break that covenant bond by their violation of Christ's polity 'and will not be reduced to his obedience', Barrow warned his puritan opponent, will be 'cast out of his favour'.[103]

Like Harrison and other Elizabethan militants, Barrow believed that the polity of the New Testament, having been prescribed by the lawgiver of the new covenant, was the subject matter of the second commandment. Any other worship was idolatry, and idolatry broke the covenant bond; for that reason alone, the separatists fled the idolatrous worship of the English church.[104]

According to Barrow, Christ had 'perfectly instructed his apostles in all things' pertaining to 'the gathering, planting and establishing of his church' during the post-resurrection appearance described in Matthew 28: 18–20. Apostolic churchmanship thus formed 'the true only foundation, the express pattern for all buildings'. It was 'exact and absolute', perpetual, immutable, and 'not to be willingly neglected or changed unto the world's end'.[105] Reflecting with remarkable accuracy the language of Travers's *Ecclesiastical discipline*,[106]

[102] Dr White has acknowledged the plausibility of my argument on this issue in his article, 'The English Separatists and John Smyth Revisited', *Baptist Quarterly*, 30 (1984), 344.

[103] Leland H. Carlson (ed.), *The Writings of Henry Barrow, 1590–1591* (London, 1966), 115–17.

[104] Leland H. Carlson (ed.), *The Writings of Henry Barrow, 1587–1590* (London, 1962), 169; *Barrow, 1590–1591*, 65.

[105] Carlson (ed.) *Barrow, 1587–1590*, 565–6, 575; *Barrow, 1590–1591*, 36.

[106] See above, n. 35.

Barrow added that since God 'set down in the mountain the perfect pattern of all things even to the least instrument, hook, or tape used therein', leaving nothing to 'the will or discretion of Moses' when dealing with the Israelites, it was inconceivable that Christ should have been 'less careful, provident, absolute, jealous' of the New Testament church.[107]

Because Barrow continued to believe that ecclesial fidelity was given its place in the Decalogue, that ecclesial fidelity was requisite for soteriological assurance, he became an outspoken critic of those disciplinarian puritans who in the 1590s had replaced their zeal for ecclesiastical purity with a pursuit of personal holiness. By focusing their sermons on the cultivation of individual piety for assurance, Barrow was convinced that parishioners remained perilously ignorant of the 'godless' system of episcopacy that threatened to undermine the religious security they so earnestly sought from puritan pulpits. Having no warning of the real dangers at hand, Barrow wondered 'what booteth this knowledge [of individual sanctification] to eternal life? Balaam with all the false prophets had, and the devils have, this faith and knowledge in as great measure as the learnedst of these ministers; yet the one is damned, the others tremble.'[108] If the godly desired genuine spiritual solace, they needed to know and practise a biblical churchmanship, as well: 'for the appeasing and assurance of our conscience, [let us] give heed to the Word of God, and by that golden reed measure our temple, our altar, and our worshippers: even by these rules whereby the apostles, those excellent perfect workmen, planted and built the first churches'.[109]

Francis Johnson, trained for ministry by Laurence Chaderton in the puritan hotbed of Christ's College, Cambridge, also emphasized the benefits of ecclesial piety for assuaging puritan anxieties about salvation. Citing the opinions of Field, Cartwright, and his former tutor, Chaderton, that the ecclesiastical laws of Christ should never be neglected, Johnson concluded that these great divines had themselves transformed Christ into a dead idol, depriving him of his rightful rule, by their continued presence in a blasphemously

[107] Carlson (ed.), *Barrow, 1587–1590*, 566–7.
[108] Ibid. 501–7. [109] Ibid. 279.

constituted institution.[110] Separation was necessary, he believed, for a guarantee of eternal security. As the separatist *Confession* of 1596, penned by Johnson, stated the matter: 'by God's commandment all that will be saved must with speed come forth from this Antichristian estate',[111] a conviction that was rehearsed on countless occasions by his separatist contemporaries.[112]

Finally, it is interesting to note that this same overriding concern for personal salvation was appropriated for their own polemical purposes by the first English baptists, who sprang from the exiled separatist community in Amsterdam in 1609. In a contrived dialogue, written by the baptist, John Murton, between a young 'searcher' named Ereunetes, and his guide, Odegos, Ereunetes asked his wiser friend to show him the way to salvation. Odegos replied that one must be in union with Christ 'by keeping his commandments . . . he that keeps his commandments dwells in him and he in him . . . thereby we are sure we know him, if we keep his commandments'. Ereunetes thought the advice helpful but not sufficient, so he urged his guide to be more specific: which commandments *must* he keep? Odegos listed six, but underscored the commandment dealing with idolatry, a sin which was afflicting many otherwise good and faithful souls who failed to practise the legitimate biblical polity, which included believer's baptism: 'for many are exceedingly deceived therein, seeing themselves blameless in the other sins . . . although they be gross idolaters'.[113]

In London the baptist leader, Thomas Helwys, pressed the same point when he told conscientious puritans that their 'great affections of zeal' in personal charity were commendable but not adequate to secure the covenant bond:

In these excellent duties very many of you greatly abound, and we cannot but with great affections look upon you and love you for them, yet know that many papists are nothing behind you in these

[110] Francis Johnson, *A treatise of the ministery of the Church of England* (Amsterdam, 1595), 31, 35.

[111] Francis Johnson, *A trve confession of the faith* (Amsterdam, 1596), art. 32.

[112] Henry Ainsworth, *The Communion of saincts* (Amsterdam, 1607), 90; John Smyth, *The Works of John Smyth*, ed. W. T. Whitley, 2 vols. (Cambridge, 1915), i, 252–3.

[113] John Murton, *A description of what God hath predestinated concerning man* (London, 1620), 125–7.

things. Therefore, let not these things deceive you as though you had all these things, because you have these.

Helwys advised they should *first* consider the importance of believer's baptism, the only true entrance into the kingdom of heaven. 'Therefore if there be any other entrance found out, it is not, nor cannot be of God . . . for no other way of salvation has Christ appointed but that men first believe and be baptized.'[114]

Significantly, it was this conviction about the indissoluble link between churchmanship and salvation that the one-time separatist, then baptist, Edmond Jessop, began to doubt when he finally renounced both anabaptism and separatism, and returned to puritan circles in order to concentrate on deepening his personal piety. He explained that, as a baptist, God had laid his providential 'rod of correction' upon him and compelled him to examine 'whether the cause (for which I suffered) would any whit avail me unto salvation'. He decided it would not, concluding that all the 'strivings . . . about forms and outward ordinations lead to nothing but contentions'.[115]

Jessop's re-evaluation of the saving power of ecclesial fidelity signalled his retreat from the ranks of pre-revolutionary puritan extremism in which church government was determined to be no 'little commandment'. While most puritans set their radicalism to one side in this way after 1590, separatists and the earliest English baptists continued to take seriously the conviction that strict attention to scriptural injunctions about church order provided a primary means of spiritual comfort and certitude. As Henry Barrow admonished his London separatist congregation from his prison cell at the Gatehouse in Westminster:

Examine your comfort by your estate and your estate by the light of God's Word; take the reed in your hand; measure your temple, your altar and your worships; if you have built upon the true foundation gold, silver, and precious stones, and that according to our Saviour's last will and testament, your works will witness to you; your work will then abide, and you have good cause to rejoice.[116]

[114] Thomas Helwys, *A short declaration of the mystery of iniquity* (London, 1612), 121–2.
[115] Edmond Jessop, 'An Advertisement', in *A discovery of the errors of the English anabaptists* (London, 1623), not paginated.
[116] Carlson (ed.), *Barrow, 1587–1590*, 112.

Henry Jacob

Between the years 1596 and 1599, Henry Jacob was engaged in a debate with the separatist, Francis Johnson, concerning the validity of the English parish churches. While conceding that they were often plagued by corrupt vestiges of Roman forms and practices, Jacob nevertheless resisted what, for a radical puritan, must have been the alluring temptation of separatism on the same grounds argued by Cartwright some years earlier, assuring Johsnon that matters of church order were indifferent and not prescribed.[117] In reply, Johnson thought Jacob's defence 'a strange divinity' because, as he pointed out, the puritan left had maintained elsewhere that ecclesiastical matters were in fact prescribed and, therefore, consequential for salvation.[118] Furthermore, Johnson reminded Jacob that Christ was 'the prophet, priest, and king of his church', and that if the godly wished to keep him as such, they must be obedient to all his commandments, including those related to the governing of his church.[119] Johnson reasoned that by remaining within the antichristian framework of episcopacy, the parish churches could not possibly 'hold the Lord Jesus, their prophet, priest, and king' and, so, could not be accounted 'true constituted churches of Christ', nor their members 'true Christians'.[120]

In return, Jacob claimed that Johnson's argument erred by failing to recognize the qualitatively different soteriological value accorded to theological doctrines, on the one hand, and ecclesiological doctrines, on the other. The two, Jacob believed, should properly be distinguished between what he called 'written' and 'unwritten' ordinances of Christ. Written ordinances pertained to theological doctrines about justification, sanctification, the resurrection, the Trinity, and so forth. They formed 'the foundation of saving faith' and 'must be in the written Word or else to be none of Christ's'. Obedience to these written ordinances was necessary for

[117] Henry Jacob, *A defence of the chvrches and ministery of Englande* (Middelburg, 1599), 12.

[118] Ibid. 16, 29.

[119] Ibid. 11.

[120] Ibid. 18.

salvation because in these matters alone 'Christ is our prophet, priest and king'.

This, however, was not true of the unwritten ordinances, such as the 'outward orders in the church'. Jacob explained to Johnson his view that, soteriologically speaking, ecclesiological reform was of little consequence since it was 'not simply of the foundation' of faith. Matters of polity were 'neither certain nor perpetual, but at the arbitrary appointment of the church and magistrate, and yet to be Christ's own nevertheless, who has left this liberty for the church to use'. In short, they were 'arbitrary and changeable, no matters of faith, nor written in the scriptures'.[121] Jacob's *adiaphora* line of reasoning in 1599, at the close of his debate with Johnson, sounded very much like the Calvinist Whitgift against a radical Cartwright—or, for that matter, the moderate Cartwright against a fanatical Richard Harrison!

But by 1604, a noteworthy reversal had occurred in Jacob's thinking about the relationship between ecclesiology, the Bible, and salvation, a reversal that he himself apparently never explicitly acknowledged. In that year, Jacob published *Reasons taken out of Gods word*, where he now argued that matters of church government were written, perpetual ordinances which, like other doctrines of the faith, were ordinarily necessary for salvation. Furthermore, he now wrote—contrary to his views in 1599—that 'all human inventions or unwritten traditions ecclesiastical are directly contrary to God's Word' because the second commandment made all ecclesial activities not founded on scripture unlawful. The New Testament contained only one form of church polity which, he now believed, it was necessary to observe for soteriological assurance: 'The right and true discipline ecclesiastical . . . is one main part of the ordinary means of salvation appointed by God for every soul.'[122] Salvation depended upon the rule of Christ in the ecclesial, as well as the personal sphere, so that

whosoever denies Christ the Saviour to be our entire and perfect prophet and spiritual king (by taking away from him some [viz., the ecclesiastical] parts of his prophetic and kingly offices, and ascribing the same unto men) he diminishes the honour and dignity of Christ,

[121] Ibid. 12–14.

[122] Henry Jacob, *Reasons taken out of Gods word* (Middelburg, 1604), 1–4, 67, 70, 51.

he impugns the foundation of saving faith and is contrary to God's Word.[123]

Throughout the corpus of Jacob's writings from 1604 to 1616, this 'mutualist' or conditional understanding of ecclesiology, in which assurance was fused with the practice of biblical polity, became an increasingly prevalent motif. The opening sentence of *Reasons* makes the point abundantly clear that the whole purpose of left-wing puritan demands for reform was to help secure 'the safety of our souls'.[124] As he explained in 1610, 'the first and weightiest matter in religion that can concern us [is] . . . to be assured that we are in a true visible and ministerial church of Christ: for out of a true visible church ordinarily there is no salvation'.[125] Three years later, he maintained simply that obedience to the discipline outlined in scripture 'is plainly the way to heaven'.[126] And by 1616, when Jacob published his final two works, the theme had become a major preoccupation of his; almost every page of those last publications offers some expression of the notion that 'the only sure way for the comfort of our souls is the practice of God's ordinances for his visible church'.[127]

Such convictions, expressed perhaps even more plainly by Jacob than by most other precisionists, were hardly innovative theologically within the broader stream of radical dissent. Behind his insistence that the assuagement of an anxious conscience could be had by visible obedience to the polity of scripture lay the well-developed framework of 'experimental predestinarianism' to which this highly principled puritan was fully committed, especially as that theology had been augmented in the works of William Perkins. Although Jacob did not share with many of his co-religionists the Cambridge puritan connection, having studied at Oxford, his theological indebtedness to the tradition of William Perkins is profound.[128]

[123] Henry Jacob, *Reasons taken out of Gods word*, 53.

[124] Ibid., 'To the high and mightie Prince James', Sig. A2.

[125] Henry Jacob, *A plaine and cleere exposition of the 2d. commandement* (Leiden, 1610), Sig. D6.

[126] Henry Jacob, *An attestation of many learned, godly and famous divines* (Middelburg, 1613), 151.

[127] Henry Jacob, *A collection of sundry matters* (Middelburg, 1616), Sig. B4.

[128] Jacob studied divinity at St Mary's Hall, Oxford, from 1563–8, after which he moved to Corpus Christi College to assume duties with the choir as precentor:

Soon after he emerged as a proponent of radical reform, Jacob constructed a brief catechism, the substance of which he copied verbatim from an earlier one written by Perkins.[129] In a much later work, *A plaine and cleere exposition of the 2d. commandement*, 1610—which had a great deal in common theologically with Dudley Fenner's 1587 treatise on the *Decalogue*—Jacob explored the theological rationale for believing that salvation was bound up with faithful obedience to the pattern of a visible church as prescribed by the Mosaic 'lawgiver' of the new covenant.[130] There he explained that saving faith could be understood from two very different perspectives: from God's perspective, salvation depended entirely upon grace so that 'no works of ours can justify us'; but from the human perspective, true faith should be 'considered simply as it is a work and a duty for us to do'. From a human vantage point, then, good works did not stand in opposition to faith, but rather 'the law of faith' should be viewed as something 'contained in the law of works', the *Decalogue*. For the believer, the presence of true faith could, therefore, be perceived in one's faithful performance of the Mosaic law. Because matters of ecclesiology were included under the second commandment, ecclesiastical obedience was a duty of faith and a necessary ingredient for acquiring assurance.[131]

Another text to which Jacob appealed was 2 Peter 1: 10, which he understood within the Perkins tradition to mean that

Andrew Clark (ed.), *Register of the University of Oxford* (London, 1887–8), vol. ii, and pt. iii, 116; Corpus Christi College, Oxford, Admissions Register, 1517–1647, not paginated. Jacob's move to Corpus in Dec. 1568 was very probably religiously significant. St Mary's was suspected of favouring the old religion, while Corpus became something of a 'nursery of the godly' in Oxford with the arrival of William Cole as President a few months before Jacob's move. Cole was an opponent of vestments and had spent the Marian years of exile in the reformed centres of Zurich, Strasburg, and Geneva. See C. M. Dent, *Protestant Reformers in Elizabethan Oxford* (Oxford, 1983), 41–3, 187.

[129] Champlin Burrage, *The Early English Dissenters* (Cambridge, 1912), ii, 153–61. See also the comparison of this catechism with one by Perkins in Walter R. Goehring, 'Henry Jacob (1563–1624) and the Separatists' (New York University Ph.D. dissertation, 1975), 241.

[130] For Jacob's view of Christ as the Mosaic lawgiver of his church, see Henry Jacob, *The divine beginning and institution of Christs true or visible ministeriall church* (Leiden, 1610), Sigs. D8, F1–2.

[131] Jacob, *Exposition of the 2d. commandement*, Sig. B1 and Sig. E7.

assurance of saving faith could be gained through obedience to all God's commandments. But with his overarching concern about churchmanship, Jacob, like Paul Baynes and other radical puritans, gave it a decidedly ecclesiological twist when he explained that, according to 2 Peter 1: 10, believers were commanded to make their 'calling and election sure by walking in the true outward way: to observe the second commandment in all the parts of it, a main part whereof under the gospel is this form of a visible church and government'.[132] Thus, while late Elizabethan puritans minimized the importance of ecclesiology in favour of the development of individual piety, Jacob came to ask, as the separatist Henry Barrow had asked his critic George Gifford in 1590, if those who thought ecclesiology indifferent could

> give assurance to men's consciences? Nay, it cannot be. At least, men standing in such state will often doubt and make question whether the spiritual blessings and graces of God in Christ be promised, or may be instrumentally wrought in them . . . This doubt, I say, at least will and must needs arise from the opinion of our adversaries. And it cannot but weaken the faith of many if, in the end, it does not wholly subvert it.[133]

He believed the same proposition applied to 'those [puritans?] who do profess and acknowledge that Christ . . . has instituted . . . a certain perpetual form of . . . church and government', yet fail to 'use and practise that which they do profess to be from heaven'. They 'truly seem to destroy the conscience and faith of the people, not unlike to the other'.[134] For Jacob, the practice of a godly discipline became 'the only true complete means to get assurance of salvation to our souls, which otherwise we, for our parts, cannot find'.[135]

Exactly why Jacob shifted his views in this way between 1599 and 1604, is, however, not clear. It is not beyond the realm of possibility that, as John von Rohr has recently postulated, the moderate puritan of the 1590s was suddenly transformed into a fervid exponent of radical ideals through

[132] Henry Jacob, *A confession and protestation of the faith of certaine Christians in England* (Amsterdam, 1616), Sig. D3. For Paul Baynes, see above, n. 81.

[133] Jacob, *Attestation*, 155–6.

[134] Jacob, 'To the Christian Reader' in *Divine beginning*, not paginated.

[135] Jacob, *Confession*, Sig. D3.

the illuminating arguments of Francis Johnson during their protracted disputation beteen 1596 and 1599. In the words of von Rohr, 'the victor's laurels for this debate went to Johnson' in 1604, when 'Jacob had begun to change his mind' and move toward a consensus with the separatist.[136] This, of course, would not be so different from the way that the 'puritan' Johnson had himself some years earlier succumbed to the persuasive logic of Henry Barrow's writings while in the very act of trying to suppress them.[137] Yet, in Jacob's case, this is highly unlikely, given both his outspoken rejection of the separatist alternative and his commitment to a radical tradition within mainstream puritanism that had already developed a rigid divine-right polemic of its own against Elizabethan traditionalists.

The more plausible explanation of Jacob's dramatic about-face is that it represents no change in fundamental convictions. Rather, it provides a picture of the two opposing sides of a puritan mind struggling to occupy a middle ground between the unacceptable extremes of outright conformity and separatist schism. The context of his confrontations with an immovable establishment after 1604 was substantially different, to his way of thinking, from his encounter with the renegade separatist, Johnson, and so necessitated an appreciably altered strategy. Without this perspective, Jacob's radical convictions of 1604 could appear to be a rather unscrupulous retraction of his previous views. But it is very likely that Jacob, given the two entirely different contexts to which he addressed himself, did not think he had forsworn his earlier 'moderate' views, nor that the difference between the moderate views he expressed to a separatist and the more radical claims he made later in the struggle for church reform were contradictory in any meaningful sense. He no doubt believed he was playing the same tune, but in a different key for a new audience.

This does not mean that Jacob remained untouched by the uncomfortable tensions between moderate and radical

[136] von Rohr, '*Extra Ecclesiam Nulla Salus*: An Early Congregational Version', *Church History* :June, 1967), 119.

[137] For Johnson's conversion to separatism, see White, *English Separatist Tradition*, 93.

puritanism. From a remark made by Jacob during his debate with Johnson, it seems that he had not been entirely successful in hiding his own radical inclinations from Johnson under the considerable pressure of the separatist's accusations. At least, this appears to be the implication from Jacob's reply to Johnson's opening assault: 'You charge an unconscionable untruth on me [when you said] . . . that I should grant and cannot deny, that all outward ceremonies and government are arbitrary at man's pleasure: I only said that our state holds that general opinion, not that I myself held it.'[138] In fact, Johnson had represented Jacob's words fairly. In his original statement, Jacob had *not* said 'our state holds', but rather, 'we hold', though he did admit at that time that 'one or two among hundreds or thousands may think otherwise'.[139]

Jacob's fumbled attempt to exonerate himself in this way from his previous *adiaphora* defence of the parish churches suggests, among other possibilities, that, however sincerely committed to acting on principle puritans like Jacob may have been, the two theoretically opposing views on ecclesiology which he embraced could always be manipulated according to the exigencies of a particular situation. Hence, Jacob found the divine-right polemic useful when confronting the bishops, as in 1604, but not while squaring off with the more militant separatists, for whom the legalistic forms of the *jure divino* defence worked more to their ideological advantage when they confronted puritans like Jacob.

So Jacob's reversal in 1604 most likely represents not so much a change of mind as a change of context, in which he now felt compelled to take a public stand on what had previously been, in his opposition to episcopacy, probably only a private conviction. If this is the correct reading of what occurred, then Johnson would certainly not have been the source of his 'new' convictions. The fact is, of course, that Jacob did not have to turn to Johnson, as von Rohr imagined, or to any other separatist for the convictions he expressed in 1604, because, as we have seen, the same concepts had been articulated just as clearly by Elizabethan puritans in the 1570s and 1580s. That, indeed, is where Johnson and most

[138] Jacob, *Defence of the chvrches of Englande*, 15.
[139] Ibid. 11–12.

separatists, along with all other Jacobean radical puritans, traced their own ecclesiological pedigree.[140] And this is exactly what Jacob did when, in 1613, he quoted directly Cartwright's famous reply to Whitgift that matters of church government are, to use Jacob's version, 'of the substance of the gospel, and that the kind of government is a matter necessary to salvation and of faith'.[141]

Another important factor in the change of Jacob's formal position between 1599 and 1604 was, no doubt, the fluctuating puritan fortunes upon the accession of James I. Rather than being affected so much by his confrontation with Johnson, as von Rohr suggests, it was more likely that the puritan failure at Hampton Court (which distressed Jacob) and subsequent deprivations (including his own)[142] acted as powerful catalysts, propelling him into his aggressive public campaign for radical reform. Curiously, although this significant shift to a *jure divino* defence of reformed ecclesiology did occur, historians who have studied the career of Jacob have either ignored or, perhaps at a loss as to how to explain it, made light of it.[143] But it was a shift of considerable importance which also indicates that in the hidden years of the 1590s, when puritan reformists had been silenced, the theological mainspring of their radicalism had not in fact been entirely discarded. What is perhaps more important, however, is that Jacob's *jure divino* argument ensured in the aftermath of Hampton Court that, while the majority of puritans continued to focus their

[140] See e.g. Lake, *Moderate Puritans*, 78.

[141] Jacob, *Attestation*, 193.

[142] Stephen Brachlow, 'The Elizabethan Roots of Henry Jacob's Churchmanship: Refocusing the Historiographical Lens', *Journal of Ecclesiastical History* (1985), 234–6, 244.

[143] Robert S. Paul failed to mention it in 'Henry Jacob and Seventeenth-Century Puritanism', *Hartford Quarterly*, 17 (1967), while Douglas Horton made the completely erroneous claim that Jacob's *adiaphora* view of ecclesiology in 1599 was the one he championed throughout his career: *Congregationalism: A Study in Church Polity* (London, 1952), 95. von Rohr noted the change, but dismissed it as a 'procedural', not a 'substantive' issue: 'The Congregationalism of Henry Jacob', *Transactions of the Congregational Historical Society*, 19 (1962), 108; see also Yarbrough, 'Henry Jacob, A Moderate Separatist and His Influence on Early English Congregationalism', (Baylor University Ph.D. dissertation, 1972), 66–70. Most recently, Goehring, 'Henry Jacob', 119–25, 142, made the vague claim that Jacob's position seemed to have changed 'in some small degree', but stressed that it was probably Johnson who changed as a result of his debate with Jacob, while Jacob remained true to his view of 1599, an interpretation which is obviously incorrect.

attention on matters of private piety, Jacob became one of a handful who now openly discussed and promoted a radical restructuring of the established church.[144]

John Robinson

In his first published apology on behalf of the separatist enterprise, *A justification of separation*, 1610, John Robinson discussed the authority which the New Testament discipline practised by the apostles now held for him as a recent convert to sectarian principles: 'It is unto me a matter of great scruple and conscience to depart one hairbreadth . . . from their practice and institution in anything truly ecclesiastical, though never so small in itself.'[145] With this rather punctilious sentiment, Robinson announced a theme he would repeatedly marshal to justify his activities as separatist pastor and apologist; at the same time, this exacting attitude marked his alliance with the legalistic theological temperament of left-wing puritan and separatist polemics. Like so many radical churchmen before him, Robinson's overriding concern centred upon the imperative of a vigilant conformity to biblical patterns in ecclesial affairs. It was a concern, he recognized, that had percolated down to the separatist tradition through the writings of Elizabethan precisionists who, although remaining within the established church, had nevertheless first articulated the biblical ecclesial model now used by the separatists.

Following the well-established formula of other radical dissenters, Robinson yoked this concern for a uniformly biblical polity with the ever-pressing issue of soteriological assurance.[146] For Robinson, assurance could be obtained

[144] Note Collinson's conclusion that 'for most church puritans' after 1604 'the presbyterian polity, or any other scheme for the extensive separation of the Church's structure, institutions and ministry, became a remote and irrelevant idea. By "reformation" they tended to mean the pursuit of a piety and a moral order of the puritan type, not the establishment of the external forms and symbols of a reformed church': *Elizabethan Puritan Movement*, 464–5.

[145] John Robinson *A just and necessarie apologie* (Amsterdam, 1625), 36.

[146] John Robinson, *A justification of separation from the Church of England* (Amsterdam, 1610), 50.

through a conscientious compliance with the commandments of Christ. The Bible was a kind of rule-book for godly living that contained definite instructions about 'how to please God in all things, unto eternal life'. Unqualified and zealous fidelity to all the demands of scripture—according to one's ability and knowledge—was 'the immediate end and use of the Word of God, and the way and means to salvation'. Assurance in the heart followed when one could 'say, with good conscience, that he has respect of all God's commandments'. Proof that one loved God came through *active*, visible obedience to God's 'good Word'. For this reason, Robinson cautioned, 'one must take heed' of what he termed a 'shadowish love of goodness and piety only in the abstract: and must love it in the concrete, where both the person, and good in him, is visible'.[147] Disobedience would move God to 'dischild' his people 'for bastards' and they would once again become 'true children of the devil'.[148] But for those who *kept* 'the law of God (written in the heart or, of stone)', God would 'assuredly keep them from hell'.[149] Obedience to both the Mosaic covenant (of stone) and the Abrahamic covenant (of the heart) were the primary instruments of spiritual comfort and security.

Robinson's advice to the uneasy puritan soul was, therefore, to obey with scrupulous attention to every detail each biblical injunction. For example, he cited the calamity suffered by the Old Testament priest, Uzzah, for breaking one rather inconsequential ceremonial law: that episode in which the unfortunate priest met his untimely death for merely touching the ark of the covenant provided the separatist with a vivid warning for his contemporaries 'that we presume not against the Lord in the least ceremony or circumstances'.[150] Only a single error, however slight, he reminded the traditionalist Joseph Hall, makes a heretic, and only 'a little leaven, whether in doctrine or manners, leavens the whole lump'.[151] This was the ethical radicalism behind the militancy of all

[147] John Robinson, *Observations divine and morall* (Amsterdam, 1625), 53, 80.

[148] Robinson, *Justification*, 44.

[149] Robinson, *Observations*, 264–5.

[150] Robinson, *Justification*, 23.

[151] John Robinson, 'An answer to a censorious epistle', in Joseph Hall, *A common apologie of the church of England* (London, 1610), 72.

separatist activity: to remain members of the established church, Robinson reasoned, would inevitably lead to the transgression of 'many Christian ordinances, to which we are most straightly bound by God's Word and our own necessities'.[152]

For Robinson, as has already been observed in the literature of other radical puritans and separatists, the figure of Christ was often portrayed in the image of the great lawmaker of the Old Testament. The Leiden separatist sometimes described Christ as a meticulous legislator, in the Mosaic tradition, who took even greater care than his Old Testament counterpart when establishing the rules of his kingdom.[153] Thus, the New Testament offered a fairly specific blueprint of ecclesiastical polity. There was one pattern for the church expressly given 'by a greater than Moses', and so plainly 'that like Habbakuk's vision, he that runs may read [it]'.[154]

This, however did not mean Robinson believed, as a contemporary critic claimed, that Christ has prescribed 'particularly every circumstance and rite' for the church.[155] Some doctrines, he said, such as infant baptism, were gathered by necessary consequence.[156] There were other matters related to the polity of the church that Robinson determined were *adiaphora*, but, following the convictions held by most radical puritans and separatists, he argued the list of those things was very short. It included such peripheral matters as anointing heads, the time and place of worship, and, as he came to believe near the end of his career, listening to sermons outside a true church.[157] The urgent point to be made, however, was not to underscore the freedom allowed in these minor areas but to recognize that altering or failing to observe Christ's ordinances for the church was considered an infraction of the second commandment, an offence which

[152] Robinson, 'An answer . . .', in Hall, *A common apologie*, 47.
[153] Champlin Burrage (ed.), *An Answer to John Robinson of Leyden* (London, 1920), 35.
[154] Robinson, *Justification*, 77, 46.
[155] Burrage (ed.), *Answer to John Robinson*, 35.
[156] John Robinson, *A defence of the doctrine propounded by the synode at Dort* (Amsterdam, 1624), 149.
[157] Robinson, *Justification*, 472; and John Robinson, *The lawfulnesse of the hearing of the ministers of the church of England* (Leiden, 1634), 57.

constituted spiritual idolatry. And that, in itself, 'most directly impeaches' the covenant bond between God and his people, and 'procures the bill of divorce'.[158]

That is why Robinson became so exercised over what he termed the 'bastardly disposition' of those puritans who thought they could 'be sure of the Father's inheritance' by cultivating personal holiness without paying sufficient attention to the public duties of the first table.[159] These people, 'as Mr. Barrow charges them', make 'parts of the holy scriptures of small moment and needless' by subordinating matters of church polity to the supposedly more consequential concerns of doctrinal orthodoxy and private piety. But for Robinson, the private and public duties of God's laws were of equal soteriological import and so 'make together a most heavenly harmony'.[160] If, as Robinson thought, Richard Bernard's intent in writing *The separatists schism*, 1608, was to offer his godly parishioners at Worksop 'satisfaction to the perplexed conscience', he did not believe Bernard succeeded because the puritan preacher altogether failed to encourage a strict fidelity to the ecclesial mandates of scripture.[161] By contrast, Robinson's advice to the troubled puritan conscience was to follow the directions of 2 Peter 1: 10, and 'in the obedience of all Christ's commandments, to make their election more sure to themselves'.[162] By '*all* Christ's commandments' he meant, of course, the ecclesiastical injunctions, as well as all others.

The matter of churchmanship was, in Robinson's view, so tied up with soteriological assurance that, like Francis Johnson and John Smyth, he was willing to say: 'we do avow it for truth' that those who do not practise the biblical church order followed by the separatists 'are no subject of Christ's kingdom'. It was, in fact, his conviction that membership in a true church often provided the only mark that scripture used to identify God's people.[163] This did not mean, as some of Robinson's contemporaries complained, that he believed

[158] John Robinson, *Of religious communion private and publique* (Amsterdam, 1614), 32–3; *Justification*, 93–4. *Observations*, 86.

[159] Robinson, *Observations*, 53; *Justification*, 24.

[160] Robinson, *Justification*, 449, 72.

[161] Ibid. 28, 35.

[162] John Robinson, *Of religious communion private and publique* (Amsterdam, 1614), 13.

[163] Robinson, *Justification*, 95; see also 100. For Smyth, see *Smyth*, ii, 354–73; for Johnson, see above, n. 110.

everyone who yet remained within the established church stood condemned.[164] Citing the conclusions of Barrow, Penry, Johnson, and Ainsworth, Robinson argued that there were undoubtedly 'hundreds and thousands' of godly people within the old order who would manage to escape divine damnation by their 'ignorance'.[165] But from a purely legal vantage point (i.e., according to the dictates of scripture), because they broke the ecclesiastical laws of God by retaining membership in a falsely constituted church, they should be *accounted* apostates.[166]

For Robinson, the formal constitution of the church was paramount. As he reminded William Ames, the external constitution of the church was that 'for which we stand and for the want of which alone we withdraw ourselves'.[167] Robinson and other separatists made much of the open wickedness, profanity, and corruption they believed permeated the parish churches. Yet those evils in themselves did not make the national church a false one. Rather, its corrupt constitution was the culprit because, in the first place, it granted membership to visibly profane people and, in the second place, it failed to provide valid biblical measures for the 'evacuation and expulsion of excrements, or other noisome things'.[168] Along with Henry Barrow, Robinson did not believe it an 'evil intolerable . . . that evil men should be suffered in the church', or that discipline was neglected, or even that there were 'personal, accidental profanations of the temple' in the English church. What he objected to was the fact that openly wicked men and women were 'compelled' into membership, that a form of discipline contrary to the scriptures was exercised, and that the very 'frame of it, in

[164] *Contra* Robert Parker who claimed that Robinson denied the covenant of grace applied to anyone in England (Parker MS, iii, 17).

[165] The issue of ignorant disobedience was an important one for separatists and puritans. The question of whether or not separatism was deemed necessary often hinged on whether they perceived the corruptions in the English church were a result of wilful disobedience or of blind ignorance. See Brachlow, 'The Elizabethan Roots of Henry Jacob's Churchmanship', 239.

[166] Robinson, *Justification*, 259; *Of religious communion*, 1, 3, 9.

[167] Christopher Lawne, *The prophane schisme of the Brownists discovered* (London, 1612), 50.

[168] Robinson, *Justification*, 83.

respect of the causes constitutive' was not of the Lord.[169] Thus, the formal constitution of any church furnished the key to its validity; its outward, legal estate proved determinative:

I do affirm that merely by virtue of a constitution there may be a true church of God though abounding (for the present) in sin and iniquity, and yet another assembly, not rightly constituted or gathered into covenant with God, no true church, though less impieties to be found in it . . . the constitution of the church that is the collection and combination of saints as matter in and into covenant with God as the form, is that which gives true being unto a church and nothing else.[170]

The validity of the church was not conferred by preaching the Word, administering the sacraments, or even the true faith of the people, but by a biblically sound constitution alone.[171]

Michael Walzer's discussion of 'constitutional politics' and the impersonal understanding of political office among radical Calvinists provides a good background against which to read Robinson's views in this regard.[172] In a sense, there was no other basis to which he could effectively appeal, since non-separating radical puritans essentially rested their case against separatism on the grounds of their experience of life together as a godly community within the parish church structure.[173] While this formal, legal definition of the church by Robinson should not be taken to indicate that separatist life was therefore devoid of meaningful communal ties and a deep, shared experience of the Holy Spirit, it does indicate that in terms of separatists' opposition to the 'moderate' tendencies within puritanism, defining the church in concrete

169 *Apologie*, 66. Barrow made much the same point in Carlson (ed.), *Barrow, 1587–1590*, 591–2.

170 Robinson, *Justification*, 81–2. Robinson voiced the same conviction as late as 1624 in his letter to the Southwark church, as appended to *Lawfulnesse of hearing*, 76.

171 Robinson, *Justification*, 88–9; 'Censorious epistle', 139; see also his answers to questions 8 and 9 in 'An appendix to M. Perkins his six principles of Christian religion', as appended to the 1644 edn. of Robinson's *A just and necessarie apologie*, where Robinson specifically rejected the notion that the Word truly preached and the sacraments administered made a true church. Jacob, of course, had made a similar point when he denied that 'saving faith' was the form of a true church. See above, nn. 121–34.

172 Michael Walzer, *The Revolution of the Saints: A Study in the Origins of Radical Politics* (New York, 1976), 81–4.

173 Lake, *Moderate Puritans*, 232–3.

legal terms provided them with what they believed to be the most effective apology for their own separatist activities, much as radical puritans themselves employed the same device in their anti-episcopal polemic.

This formal, almost legal status of the church constitution in Robinson's ecclesiology was one reason why he, like other Jacobean radicals and separatists, rejected the argument of those godly puritans who claimed that an evangelical preaching ministry was more valuable to the cause of the gospel than campaigns for a reformed ecclesiastical order. 'The forward sort will magnify preaching, but . . . with an evil eye to the right gathering, lawful government . . . in the church. Well, the Lord sees this halting . . . and will avenge the quarrel of his very meanest ordinance and least commandment upon all these deceitful workers.'[174]

For the same reason, Robinson insisted that the validity of a ministerial office rested on statutory, rather than spiritual grounds. The puritan vicar Richard Bernard defended the authenticity of his ministry within the parish system on the basis that, however corrupt the structures of the established church might have been, his ministry nevertheless effectively converted sinful men and women to saving faith. Robinson did not deny the gospel power of Bernard's ministry, only that this in itself was not the proper foundation for 'a true office of ministry'.[175] That depended solely upon a lawful calling according to scriptural prescriptions regarding the election of church officers.[176] In precisely the same way, Robinson defined religious communion in purely legal terms: 'communion is a matter of order and relation, standing in the orderly combining of the graces of God in two faithful persons or more'.[177] Neither the piety nor the profanity of an individual determined the validity of religious communion, only the legal standing of the individual within a true church.[178]

Robinson thus stressed the soteriological worth of ecclesial

[174] Robinson, *Justification*, 72; cf. also, Ames, *Reply to Dr. Morton's generall defence*, Sig. A2, 87.

[175] Robinson, *Justification*, 11.

[176] John Robinson, *A manvmission to a manvdvction* (Amsterdam, 1615), 10.

[177] Robinson, *Justification*, 437.

[178] Ibid.; 'Letter to Ames', in Lawne, *Prophane schisme*, 50; cf. also, *Smyth*, i, 262.

obedience and, in relation to those who defended the parish churches on the grounds of the presence of orthodox faith, defined the legitimacy of a church in statutory terms; however, events within the exiled communities of English radical churchmen in Holland altered this emphasis to a degree on three occasions.

First, the anabaptist threat posed by John Smyth and Thomas Helwys caused a noticeable, if momentary, shift in Robinson's thinking about the link between soteriology and ecclesiology and the Mosaic models of Christ. In his controversy with Helwys, published in 1614 as one of the five tracts that comprised *Of religious communion*, Robinson retreated significantly from the notion that membership in a true church order had anything to do with salvation. 'Yet it must always be remembered', Robinson now reminded the anabaptist, 'that our question is not about peremptory salvation or condemnation of any, but about their admission, or not admission into the visible church. And strange it is for this man to make it all one, to be saved and to be of the visible church.'[179] This, of course, did not formally contradict what he had said earlier. Robinson, like all separatists, never claimed 'peremptory' or absolute knowledge about salvation—but then, in all fairness, neither did the baptists. What Robinson's statement to Helwys does represent, however, is a subtle shift in emphasis, the very same shift we observed earlier among Elizabethan and Jacobean left-wing puritans. He had moved from the positive claims of radical ecclesiology about the soteriological value of obedient churchmanship, which he used when engaged with puritan opponents. He now emphasized the uncertainties all Calvinists agreed were concealed in the dark, inscrutable mysteries of predestination, which English radical Calvinists inevitably employed whenever those more radical than themselves forced them to be less categorical in their dogmatic claims about matters of church polity.

A decade later, a second change occurred when Robinson was traversing much the same ground with the English baptist, John Murton. In this instance, Robinson backed

[179] Robinson, *Of religious communion*, 95.

away from his earlier claims about the Mosaic nature of Christ's work in ecclesial affairs; indeed, he now *contrasted* Christ and Moses, grace and law. While the first English baptists, as the separatists and other radical puritans before them, had discussed the Abrahamic covenant in conditional, Mosaic terms,[180] Robinson now stressed the opposition of Abraham and Moses, and the unconditional nature of the Abrahamic covenant. He explained that the Mosaic law could not save; rather, it revealed the fruitlessness of human effort and the need for complete reliance on the grace of God.[181]

But the juxtaposition of law and grace, Moses and Christ, seems to have been a polemic Robinson raised only in the face of the baptist threat, just as radical puritans would conveniently change their *modus operandi* when forced to confront the menace of separatism.[182] While in controversy with puritans and others to his right, Robinson would minimize the unconditional dimensions of the covenant relationship. For example, a year after his skirmish with Murton, and in a context entirely free from the anabaptist controversy, he said that God would surely save only those who obeyed his law 'written in the heart or, of stone'.[183] Years earlier, when he wrote *Of religious communion*, Robinson pictured Christ in Mosaic imagery and argued that infractions of New Testament ecclesiology constituted religious idolatry, according to the second commandment. He made this claim, however, not in the sections of that work dealing with the anabaptism of Helwys, but, significantly, only in his dispute with non-separating puritans.[184] 'Mutualist' theology, as we have noted about the English radical tradition as a whole, seemed to be a useful tactical weapon for Robinson against those more conservative than himself, but a liability when he confronted those who had moved into deeper waters of dissent.

[180] See above, nn. 38–49, 97–116; and ch. 4, below.

[181] Robinson, *Defence of the synode at Dort*, 167–72.

[182] This particular shift of argument when faced with anabaptism was not unique to Robinson among the separatists. The puritan, John Burgess, noted in 1610, for example, that Richard Clifton was forced to reassess the role of the Mosaic law when arguing with the anabaptist, Smyth. See Burrage, *Answer to John Robinson*, 35. This in general seems to be true of the separatist polemic with anabaptists; see ch. 4, below.

[183] Robinson, *Observations*, 264, as quoted above, n. 148.

[184] Robinson, *Of religious communion*, 31–3.

Finally, a third small but significant deviation in emphasis occurred in response to what he perceived to be a decline in personal holiness among the separatists exiled in Holland. While the separatists always stressed the importance of ecclesiastical purity, Robinson came to believe in his later years that there was an increasing neglect of the social personal duties of both tables in the Decalogue by many of the saints. Such neglect was, according to his own explanation, the primary reason behind his well-known modifications concerning religious communion and listening to sermons. Other factors, of course, may also have played a part in moderating his separatism in this way. G. F. Nuttall has suggested that his radicalism abated while he was in Holland because the pressure of persecution had been greatly reduced.[185] This argument is given some support in Robinson's introductory words to his last work, *The lawfulness of hearing of the ministers of the church of England*, published posthumously in 1634, where he talks of having previously overvalued some matters 'for which they have suffered trouble and affliction formerly'.[186] On the other hand, B. R. White has suggested that the change expressed in *Lawfulness of hearing* may have occurred in response to the anabaptist threat posed by the followers of John Smyth.[187] Although this is possible, there is simply no evidence in that treatise to indicate Robinson had been concerned about the dangers of anabaptism, and it seems unlikely he would have waited fifteen years after Smyth's secession from the ranks of separatism to react in that way.

While either of these explanations could have played some part in the alteration of his views on the matter of listening to puritan sermons, it is clear that Robinson himself discussed the matter of religious communion with parish churches in the context of his worries over the many failures he recognized in the personal piety of his separatist coreligionists. When he wrote *Of religious communion* in 1614, advocating private religious communion with godly members of English parish churches, he did so partly in response to the allegations made

185 G. F. Nuttall, *The Puritan Spirit* (London, 1967), 60.

186 Robinson, *Lawfulnesse of hearing*, 9–10.

187 White, *English Separatist Tradition*, 158–9.

by Christopher Lawne about the dubious moral conduct of Daniel Studley and others who had caused such a scandal among the exiled separatists.[188] While Robinson argued that Lawne's report grossly exaggerated the sad facts of the case surrounding Studley's lascivious affairs, he was willing to admit that, in their zeal for purity of polity, a number of separatists had 'undervalued' and 'neglected' the personal graces that were being so carefully nurtured by godly puritans. As a result, God had caused those improvident separatists to fall 'into such personal sin and evils (notwithstanding their advantage in the Lord's ordinances) as from which (without this help) many thousands of them [in the church of England] have been preserved'.[189] Robinson evidently believed that contact with these saints still captive in Babylon, who had nevertheless made the cultivation of personal godliness their special concern, could help redress the balance for the more ecclesiologically orientated separatists.

Robinson expressed the same conviction, only with even greater urgency, in *The lawfulness of hearing*. He addressed the book to those separatists 'who . . . think to cover and palliate their own both grosser, and more proper and personal corruptions under a furious march . . . against the failings . . . in matters of church order'.[190] By occasionally drinking at the fountain of godly parish preachers, these wayward separatists would, presumably, be reminded of their private religious duties listed in the second table of the Mosaic law. The importance of maintaining *both* tables, while never completely neglected in his previous works,[191] thus became a more pronounced feature in some of Robinson's later writings.[192]

[188] Lawne, *Prophane schisme*, *passim*. For the notorious career of Daniel Studley, an elder in Francis Johnson's Amsterdam congregation, see White, *English Separatist Tradition*, 96–109, 153.

[189] Robinson, *Of religious communion*, 5.

[190] Robinson, *Lawfulness of hearing*, 11–12.

[191] e.g., see above n. 157.

[192] In *Observations*, for example, he had stern words for 'civil hypocrites' who observed the second table but neglected the first. But he appeared even more concerned about the 'religious hypocrites' who had great zeal for 'church . . . and chamber religion . . . which is not accompanied in the house and streets with loving kindness and mercy and all goodness towards men'. For assurance of salvation, Robinson emphasized that both tables must be observed, not only the first: Robinson, *Observations*, 41–2, 77–8.

Yet Robinson, for all his modifications on these significant issues, remained a separatist. While representing a significant shift in emphasis, his convictions about private communion and 'listening' in puritan parishes could not replace, if he were to remain faithful to separatist ideals, what he continued to believe about the necessity of ecclesial obedience for soteriological assurance. Near the end of *Lawfulnesse of hearing*, Robinson made this manifestly clear when he warned that those who avoided practising Christ's ordinances for the church will 'be called little, that is, be indeed none in the kingdom of heaven'. With sentiments that had already been matured within the broader context of radical puritan and separatist dissent, Robinson concluded that obedience to a godly discipline was still

> necessary for our sound and entire comfort with the Lord our God, that our obedience be entire in respect of all his holy commandments . . . That so we may have our part in the testimony given by the holy ghost of Zachary and Elizabeth: which was, that they were righteous before God, walking in all the commandments and ordinances of the Lord, blameless.[193]

Thus, the point of his writing *Lawfulnesse of hearing* was, in Robinson's mind at least, not to signal a retreat from separatism by encouraging a *rapprochement* with the puritan element in England, as many historians have suggested; rather, it was a pastoral one by which he wished to remind the ecclesiologically zealous separatists of their duties to '*all* the commandments', the *personal* as well as the *ecclesiastical*.

By this new emphasis, he may have come back part way in the direction of mainstream puritanism, which in the years after 1590 accentuated the value of personal piety rather than ecclesial purity. But as an exercise devoted to the encouragement of individual graces among the Leiden separatists, it probably should not be taken to indicate, as John Cotton claimed some years later, that Robinson had returned '*more* than half way' to communion with the church in England: that was clearly not Robinson's intention. While Robinson may have found it pastorally necessary to stress the personal side of piety in his last work, he never relinquished his

[193] Robinson, *Lawfulnesse of hearing*, 59, 61–2.

commitment to the necessity of visible obedience to the second commandment through separation from a falsely constituted English church for the sake of salvation assurance. It remained as much the theological dynamic of Robinson's continued life in separatism as it had always been the religious logic behind left-wing puritan activism for reform.

2

HISTORY AND THE FUTURE

Elizabethan Radical Puritans

THE sixteenth century in England was a period in which people increasingly came to expect and, indeed, often found sweeping changes in politics and religion. G. F. Nuttall has suggested that a key to understanding the mood of radical puritans is to realize that they 'believed themselves to be living in a remarkable age, a new age, perhaps the last age'.[1] Interest in the Apocalypse, of course, was never entirely missing from previous epochs in the history of Christianity. Eschatological expectations ran especially high during the first three centuries of persecution and martyrdom in the early church. Yet even after Christianity became a legal religion under Constantine and state persecution ended, the apocalyptic dimension of Christian faith occasionally resurfaced throughout the medieval era in a variety of forms among radical sectarian groups. Norman Cohn has observed that, despite official suppression of radical millennial hopes by medieval ecclesiastics and theologians, 'at times of general uncertainty or excitement people were always apt to turn to the Book of Revelation and the innumerable commentaries upon it'.[2] Nevertheless, the sense of historical crisis and conflict that accompanied the outbreak of the reformation in England, as well as on the Continent, only served to heighten a widespread awareness of apocalyptic themes in the gospel among sixteenth- and seventeenth-century Protestant and Roman Catholic theologians alike.

In perhaps something of a similar way, the rapid change and catastrophic events of the twentieth century have aroused the attention of modern biblical scholars to apocalyptic motifs

[1] G. F. Nuttall, *The Holy Spirit in Puritan Faith and Experience* (Oxford, 1946), 102.
[2] Norman Cohn, *The Pursuit of the Millennium* (London, 1962), 15.

in scripture and, in more recent years, have helped fuel a growing sensitivity among puritan historians to the significance of the eschatological visions that formed so much of the conceptual backdrop for early English dissent.[3] Much of the attention of puritan scholars has centred on the millenarianism of Civil War sectaries which was so effectively wielded as a weapon for social and political revolution. But it has also been increasingly recognized that eschatological speculations and visions were a much more general cultural phenomenon of the period, with roots that reached back into the late medieval world, deeply influencing the thinking of the sixteenth-century reformers.[4] Luther, Melanchthon, and Calvin all shared a belief in Christ's imminent return, the two German reformers being fully convinced that the climax of history would occur before the turn of the seventeenth century. At the same time, in England a 'developing eschatological consciousness' began to emerge in the writings of early English reformers like John Bale, Hugh Latimer, and John Bradford. By Elizabethan times, eschatological stirrings and expectations had become deeply ingrained in the contemporary outlook and interest in them steadily mounted throughout the 1570s and 1580s.

The radical activity of left-wing puritans during the reign of Elizabeth was, to a considerable extent, motivated by this prevailing eschatological climate.[5] John Foxe, the pre-eminent

[3] Examples include B. S. Capp, *The Fifth Monarchy Men* (London, 1972); William Lamont, *The Godly Rule* (London, 1969); Christopher Hill, *Antichrist in Seventeenth-Century England* (Oxford, 1971); Peter Toon, *Puritans, the Millennium and the Future of Israel* (London, 1970); Byran W. Ball, *A Great Expectation* (Leiden, 1975).

[4] Four recent studies of the subject have focused largely, though not entirely, on apocalyptic thought in Tudor England. See V. Norskov Olsen, *John Foxe and the Elizabethan Church* (Berkeley and Los Angeles, 1973); Paul Christianson, *Reformers and Babylon: English apocalyptic visions from the reformation to the eve of the civil war* (Toronto, 1978); Richard Bauckham, *Tudor Apocalypse*, Courtenay Library of Reformation Classics, no. 8, ed. G. E. Duffield, (Appleford, 1978); Katherine R. Firth, *The Apocalyptic Tradition in Reformation Britain 1530–1645* (Oxford, 1979); see also, John M. Headley, *Luther's View of Church History* (New Haven, Conn., 1963), 153, 265; and B. S. Capp, 'Godly Rule and English Millenarianism', in Charles Webster (ed.), *The Intellectual Revolution of the Seventeenth Century* (London, 1974), 389.

[5] e.g., Peter Lake, 'The Significance of the Elizabethan Identification of the Pope as Antichrist', *Journal of Ecclesiastical History*, 31 (1980), 161–78, argues that puritan theology about the Antichrist 'served to generate an activist, reforming attitude in the face of contemporary social and political reality', whereas traditionalists, while sharing many of the same theological views, did not allow doctrines about the Antichrist to dominate their perception of contemporary affairs: ibid. 175.

Elizabethan historiographer whose *Acts and Monuments* were 'written in the charged atmosphere of the last days',[6] undoubtedly made the single most important contribution to the eschatological outlook of the radicals through the prophetic interpretation he gave to the history of the church under persecution, though as suggested below, radical puritans appear to have modified Foxe's vision at certain significant points. Foxe was, as Katherine Firth has recently written, 'the first British author to write a Protestant apocalyptic history that attempted to explain changes in time in terms of an unfolding pattern of events'.[7] It was to Foxe's scheme of history that the more forward puritans were largely committed, a scheme that provided them with the interpretative framework for understanding the remarkable events of the Reformation in which they found themselves now playing such a propitious role.

Like Foxe, Elizabethan radical puritans believed that throughout the centuries the church had been caught in a cosmic conflict between light and darkness, Christ and Antichrist.[8] Left-wing puritans believed that after the initial light of the gospel had illuminated the church in the apostolic age, the institutional church very soon became enveloped in antichristian darkness through the escalation of Roman episcopal authority, especially in the years following the conversion of Constantine. But the momentous changes wrought in more recent times through the protestant reformers and the many pre-Reformation advocates of reform suggested that new light from the gospel was, for the first time since the halcyon days of the primitive church, being shed abroad once again; and it appeared certain to the more advanced puritans that, under these signs, God was about to bring the long eschatological struggle of the past sixteen centuries to a sudden and resounding climax in their own time, rewarding the obedient and punishing the recalcitrant in a day of divine

[6] Olsen, *John Foxe*, 99.

[7] Firth, *The Apocalyptic Tradition*, 110.

[8] For Foxe's conceptualization of church history as 'the age-long contention of Christ and Antichrist', see William Haller, *Foxe's Book of Martyrs and the Elect Nation* (London, 1963), 137. However, the 'elect nation' interpretation of Foxe has been repudiated by the recent studies of Olsen, *John Foxe*; Firth, *Apocalyptic Tradition*; and Bauckham, *Tudor Apocalypse*.

judgement that was near at hand. To a large extent, salvation from this impending doomsday gave radical puritans the impetus for their tireless campaigns for reform. The threat of imminent destructon for the disobedient, combined with the hope of future glory for those who faithfully submitted to the ecclesial mandates of scripture, increased the conviction among advanced puritans that radical change was urgent and must be pursued at all costs, even in the face of the most cruel and inhumane punishment. Indeed, the repressive policies of the English hierarchy from Whitgift to Laud only served to intensify the resolve of many radicals because they were convinced, as Foxe's martyrology had so vividly underscored, that persecution of the saints provided a reliable sign that the iniquitous Antichrist was in his last, panic-stricken death-throes and that the final vindication of the gospel was about to be achieved with the triumphant personal return of Christ.

In reformed theology, the advent of Antichrist in the early church was linked primarily to the gradual and, at first, imperceptible development of papal authority.[9] Calvin wrote, 'there is no doubt that from slight beginnings the Romanists have little by little made great increases. For they could not climb so high with the first step. But at one time they secretly advanced themselves by craft and by devious arts, so that no one could have foreseen what would happen until it happened'.[10] Cartwright, citing Eusebius, argued that while the apostles lived 'the church remained a pure virgin'; soon after they passed away, however, 'the placing of wicked error began to come into the church'. He may have been unclear as to exactly when the purity of the primitive church became thus polluted, but Cartwright was at least certain that even before the turn of the first century the 'Antichrist was corrupting the church'.[11] Pride, personal ambition, and lack of selfless care for the church, Walter Travers explained, led the earliest

[9] For the Antichrist legend in medieval and sixteenth-century reformation thought, and the identification of the Antichrist with the pope and the Turks, see Bauckham, *Tudor Apocalypse*.

[10] John Calvin, *Institutes of the Christian Religion*, ed. J. T. McNeill, trans. F. L. Battles (London, 1960), bk. 4, ch. 11, s. 10.

[11] Thomas Cartwright, *A reply to an answere made of M. Doctor Whitgifte* (n.p., 1574), 73–4. John K. Luoma, 'Who Owns the Fathers? Hooker and Cartwright on the Authority of the Primitive Church', *Sixteenth Century Journal*, 8 (1977), 50.

bishops to inflate their judicial authority 'little by little', initially by reserving the name of bishop only for the moderator of an assembly of ministers,[12] then by 'negligence and ignorance'. In this way, he believed that the authority for church discipline had gradually been transferred from its original *locus* in the whole congregation to an individual. 'But afterward, that darkness increasing, and covering all the church . . . the tyranny grew greater and increased still, and brought under subjection of one man all the churches which were in a whole diocese.' By degrees, the Antichrist usurped more power with the establishment of 'Metropolitans' or 'Archbishops'; then the jurisdiction of the church universal was reduced to only four 'Patriarchs'. Finally, 'Antichrist by these stairs went up to the throne of God and sat him down in the midst of the churches' hidden under the guise of the pope.[13]

Once the Antichrist had become entrenched in this way at the centre of the church at Rome, he virtually ruled unchecked until a movement toward reform commenced, at first haltingly with the advent of Wycliffe and Huss, but then more fully in the work of Luther, Calvin, and the Henrician reformers in England. They were all 'extraordinary' lights, 'new apostles', as Travers called these harbingers of the last age.[14] Yet the Elizabethan radical puritans believed that the early reformers, while acting nobly as God's chosen instruments for reform, did not entirely liberate the church from the dark oppression of the Antichrist: 'Luther, Bucer, and Melanchthon were good men', wrote one unidentified puritan in 1573, 'and yet . . . good men carry in them the note of the corruptions of those times wherein they live'.[15] They were revered by the radicals

[12] Walter Travers, *A full and plaine declaration of ecclesiastical discipline* (n.p., 1574), 181–2: Travers explained that before that time, the name bishop was, according to Acts 20, common to all ministers.

[13] Ibid. 182–3. 'This', concluded Travers, 'is the true history of the confusion of ecclesiastical offices.'

[14] Ibid. 135. With these appellations, Travers was echoing Foxe and continental reformed tradition. See Olsen, *John Foxe*, 66; Walter Travers, *An harmony of confessions of the faith of the christian and reformed chvrches* (London, 1643), 254.

[15] Albert Peel (ed.), *The Seconde Parte of a Register* (Cambridge, 1915), i, 96. See also the critique of the fathers and martyrs of the English Church (Cranmer, Latimer, Ridley, and Hooper) by the puritan, Edward Dering, in Patrick Collinson, *A Mirror of Elizabethan Puritanism, The Life and Letters of 'Godly Master Dering'* (London, 1964), 27.

for their recovery of sound doctrine but not so warmly praised for their churchmanship because they had failed, or, more accurately, had not discerned the need to oppose many of the ecclesiastical corruptions of Rome.

Radical puritans were quick to add, however, that the early reformers were not thereby at fault for failing to reorganize the church according to the biblical pattern. They had not opposed several corrupt elements of Roman polity only because the Spirit of God had not yet granted them a full measure of light regarding those ecclesiastical matters. God, they believed, had been carrying out a reformation of the church in stages, progressively revealing further knowledge of the divine intentions through the course of time. For that reason, puritan precisionists argued that, in spite of the ecclesiological bankruptcy of the early reformers, they would not suffer damnation in the coming day of perdition because they had erred out of ignorance, not wilfully: the first protestants would thus be spared condemnation because they wholeheartedly embraced the full measure of light Christ had revealed in their day.[16]

By the Elizabethan era, however, this situation had changed. The radicals believed that people could no longer plead the ignorance of the original reformers because further light had been granted to English protestants at home and abroad during the Marian persecution;[17] now that this knowledge was widely available through the puritan press, failure to follow it would lead to certain and eternal destruction. The principle was laid down unequivocally by William Fulke in his Hampton Court sermon of 1570:

The effect is in few words: that horrible, intolerable and eternal torments remain for all them that now especially, when Babylon is now discovered, will have anything to do with her damnable errors and pernicious doctrine. For howsoever ignorance before her fall, though it were inexcusable, yet seemed to diminish the greatness of the crime. Now that her wickedness is openly displayed, no pretence

[16] This line of reasoning was not the property of puritans alone. Traditionalists like Richard Hooker relied upon the same basic argument to defend their forerunners in the Church of Rome. Richard Bauckham, 'Hooker, Travers and the Church of Rome in the 1580s', *Journal of Ecclesiastical History*, 29 (1978), 44.

[17] Peel (ed.), *Seconde Parte*, ii, 84.

can save men from the extremity of God's wrath, if they will still obstinately continue in her heresies.[18]

Obstinacy, rather than prelatical pride or even tyranny, was in a precise sense the real problem with those bishops of the English church who opposed puritan ecclesiastical reform. Their obstructionist policies were so appalling precisely because, despite the new light of the gospel that was now in the world and widely disseminated by godly preachers and publications, the prelates continued to commit the most 'filthy fornication' with Babylon's idolatrous religion.[19]

The recent history of the church of England was also of special interest to left-wing puritans, and it is here that discernible differences between the radicals and Foxe began to appear. Travers sketched the pattern of reform under the early Tudor monarchs in the following way: 'For a long space before [Henry VIII came to power, the English church] had lain dead . . . without any life.' Under Henry, 'diverse notable men rose up [who] . . . got at the last some life into it' by recovering 'certain articles of sound doctrine'. Then under Edward VI, the church 'was fully revived and recovered' except that she 'used no exercise to get her colour and strength again', and so retained that 'form of governing . . . whereunto it had been accustomed under popery'.[20] With the accession of Mary, the church was once again flung headlong into antichristian darkness. It would have been 'utterly destroyed' except that God, through the agency of Queen Elizabeth, 'quickened it being more than half dead, and raised it up like Phoenix out of the ashes again'. But significantly, Travers pointed out that Elizabeth's reform was incomplete in that she

[18] William Fulke, *A sermon preached at Hampton Court on Sunday being the 12. day of November, in the year of our Lord, 1570* (London, 1570), Sig. H2.

[19] With this in mind, it is interesting to note Travers's apparently atypical critique of the pre-Marian English reformers who, he said, 'were so wholly bent unto doctrine that they never thought of discipline . . . which, whether it were done by reason of the ignorance of those days, or of negligence, or for ambition and vainglory, or because they thought that popish discipline might be tolerated for a time' was, nevertheless, a 'great hindrance and discommodity of the church': Travers, *Ecclesiastical discipline*, 15–16. While most Elizabethan puritans revered the faith of the first English reformers, Travers's remark about the possible ambition and vainglory suggests that he, at least, may have had some doubts about their sincerity.

[20] Travers, *Ecclesiastical discipline*, 3–4. For a similar assessment of the reform under King Edward VI, cf. Peel (ed.), *Seconde Parte*, ii, 84.

had failed to abolish entirely a 'popish tyranny' among her prelates and establish a biblically grounded order for the church.[21] By saying this much, Travers diverged slightly from the pattern established by Foxe, the latter having underscored the effectiveness rather than the deficiencies of Elizabeth's reformation. In so doing, Travers appears to anticipate the historiography at the turn of the century of post-millennialists such as John Napier and Thomas Brightman. While Foxe, Napier, and Brightman all agreed that the Queen had played a God-ordained role in the Reformation, only Napier and Brightman suggest, as Travers had implied before them, that 'her established church could still become the seat of Antichrist'.[22]

With Napier and Brightman's publication of commentaries on the eschatological implications of the prophetic books of Daniel and Revelation at the turn of the seventeenth century, as well as those by Joseph Mede in 1627, a new and radically transformed understanding of the Parousia was, according to many modern scholars, inaugurated in English protestant thought.[23] It was in their writings, and not those of Foxe, that seventeenth-century apocalyptic expectations of the millennium as a future golden age on earth were beginning to surface.[24] John Foxe had worked within the conventional 'amillennial' eschatological framework, originally developed by Tyconius and Augustine at the end of the fourth century, that dominated medieval eschatology and formed the eschatological perspective of the magisterial reformers. According to this view, the millennial reign of Christ described in Revelation 20 was a spiritual reality that commenced, as Foxe explained it, at the victory of Constantine and ended,

[21] Travers, *Ecclesiastical discipline*, 3–4.

[22] Olsen, *John Foxe*, 78–9, 83. For a list of puritan grievances concerning antichristian elements in the Elizabethan church, see Hill, *Antichrist*, 43–8.

[23] Ball, *Great Expectations*, 80–7; Toon, *Puritans, the Millenium*, 27–31; Robert Clouse, 'The Apocalyptic Interpretation of Thomas Brightman and Joseph Mede', *Bulletin of the Evangelical Theological Society*, 11 (1968), 181–93; see also Clouse, 'Johann Heinrich Alsted and English Millenarianism', *Harvard Theological Review*, 62 (1969), 189–207; and Clouse, 'John Napier and Apocalyptic Thought', *Sixteenth Century Journal*, 5 (1974), 101–14.

[24] Olsen, *John Foxe*, 83–4: 'Thus there is a great gulf between Foxe and Brightman, and not the former but the latter is the ancestor of the apocalyptic hopes of the men of the 1640s.'

according to his calculations, in the fourteenth century. Thus, from the amillennial perspective, the millennium belonged wholly in the past while the future promised not a thousand-year earthly reign of Christ but the sudden end of history and the inauguration of eternity in a world yet to come. Neither Napier nor Brightman were thoroughgoing millennialists, but transitional figures, who nevertheless significantly transformed this accepted Augustinian amillennial eschatology by teaching a double millennium: one in the past (as the modified Augustinians early in the seventeenth century understood it) and one in the future that, as Brightman believed, had in part already begun in 1300 and would be more fully revealed in the near future.[25]

While the evidence is admittedly vague, it appears that a few radical churchmen of the Elizabethan period may also have departed from Foxe's Augustinian amillennialism in just such a way by entertaining hopes of what they called the 'latter-day glory', a hallmark of millenarianism in the next century.[26] This, at least, seems to have been the implication of a statement issued in an anonymous Elizabethan puritan petition addressed to the Queen. The petition prophesied that if Elizabeth should back the cause of reform, 'then shall the latter blessing fall upon your Highness as the latter rain from heaven, and surmount the former graces that already you have received, so that you shall be astonished and wonder that the Lord should yet find out ways to enlarge himself towards you'.[27] This is not, of course, a full-blown millennialism in the seventeenth-century sense, but it does at least indicate that already by the 1580s, some radical puritans were anticipating what Dr Bauckham has recently described as 'the trend

[25] To complicate the matter further, Brightman's description of this second, future millenium was rich enough to provide seed for both the post-millennialists (the belief that the millennial reign of Christ is a period *before* the return of Christ) and the pre-millennialists (the belief that the millenniun is a period that *follows* Christ's return) of the 1640s and 50s. See Ball, *Great Expectations*, 161–2, 168, 172; and Bauckham, *Tudor Apocalypse*, 223–4.

[26] On the theme of an expected latter-day glory, see Toon, *Puritans, the Millenium*, ch. 2.

[27] *A parte of a register countayning sundrie memorable matters, for the reformation of our church* (n.p., 1593), 320. For other ways in which radical puritans appear to have departed from Foxe, see Olsen, *John Foxe*, 152–60, 209.

toward optimism' that evolved in English apocalyptic thought during the 1590s following the defeat of the Armada.[28]

But this optimistic side of Elizabethan radical puritan eschatology was rarely unveiled, especially in the period before 1588. Instead, left-wing puritans focused their eschatological speculations on warnings of impending doom: the full wrath of God's vengeance was soon to be poured out upon the Antichrist and all his followers. They repeatedly raised the apocalyptic alarm and declared that unless the church hierarchy 'speedily' repented and returned to the apostle's discipline, the bishops would 'kindle the wrath [of God] against us where with all England . . . may shortly be set on fire'.[29] No one knew exactly what form this divine calamity would take, but biblical apocalyptic literature held portents of such terrifying events that, as one group of puritan laymen wrote, '[it] doth make our ears to tingle'.[30] While there are a few examples from the Elizabethan period of 'false prophets', who attempted to predict the exact dates of future apocalyptic events, radical puritans were uniformly unwilling to be too precise about when they believed these dreadful events would occur. Nevertheless, the feeling was running high, especially during the 1570s and 1580s, that signs of an imminent judgement were everywhere. As early as 1566, a communiqué from the Scottish reformed party warned the prelates of England that 'the days are evil, iniquity abounds, Christian charity is waxen cold and therefore we ought more diligently to watch, for the hour is uncertain when the Lord Jesus shall appear'.[31] In the 1580s, Dudley Fenner was convinced that 'the Lord has almost drawn out his wrathful sword' against England, while a contemporary puritan supplication to Parliament warned that England had 'fallen into the last and worst age', and that if Parliament failed to reform the church, 'God knows how great a multitude of us might be lodged in hell, and there cry and curse without ceasing, in the midst of the flames of eternal fire, before another parliament were assembled'.[32]

[28] Bauckham, *Tudor Aocalypse*, 173–80.

[29] Travers, 'Epistle', *Ecclesiastical discipline*, Sig. A3.

[30] *Parte of a register*, 231.

[31] Ibid. 127. For Elizabethan 'false prophets', see Bauckham, *Tudor Apocalypse*, 185–207.

[32] *Parte of a register*, 217, 271.

With rising expectations of the imminent return of the Lord, left-wing puritans were undoubtedly even more encouraged to take on the militant posture they assumed in the years before 1590. That appears to have been true for the London puritan preacher of St Clements without Temple Bar, Robert Johnson, when he stood before the High Commissioners in 1573. When the Bishop of Lincoln demanded that he subscribe and cease his public denunciation of the established church, Johnson refused to comply on the basis of his Apocalypse-based fear of the impending day on which he should find himself answering before a divine court:

> if I consent to this muzzling I can not see before God how I should or can answer it [in the day of coming judgement]: therefore the fear of this likelihood in these perilous days, full of confusion, is another argument that stays me from giving either promise by word or by subscription of hand, to hold my peace against the government of the Church as it is.[33]

Within a month or two Johnson was dead, the fourth puritan that year to fall victim to disease as a prisoner of conscience in the notoriously wretched prisons of London.[34] Coupled with their ecclesiastical legalism, the eschatological militancy of puritan extremists like Robert Johnson engendered the cause with a religious fervour that made them determined to oppose antichristian tyranny at all costs, even at the risk of limb and life.

As the years passed, however, and their efforts for national reform met with continued failure, some Elizabethan radical puritans found themselves compelled, in the urgency of the apocalyptic times in which they lived, to separate entirely from the established church in order to disentangle themselves from an institution that obstinately remained the instrument of Antichrist. Given the commonplace puritan conviction that the English prelacy was little more than an insidious extension of Antichrist's reign in the world,[35] complete separation was a reasonable, if none the less socially painful, step for some radical puritans to take. When the absolutism of those

[33] Ibid. 95–6.
[34] Patrick Collinson, *The Elizabethan Puritan Movement* (London, 1967), 152.
[35] Peel (ed.), *Seconde Parte*, i, 86.

puritans who would, as they put it, 'not so much as communicate with the tail of the beast',[36] was combined with their apocalyptic fears of the 'horrible torments' to be suffered by those who wore the mark of the beast,[37] ecclesiastical separatism seemed the only sure way to avoid the terrible wrath of God's impending judgement.

While that would be the path taken by a few, especially during periods of intense pressure and persecution from the authorities, with the dissolution of the puritan movement in the 1590s many more were inclined to turn their attention away from apocalyptic speculation at a time when they were also giving up the quest for ecclesiastical reform; in the mood of those quiet years before the accession of James I, they devoted their energies to the development of an individualistic eschatology centred on the pursuit of a personal salvation that would occur outside history in eternity.[38] Meanwhile, the apocalyptic tradition in England was to experience the beginnings of a major reinterpretation that would redirect interest from searching into and identifying patterns of the past, which typified the historical preoccupations of Foxe's eschatology, to giving greater attention to a biblical vision of the future, a change of focus that was eventually to pave the way for the outbreak of millenarianism among the Civil War sectaries.

The early Jacobean non-separating congregationalists and separatists who were active between the Elizabethan and Caroline periods appear to exhibit something of the impact of both of these tendencies. The decline in apocalyptic interest among some puritans at the end of Elizabeth's reign is evident in the way that eschatological speculation seems not to dominate the writings of Jacobean radicals to quite the same extent as it had in the works of their puritan antecedents of the 1570s and 1580s; yet there are indications that they had absorbed a good deal of the Elizabethan apocalyptic tradition. At the same time, there is significant evidence that some of the early Jacobean radical puritans and separatists were beginning to embrace the optimistic hope in a future period of earthly

[36] W. H. Frere and C. E. Douglas (eds.), *Puritan Manifestoes* (reprint edn., London, 1954), 36.

[37] *Parte of a register*, 306.

[38] Bauckham, *Tudor Apocalypse*, 210.

glory and bliss that characterized the eschatological concerns of several protestant theologians during the first quarter of the seventeenth century.[39]

Jacobean Radical Puritans

While the writings of Jacobean radical churchmen offer disappointingly little evidence reflecting the details of their periodization of church history, it is clear that—like John Foxe and sixteenth-century protestant reformers in general—all of them believed the present epoch to be the last one; theirs was the terminal generation, or, as Robert Parker simply wrote, they were witnessing in their day 'the last age of the world'.[40] Ever since Wyclif, Huss, Luther, and Zwingli—God's 'extraordinary' agents of reform—began to restore the gospel,[41] the Antichrist had become more visibly active: Satan, 'knowing his time to be short', William Bradshaw observed, was stirring up trouble throughout the church 'about unprofitable and popish ceremonies'.[42]

So the apocalyptic warnings were once again sounded in puritan manifestos urging the prelates and people not to meddle with the whore of Babylon, 'but to go out of her my people . . . that you may not be partaker of her sin, and that you receive not of her plagues'. This fear of impending disaster from on high impelled the more rigorous of the godly to disentangle themselves from 'all superstitions and idolatrous ceremonies of that whorish synagogue' that continued to be practised in many assemblies within the established church.[43] While a separatist disposition is clearly evident in this concern over the potential antichristian contamination arising from indiscriminate religious communion, the figure of the Antichrist actually cut both ways in left-wing puritan usage. It served not only to galvanize their opposition to profane elements in the established church, and to help identify the

[39] Katherine Firth, *Apocalyptic Tradition*, 249–53.

[40] Parker MS, ii, 2.

[41] William Ames, *The marrow of sacred divinity*, 147, in *The workes of the reverend and faithfull minister of Christ William Ames* (London, 1643); also Parker MS, ii, 14, and the marginal notes by Junius in the *Genevan Bible* (Frankfurt, 1599), for Rev. 14, where the three angels are identified with Wyclif and the early reformers.

[42] Bradshaw, *Several treatises*, 90.

[43] *Several treatises*, 116; 92–4.

godly community within that institution; it could also function as an instrument of integration, keeping the godly firmly within an ecclesial structure that, although corrupt, was not indissolubly so.[44]

As noted in the previous section, at the close of the sixteenth century, divergence from Foxe's view of church history is evident in English protestant apocalyptic theology with the modified Augustinian eschatology that evolved in the writings of John Napier and Thomas Brightman. Both rejected Foxe's description of a golden era for the church during the Constantinian period and also diverged appreciably from his amillennial schemata. Foxe viewed the millennium mentioned in Revelation 20 as the period from 300 to 1300, between the reign of Constantine, when Satan was bound, and the pontificate of Boniface VIII, when he was loosed in order to commence his persecution of Wyclif and Huss; but Napier and Brightman emphasized that while also believing Satan had been restrained during the post-Constantinian era by means of heathen rulers he nevertheless managed to reign in the church through the instrumentality of the Antichrist, so it could be said that 'the beast was born together with Constantine'. They also anticipated, unlike Foxe, a future millennial age of happiness when the church would experience increasing peace and prosperity following the defeat of Antichrist in Rome and the restoration of the Jews. Brightman, in particular, believed this period had already begun in 1300, though it remained largely hidden. His conviction was, however, that the millennial reign of Christ was in recent days gradually gaining strength, 'whereby continuance of the truth is promised for a thousand years' and 'does get ground and strength every day more, blessed be God for it'. Thus the New Jerusalem would be established, Christ would return in person, Jerusalem 'shall be translated at length from earth to heaven', and eternity inaugurated.[45]

[44] Peter Lake, 'William Bradshaw, Antichrist and the Community of the Godly', *Journal of Ecclesiastical History*, 36 (1985), 570–89.

[45] Thomas Brightman, *A revelation of the revelation . . . opened clearly with a logicall resolution and exposition etc.* (Amsterdam, 1615), 824, 559, as quoted in Clouse, 'The Apocalyptic Interpretation of Thomas Brightman and Joseph Mede', *Bulletin of the Evangelical Theological Society*, 11 (1968), 185–6; and Firth, *Apocalyptic Tradition*, 174.

Although Brightman was esteemed by many within the broader puritan community for his erudition, the 'post-millennial' views suggested by his writings were not always so warmly received early in the seventeenth century, even among many of the more advanced puritan writers. For example, John Cotton, who had been conducting experiments in radical churchmanship at St Botolph's in Boston as early as 1615, expressed grave misgivings about the doctrine;[46] similarly, Keith Sprunger has argued that the non-separating congregationalist William Ames remained entirely unmoved by the developing chiliastic eschatological climate.[47] In this, as in so many other respects, Ames appears to reflect the disposition of William Perkins whose 'lack of apocalyptic fervour', according to Dr Bauckham's assessment, 'marked him out from so many of his contemporaries'.[48] This is also true of Robert Parker, who quite specifically repudiated the millenarian heresies of the early church fathers, in particular the eschatology of Irenaeus, whose pre-millennialism is well documented.[49]

Nevertheless, despite Parker's disparaging view of Irenaeus and second-century pre-millennialism, a criticism commonplace within the reformed tradition, it is noticeable elsewhere in his *De politeia* that Parker himself appears to have broken with the Augustinian amillennialism of Foxe and embraced something very much like the millennial framework laid out by Brightman. Written just six years after Brightman first published *Apocalypsis apocalypseos* (1609), Parker's *De politieia* is perhaps unique in the literature of Jacobean radical ecclesiology for its remarkable agreement with Brightman's eschatology. At least there seems to be no other clear evidence among the Jacobean non-separating congregationalists of this inclination, though it is possible that the rejection of millennialism by Ames cited in Sprunger's biography of the puritan casuist is vague enough that it could be interpreted in amillennial, pre-millennial, or post-millennial terms. More-

See also Bauckham, *Tudor Apocalypse*, 223–4; and Christianson, *Reformers and Babylon*, 101–7.

[46] Olsen, *John Foxe*, 85.

[47] Keith L. Sprunger, *The Learned Doctor William Ames* (Urbana, Ill., 1972), 185.

[48] Bauckham, *Tudor Apocalypse*, 173.

[49] Parker MS, ii, 4, 8. On the millennial views of Irenaeus, see J. N. D. Kelly, *Early Christian Doctrines* (New York, 1958), 465 ff.

over, Ames had nothing but praise for Brightman, though typically, given his general silence on the subject of eschatology, he did not comment on Brightman's apocalyptic system.[50]

Robert Parker's views were, by contrast, considerably more developed than Ames's, and suggestive of at least a rudimentary form of pre-millennialism. Not only did Parker cite Brightman's commentary on the Apocalypse with approval, he also appears to have adopted Brightman's view of church history and so, in some respects, predates the millenarian interest of, for example, the distinguished London Independent pastor, Thomas Goodwin. Parker's millenarian views remained, however, largely unnoticed until the 1650s, when Sir John Wray published two apocalyptic tracts by the radical Jacobean churchman, *The mystry of the vialls opened*, 1651, and *An exposition of the powering out of the fourth vial*, 1650.[51]

Following the accepted periodization of orthodox protestant historiography, Parker declared that Antichrist had made significant advances during the earliest centuries of the church: even while 'the apostles yet lived, the mystery of iniquity' was at work building the foundations of his temple, so that by the close of the first century 'the spirit of Antichrist began to boil out'.[52] But unlike Foxe, who prized the Constantinian era as 'the flourishing age of the church',[53] Parker inclined toward the view of the Elizabethan radicals, as well as Thomas Brightman, who often described the state of the church under Constantine in more disapproving terms. Parker believed that by 'Constantine's days' the church had already 'decayed' and 'much declined' from its primitive

[50] See Ames's 'Preface' to William Bradshaw, *English puritanisme, containing the main opinions of the rigidest sort of those that are called puritans* (n.p., 1604), not paginated; Ames, *A fresh suit against human ceremonies* (Rotterdam, 1633), ii, 502; *Reply to Dr Mortons particular defence*, 9, 27.

[51] For Thomas Goodwin's fascination with the topic while still at Cambridge in the 1620s, see Ball, *Great Expectation*, 165. Parker's millennialism is also discussed in Frank Benjamin Carr, 'The Thought of Robert Parker (1564?–1614) and His Influence on Puritanism Before 1650' University of London Ph.D. thesis (1964), 256–60.

[52] Parker MS ii, 8. This concurs with, for example, Junius, who believed that 'the dragon . . . went about to molest the new birth of the church' in AD 36. See n. 1, for Rev. 20, in the *Genevan Bible*.

[53] *Actes and Monuments* (London, 1563), 0, as quoted in Olsen, *John Foxe*, 68.

purity.[54] Under the first Christian emperor 'episcopal prelacy increased . . . and the churches' discipline' became 'miserably polluted'. Then, specifically citing Brightman's commentary on the Apocalypse, he concluded that 'Constantine himself became an adversary' of the church.[55] After casting doubts, in this way, on the first Christian Roman emperor, whom Foxe had exalted as the paradigm of the godly ruler, Parker appears to circumvent entirely the need expressed by Brightman and others for an imperial instrument to dethrone the man of sin:[56] rather than James I, it was, according to Parker, the godly ministers 'by whom the Lord hath overthrown him [Antichrist] as Paul foretold by the breath of his mouth in their ministry'.[57]

Parker sensed that the complete destruction of Antichrist was close at hand and would occur, he believed, at the second coming of Christ, 'which I judge to be at the Jews' conversion', an event 'whereto we come near'.[58] In opposition to sixteenth-century reformed eschatology, however, he also appears to have modified the traditional Augustinian view that the millennium of Revelation 20 referred only to the period beginning with Constantine; he accomplished this by placing a second new millennium, as Brightman had, in the present era while also maintaining a vestige of the traditional view. Christ's return and the destruction of Antichrist are 'in some sort begun in our age'. 'To our times also and not to the fathers belongs the resurrection [of the] apocalypse 20: 4–5, wherein the church reigns with Christ one thousand years.'[59] Finally, Parker shared Brightman's conviction that the advancing eschaton was intimately bound up with the issue of ecclesiology and the struggle for reform in England. The millennium would arrive in maturity, he believed, on the shoulders of the reformed discipline advocated by the more

[54] Parker MS, ii, 9. [55] Ibid. 10.

[56] See Christianson, *Reformers and Babylon*, 41, 102, for Brightman's views on the role of a godly prince.

[57] Parker MS, ii, 16.

[58] Ibid. 15, 16. Proponents of a latter-day conversion of the Jews as a sign of the end times were widespread in protestant writings. See Ball, *Great Expectation* 107, n. 129.

[59] Parker MS, ii, 16. This is close to Brightman's vision of the second millennium, as expressed in *A commentary on the canticles*, in which 'the seeds of a coming millenarian emphasis are plainly evident'. Ball, *Great Expectation*, 172.

conscientious puritans, while the English episcopacy would suffer the fate of Laodicea:

> As for time to come, Christ promises under the type of Philadelphia, that Geneva shall not decay or wither, and shall hold the key of David, that is, the discipline unto the conversion of the Jews and become one with them: which promise is proper to the church set out by Philadelphia, whereas Laodicea shall be cast out as vomit not to be resumed.[60]

In this, as in so many other respects, Parker accurately mirrors the convictions of Brightman's commentary on the Apocalypse. Brightman believed the reformed discipline of Geneva represented the church of Philadelphia among the seven churches of Asia Minor, as described in the Apocalypse, while the church in England found its parallel in the image of Laodicea.[61] Nevertheless, Parker's eschatology, although more fully expressed than any of his contemporaries within the left-wing of the puritan movement, was not a comprehensive statement of a millennial system; at the same time, it is suggestive of a drift toward the pre-millennial chiliasm that was to characterize future radical puritan rhetoric at the outbreak of the Civil War.

Elizabethan and Jacobean Separatists

Against an apocalyptically shaded history of official persecution and repression, Elizabethan and early Stuart separatists conceived and played out their illegal ecclesiastical experiments within the eschatological climate of confrontation and crisis that prevailed in the circles of left-wing puritanism. As early as the 1570s, a belief in an imminent divine judgement of England, due to her antichristian church order, underlay the separatism of the small underground London congregation of which Richard Fitz was pastor.[62] Having imbibed the potent notions of the evolving English apocalyptic tradition, their imaginations were fired by the prophetic

[60] Parker MS, ii, 8.

[61] Christianson, *Reformers and Babylon*, 102.

[62] B. R. White, *The English Separatist Tradition* (Oxford, 1971), 30.

utterances of the gospels, Old Testament prophecies ('though more darkly, and as afar off') found in Isaiah, Nahum, Daniel, Ezekiel, and Joel, along with the writings of the apostles who 'gave much more evident and plain warning of these things'. But chief among them all, as Henry Barrow explained, was 'that heavenly book of the Revelation' where 'all these things are most particularly and most lively described'.[63] It was there that the separatists found a framework for understanding the flow of church history from apostolic times to the present and their uniquely ordained role within this unfolding divine drama.

Following the mainstream of English protestant interpretation, the separatists linked the rise of Antichrist in the church with the evolution of episcopal and papal power in Rome. Although a graduate of Clare College, Cambridge, Henry Barrow (like Browne and other radical puritans) held a certain contempt for the 'vain affected arts' of Oxbridge degrees in divinity.[64] Nevertheless, he admitted that, while he did not possess the theological learning and 'cunning to derive' the 'genealogies and pedigrees' of papistry, he believed he understood the story as well as anyone from simply reading 'that old book of God's Word. There indeed I remember Revelation 9 that I read of a star that fell from heaven unto the earth'. The event, thought Barrow, signalled the first appearance of the Antichrist, which the separatist judged occurred at the destruction of Jerusalem in AD 70.[65] Gradually, the power of the Antichrist matured and his presence became fully and visibly enthroned in Rome under the cloak of the papacy

[63] Henry Barrow, *The Writings of Henry Barrow, 1587–1590*, ed. Leland H. Carlson (London, 1962), 271–2; *The Writings of Henry Barrow, 1590–1591*, ed. Leland H. Carlson (London, 1966), 34.

[64] *Barrow, 1587–1590*, 344–5, 266; Robert Browne, *The Writings of Robert Harrison and Robert Browne*, ed. Albert Peel and Leland H. Carlson (London, 1953), 481. Barrow did not categorically reject the universities (*contra* F. J. Powicke, *Henry Barrow, Separatist (1550?–1593) and the Exiled Church of Amsterdam 1593–1622* (London, 1900), 115), any more than Field, Wilcox, and Travers. Frere and Douglas (eds.), *Puritan Manifestoes*, 98; Travers, *Ecclesiastical discipline*, 142–3. Like all radical puritans, Barrow had a healthy respect for 'any lawful arts or necessary sciences, any holy exercises or schools of institution': *Barrow, 1590–1591*, 223.

[65] *Barrow, 1587–1590*, 271; Henry Ainsworth and Francis Johnson, 'To the Kings Most excellent Maiesty' in *An apologie or defence of svch trve Christians as are commonly (but vnjustly) called Brownists* (Amsterdam, 1604), not paginated; Thomas Helwys, *A mystery of iniquity* (London, 1612), 84.

through whom he spread his 'abominable desolation and havoc' across Christendom. The separatists believed all this had been plainly 'foreshown' in the imagery of the three beasts from Relevation 13. John Wilkinson, the Colchester separatist leader, who very likely died in prison while writing the only surviving separatist commentary on the Apocalypse,[66] speculated that the first beast represented the advent of episcopal power in the early life of the church when 'the prelacy and priesthood of many nations, as patriarchs, cardinals, archbishops, bishops . . . did usurp and take on them the office of Christ Jesus in making laws and canons . . . to be of all men observed and obeyed'. The second beast he reckoned to be a figure of the Pope, 'which thing was effected and came to pass when Phocas being Emperor, he promoted Boniface, then prelate of Rome, to be universal bishop' in AD 603. The third beast, cast in the 'image of the first beast', represented for Wilkinson not merely the popish remnants that yet survived in some aspect of the established church, as radical puritans claimed, but the English church constituted in its entirety.[67]

Wilkinson shared with Calvin and the wider reformed tradition a conviction that the kingdom of Antichrist could be identified by way of the corruptions that had crept into the polity and ceremonial practices of the church.[68] It was part of the very character of the Antichrist to establish some form of church government of his 'own making', and so 'usurp the name of the church of Christ' by either adding to or taking from the divine order of the church given in the New Testament. This was also true of those who, as the separatist quaintly put it, 'worshipped the beast' by their involvement with a church that maintained even the vestiges of Roman

[66] For Wilkinson's career and imprisonment, see Champlin Burrage, *The Early English Dissenters* (Cambridge, 1912) i, 192–4.

[67] John Wilkinson, *An exposition of the 13 chapter of the revelation of Iesus Christ* (Amsterdam, 1619), 4, 20, 23. While there was some difference of detail, most separatist apologists described a similar pattern. Helwys, for example, believed the second beast was the English church, not Rome: *Mystery of iniquity*, 15–16. He did not comment on the third beast. For Barrow on Rev. 13, see *Barrow, 1587–1590*, 174–5, 337–9; *Barrow, 1590–1591*, 34–5.

[68] For example, Calvin explained that it 'behooves us . . . to see what was formerly the true use of ecclesiastical jurisdiction and what great abuse crept in . . . if we wish to overturn the Kingdom of Antichrist': *Institutes*, bk. 4, ch. 11, s. 5.

rites and rituals.[69] Thus, anyone who knowingly participated, however guardedly, in an ecclesiastical institution that continued to observe human ceremonies was bound to suffer the terrible judgement of God. Browne, for example, forewarned the godly that, despite their scrupulous attention to matters of personal piety, their false worship would lead to a fate worse than 'Sodom and Gomorrha', while Ainsworth predicted that the idolatrous worship in the church of England would procure a 'heavy doom' and 'provoke God to wrath' against those who remained within her.[70]

Understandably, separatists like Browne and Ainsworth believed that the whole tottering edifice of the English episcopal hierarchy, which bore the 'mark of the beast', would be the direct target of God's vengeful wrath; but monarchs, magistrates, and entire nations—papists, protestants, and puritans alike—were all included in the doomsday predictions of the separatists.[71] While Johnson identified the reformed churches of Europe as 'the sun and moon, the lights of the world', he nevertheless cautioned that the many antichristian corruptions that yet lingered in those church threatened 'some heavy judgement of God'.[72] It was the erstwhile separatist, John Murton, who, upon his return to England as a baptist, gave King James I and his minions of justice the solemn warning that 'the Lord Jesus Christ . . . shall judge all judges according to their works without respect of persons, and therefore [they] are commanded to kiss the Son lest he be angry and they perish in the way'.[73] By using examples from scripture, the separatists called down the same dire judgements upon the world around them, judgements they found so vividly portrayed in the prophetic books of the Bible. This was especially true when they turned to the vision of Armageddon in the Apocalypse, where they noted that God would soon

[69] Wilkinson, *Revelation*, 13–17.

[70] *Browne*, 76, 78, 200; Henry Ainsworth, *An arrow against idolatry* (n.p., 1640), 13.

[71] *Browne*, 206; *Barrow, 1587–1590*, 129, 234, 242, 553, 604–5; Francis Johnson, *A treatise of the ministery of the Church of England* 133; (Amsterdam, 1595), 133; Preface to *A trve confession of the faith* (Amsterdam, 1596), not paginated; Ainsworth and Johnson, 'To the Kings Most excellent Maiesty' in *Apologie*, not paginated.

[72] Francis Johnson, 'To the Christian Reader', in *A Christian plea conteyning three treatises* (Leyden, 1617), Sig. A3.

[73] John Murton, 'To the Reader', *Obiections answered by way of dialogue* (n.p., 1615), not paginated.

pour out his 'vials' upon the earth and begin 'the battle of that great day of God almighty' when the kings of the earth would, with the Antichrist, 'make war against the lamb and besiege the beloved city and the tents of the saints round about'. In the end, Christ and his saints would emerge victorious and the enemies of Christ would find themselves mercilessly flung 'alive into that lake of fire burning in brimstone'.[74]

In the minds of some separatists, it seemed as if the events leading up to this dreadful climax were already well under way toward their fulfilment. As Johnson explained, anyone who read 'with a single heart' the book of Revelation and 'compared with it the events of things partly come to pass already' would realize that the days of Antichrist were numbered.[75] Indeed, it was generally held by the separatists that the 'vials' of God's judgement 'in this latter age' had already been poured out upon the Antichrist in the writings of the 'Lutherans, Calvinists, Zwinglians, etc.', as well as in their own. Henry VIII, Edward VI, and Elizabeth I had also acted as instruments of God's judgement by abolishing the monasteries and routing the Roman Catholic clergy, thereby sending them 'into the bottomless smoking lake from whence they came'.[76] Other signs which showed that 'the days of greatest tribulation' were coming to pass before their eyes included a fresh outbreak of religious factionalism across the land (and, as Francis Johnson observed, even within their own separatist ranks!), as well as the persecution, imprisonment, banishment, and the occasional execution of their protestant co-religionists who had preached against Antichrist.[77]

Exactly what form the separatists believed this judgement would take is difficult to discern with any precision. In common with radical puritans, they were inclined to compare the present situation of their episcopal and puritan adversaries with Old Testament examples of the idolatrous Israelites, who

[74] *Barrow, 1587–1590*, 338; *Barrow, 1590–1591*, 35–6.

[75] Johnson, *Ministery*, 36.

[76] John Smyth, *The Works of John Smyth*, ed. W. T. Whitley (Cambridge, 1915), ii, 341; *Barrow, 1590–1591*, 35–7; Johnson, Preface to *True confession*, not paginated; Ainsworth and Johnson, Preface to *Apologie*, not paginated; *Browne*, 104.

[77] Sabine Staresmore, *Certain notes of M. Henry Ainsworth His Last Sermon* (n.p., 1630), Sig. A2; Helwys, *Mystery of Iniquity*, 85; Johnson, Preface to *True Confession*, not paginated.

physically suffered the wrath of God through plagues and foreign armies. The classic example was the story of how God brought 'desolation' upon the people of Israel when 'Jerusalem was broken up by the Babylonians, the temple burned, the people killed, and the rest carried prisoners into Babel'.[78] Such examples took on new urgency and realism in the wake of the growing military threat from the Counter-Reformation during the decade before the Armada and the period leading up to the outbreak of the Thirty Years War in 1618. Six years earlier, in 1612, Thomas Helwys wrote:

> Who can remain ignorant of these days and times and what ignorance is it, not to know that these are even the days and times here prophesied of. Have not wars and rumours of wars been heard of? has not nation risen against nation, and realm against realm? have there not been famines, and pestilence, and earthquakes in diverse places?[79]

The separatists understood the prophetic passages of the Bible in a historical fashion. They did not expect a simply spiritual judgement to descend from on high, but one that could equally as well include some form of physical devastation, as it seems Harrison was thinking when he warned: 'So let us take heed, that we do not so long eat and drink of the spoil and dance in security, until that David, Christ Jesus, come at [us] unawares, and take away all, and our lives therewith also, in most just judgement.'[80] Nevertheless, separatist warnings of an approaching judgement were not always taken by them to mean a physical destruction, as borne out by their belief that God's wrath was already being poured out through the 'weighty arguments' of their own publications.[81] Hence, when Barrow warned his opponents that Christ 'is coming with thousands of his saints' to war against the idolaters, he may not have necessarily intended a literal battle so much as a spiritual war of ideas. Thus he explained to Gifford, Christ and his saints would fight the beast 'mounted upon the white horse of his Word'.[82]

78 Ainsworth, *Arrow against idolatry*, 37.
79 Helwys, *Mystery of iniquity*, 3.
80 *Browne*, 76; note also Christianson, *Reformers and Babylon*, 65.
81 Johnson, Preface to *True Confession*, not paginated.
82 *Barrow, 1587–1590*, 533; *Barrow, 1590–1591*, 35.

While in this way the Book of Revelation served the separatists as a basis for prophecies of doom, it also held the promise of a period of glory and tranquillity for the true churches of God when Christ would reign with his faithful ones in perfection, an event that would occur after the fall of Antichrist but before Christ gave his church over to God the Father. While this optimistic note of a 'latter-day glory' was to be expounded and popularized with some success by Thomas Brightman in 1609, it is evident that the concept had already taken root much earlier in the writings of some separatists in much the same way that it had among the Elizabethan and Jacobean radical puritans discussed above.[83] As early as 1595, Johnson predicted that after the Lord destroys Antichrist, he will 'reign in his church by his own offices and laws, with his crown of glory upon his head and his sceptre of righteousness in his hand, until he give up the kingdom to God even the Father, that God may be all in all'.[84] A similar millenarian note was sounded by Ainsworth in 1607, when he explained that 'the Son of righteousness' will come to those who opposed Antichrist,

> with health under his wings, and they shall tread down the wicked as dust under the soles of their feet. Thus the redeemer will come unto them . . . and he will leave in the midst of it an humble and poor people, and they shall trust in his name, and the remnant of Israel shall do no iniquity nor speak lies.[85]

A decade later, Wilkinson hinted that oppressed saints could expect an earthly millennial reign with Christ, a conviction that was undergirded by his belief that a 'time of refreshing' was near,[86] while John Murton believed the Lord had already begun to 'destroy Antichrist's cruel kingdom'.[87] In his last book, Johnson expressed some doubt as to exactly when the latter-day glory would be fulfilled. In the preface, he wrote that only time would tell when 'the Lord of hosts shall reign in Mount Zion and in Jerusalem, and before his ancients gloriously . . . at the conversion of the Jews to the Christian

[83] For radical puritan views, see above nn. 26–8, 45.
[84] Johnson, *Ministery*, 36.
[85] Henry Ainsworth, *The communion of saincts* (Amsterdam, 1607), 289.
[86] Wilkinson, *Revelation*, 18, 37; Christianson, *Reformers and Babylon*, 110–11.
[87] Murton, 'To the Reader', in *Dialogue*, not paginated.

faith (which now hastens on)'. Later, however, he suggested that this might occur even before the Jewish conversion.[88] But whenever it was to be fully accomplished, Johnson, like Murton, believed that it was 'in part already fulfilled', though 'yet more fully to be effected'.[89] If this was the general conviction of the separatists, as it appears to have been, then the idea so often and deliberately expressed in the writings of Smyth, Ainsworth, and other separatists that Christ was immediately present and 'most lively seen' in the congregations of the separatists[90] takes on richer meaning and perhaps offers a glimpse into their vision of life in the latter-day glory; at that time Christ would reign on earth through disciplined churches like their own.[91]

Henry Jacob

Turning from the separatists to the Jacobean semi-separatist, Henry Jacob, one of the obvious curiosities of Jacob's ecclesiology is that, while standing more than knee-deep in the puritan stream of radical dissent, he rarely used the militant rhetoric of eschatological judgement which so permeated the writings of the separatists and of many of his predecessors within the Elizabethan radical puritan movement. Jacob, it seems, was more inclined to demand radical change in the classical language of reformed soteriology discussed in the previous chapter than in the threatening words of Old Testament prophets or the horrific imagery of biblical apocalyptic. Neither is there any evidence that Jacob gravitated

88 Francis Johnson, *A Christian plea conteyning three treatises* (Leiden, 1617), Sig. A3, 245. On the importance of the conversion of the Jews in seventeenth-century millennial expectations, see Toon, *Puritans, the Millenium*, 23–4.

89 Johnson *Ministery*, 36.

90 Johnson, *True confession*, art. 18; Ainsworth, *Communion*, 203; Smyth, ii, 414–15. The concept of Christ's presence was not unique to the separatists but part of the common currency of reformed rhetoric. e.g., see *Harmony of confessions* (London, 1634), 206; Travers, *Ecclesiastical discipline*, 192.

91 Separatist discussions of a future period when Christ would reign with his saints were not sufficiently developed to determine for certain whether they envisaged a spiritualized advent of Christ characteristic of post-millennnialism or a literal advent characteristic of pre-millennialism. For the distinction between post- and pre-millennialists on this point, see Ball, *Great Expectation*, 169–71.

toward the 'optimistic' millenarianism of Thomas Brightman which Jacob's co-religionist, Robert Parker, found so attractive. While he was aware of Brightman's commentary on Revelation,[92] Jacob showed no interest in the latter's passion for future chronology, but rather shared with William Ames, William Bradshaw, and other non-separating congregationalists of the Jacobean era (with the exception of Robert Parker), the distinction of remaining relatively silent on the subject of eschatology.

This may in part be due to the tendency of protestant divines in the first decade of the seventeenth century, noted by Katherine Firth, to leave apocalyptic speculation more and more in the hands of specialists, as the entire tradition became a highly sophisticated enterprise in which the mysteries of biblical prophecy could be discerned successfully only by skilled historians, linguists, and mathematicians. Thus, while the popularity of apocalypticism increased, she observes that it was on the wane among many of the more theologically trained ministers. The reason for this anomaly is not that puritan preachers became indifferent to the topic so much as that they believed the intricacies of the matter put the subject beyond their grasp. As Dr Firth has described it, 'the tradition had become top-heavy, weighed down by too many theories attempting to cover too much material' and 'so sophisticated that only the greatest minds could comprehend the complexities of language, history, chronology, and divinity necessary to pursue its development'.[93]

Whether or not this explains Jacob's relative disregard of the subject, it is nevertheless possible to piece together from passages scattered throughout Jacob's writings an eschatological vision that accurately reflects what Richard Bauckham has termed the 'historicist exegesis' of the Apocalypse that concurs with the eschatological interests of John Foxe and the Elizabethan puritan movement, especially in the period before the 1590s. This tradition directed its attention to a study of the past, and employed the Apocalypse primarily as an interpretive tool for tracing the course of the true church

[92] Henry Jacob, *An attestation of many learned, godly and famous divines* (Middelburg, 1613), 126.

[93] Firth, *Apocalyptic Tradition*, 179, 202.

throughout history—a church which appeared often only as a small, persecuted remnant—and for plotting the parallel event of the Antichrist across the centuries.[94]

The eschatological concerns of Jacob, limited as they appear to have been, were historically oriented in just such a way. For Jacob, the papacy represented the stronghold of Antichrist; but as a puritan radical, he perceived that the influence of this wily man of sin had, since medieval times, reached far beyond Rome into the very heart of the church in England, touching in his own day many otherwise godly individuals even within the puritan sector itself. The rise of Antichrist began, so he believed, during the initial centuries of the Christian era; the first visible sign that this mystery of iniquity had actually infiltrated the ecclesiastical machinery of the patristic church occurred when Dionysius became Bishop of Alexandria in the fourth century. Jacob identified Dionysius as the first 'diocesan ruling bishop', because he abolished the parity that had marked the relationship between ministers in the early church and took for himself 'more power than any of the rest of the ordinary pastors (though yet not any sole power)'.[95] The next and even more disturbing step happened shortly after the death of Augustine of Hippo in the fifth century when, he claimed, 'diocesan lord bishops' first appeared. Jacob averred that the prelatical offices in the English church in his own day were patterned after these original lord bishops of the patristic church because each English prelate in the Jacobean church 'ruled ordinarily in his diocese by his sole power'. It was not, however, until 'about 600 years after Christ' that the enemy of Christ openly revealed the extent of his perverse powers in the establishment of the 'catholic or universal bishop' at Rome during the pontificate of Boniface III, though he 'came not to his absolute greatness till diverse hundred years after'.[96] At that time the 'Antichrist began the desolation of abomination,

[94] Bauckham, *Tudor Apocalypse*, 15, 19, 29–31, 43–5.

[95] Henry Jacob, *Reasons taken out of Gods Word* (Middelburg, 1604), *Reasons* 7–8; *Attestation*, 273.

[96] Jacob, *Reasons*, 8; *Attestation*, 276; *A declaration & plainer opening of certaine points in the divine beginning* (Middelburg, 1611), 24–5.

which since has been everywhere set up, and with strong hand maintained'.[97]

Following the accepted protestant formula, Jacob believed that God had recently commenced the gradual overthrow of Antichrist through the heroic efforts of reformers like Luther and Zwingli, and that he and his early Jacobean contemporaries were thus living in the 'latter age'.[98] Among those who had taken an active role in advancing 'the light of the gospel' into what had become the nefarious domain of the Roman Antichrist, Jacob included Calvin, Beza, Bucer, Vermigli, Viret, Farell, Bullinger, Ursinus, and Junius on the Continent, the Marian martyrs and, of late, earnest puritans such as William Whitaker and Thomas Cartwright in England. All of these and many more true 'lights of religion' Jacob categorized as those 'who have been our masters and teachers in this matter of the church constitution and government'.[99]

But while Jacob recognized these stars on the religious horizon as 'learned, godly, and famous divines', he nevertheless believed—like other radical puritans and separatists—that some of them had erred in their judgements about ecclesiological matters to the extent that 'the mystery of iniquity (that is Antichrist) [was] advancing itself daily very much even by them'.[100] As early as 1599, during his altercation with the separatist Francis Johnson, Jacob willingly recognized that the three English protestant martyrs, Cranmer, Ridley, and Latimer, had perpetuated many of the ecclesiastical defects inherited by the English church from Rome; but because Jacob had, at the time of his controversy with the separatist, adopted an *adiaphora* defence of the established church,[101] he did not consider these corruptions of the three martyrs a serious matter. It was Johnson, he said, whose rigorist demands about the essential nature of ecclesiology put the separatist in a precarious position; for by saying that the practice of a biblical polity was necessary to salvation, Johnson, he argued, had implicitly damned the renowned

[97] Jacob, *Attestation*, 67. This reconstruction of the rise of Antichrist agrees favourably with Foxe, who calculated that the process culminated with the loosing of Satan from the pit in about the year AD 1000. Olsen, *John Foxe*, 67.

[98] Jacob, *Attestation*, 29.

[99] Ibid. 52.

[100] Jacob, *Reasons*, 54.

[101] See above, ch. 1.

martyrs. Johnson's escape was to adopt the 'further light' defence invoked by earlier separatists and other radical puritans when faced with the same charge: even though the worthy martyrs died while holding 'grievous errors' about church polity, Johnson reasoned that they 'yet notwithstanding died most constantly for the truths which they saw and testified, some for one, and some for another, as God manifested the truth unto them, as may be seen at large in their several histories in the *Acts and Monuments*'. But now, because further light about the nature of the church had been revealed by the Spirit through God's word, Johnson argued that the errors of the martyrs could no longer be used as an excuse for failing to practise a fully reformed polity.[102]

When Jacob himself began openly working for fundamental reforms in the English church in 1604, following the disappointments of the Hampton Court conference and Bancroft's renewed campaign to enforce conformity, Jacob adopted the same apology of ignorance traditionally employed by radical puritans and separatists in order to defend the innocence of the Marian martyrs. While he now admitted that his radical convictions about the essential nature of ecclesiology implied that 'our late blessed martyrs, Cranmer, Ridley, Latimer, Ferrar, etc.' had erred 'in faith to salvation', he nevertheless believed they should be judged

> as faithful servants of Christ according to that measure of light wherein they lived . . . True it is they erred in . . . external parts pertaining to Christ's prophecy and kingdom through the common sway of the times then: the mystery of iniquity (that is Antichrist) advancing itself daily very much even by them, and by these their errors, though they for their parts were unwitting and unwilling. The case thus standing with them, we are not to doubt but these their errors (though of themselves very great) were graciously pardoned in Christ: chiefly considering that these matters were not then examined nor anything looked into; which with us now these 40 years have been much debated, tried, and sifted.

Just as Johnson had asserted in 1599, Jacob now argued that with the appearance of more light in these latter days there was 'no excuse' for those who failed to continue the work of

[102] Henry Jacob, A. *Defence of the churches and ministery of Englande* (Middelburg, 1599), 32, 13.

reform.[103] The light of the gospel, having recently revealed the true extent of the restoration needed in the church, had progressively dawned across the land, and Jacob was convinced that further light would be graciously shed upon the hearts and minds of those who were open and receptive to it: 'the truth . . . has appeared to the world ever since the discovery of Antichrist more clearly than it did for many years before: so doubtless it will more and more appear still and be made further manifest to all men even where the gospel is received'.[104] Jacob's dynamic understanding of the progressive work of the Spirit, who rolled back the heavy layers of antichristian darkness that had encrusted the church of Christ for centuries and who increasingly illuminated the minds of men and women of good will and true faith, was a conviction widespread in left-wing puritan and separatist eschatology. More than a decade later, this doctrine would be immortalized by John Robinson in his celebrated farewell to the Plymouth-bound pilgrims at Delftshaven in 1620. Jacob's own use of the theme, along with his contemporaries, indicates that it was hardly original to the pilgrim pastor but had become, by then, a pervasive and potent image in the puritan mind.

John Robinson

Robinson's understanding of history and the future formed an important element of the conceptual context from which he approached the Bible in the process of working out his ecclesiological convictions. While aware of Brightman's seminal commentary on Relevation, Robinson, like Jacob, showed no discernible interest in the emerging fascination with millenarian prognostication that was exerting its influence on turn-of-the-century puritan apocalypticism. Like most separatist and radical puritans, Robinson's eschatology reflected primarily the historiographical heritage of John Foxe, though not without some modifications.

Concerning the periodization of church history, Robinson believed that within 'a few ages' following the establishment of

[103] Jacob, *Reasons*, 54–5.
[104] Jacob, *Attestation*, 18.

the primitive church, Antichrist visibly corrupted the churches of Christendom.[105] This did not happen all at once; rather, the Antichrist 'did in time and by degrees so universally corrupt and confound both persons and things as that God could no longer be said to dwell there by his visible presence and promises'.[106] Close to Foxe's view of English church history, Robinson believed there had been at one time true churches in England, pure in doctrine and practice like the first church at Rome: 'That there was at Rome a true church beloved of God, called saints by giving obedience unto the faith, is apparent: . . . So for England, I will not deny but there were at the first true churches planted in it by the preaching of the gospel and obedience of faith.'[107]

But following Rome's defection to Antichrist, Robinson claimed the consequences of this calamity were far more catastrophic for the church in England than Foxe appears to indicate. The martyrologist explained that while the fall of the Roman church involved succeeding generations of the English people in recurring battles with Antichrist which left them 'in such misery and desolation as yet to this day remaineth', a true church in England yet survived this evil onslaught in at least a hidden form.[108] Robinson, however, paints a more categorical and darker picture of the results, contending that the covenant bond itself, between God and the church in England, as well as with Rome, had been entirely dissolved: 'so did the Lord . . . break the covenant on his part and gave her as an harlot, a bill of divorce and put her away, and her daughter England with her, amongst the rest'.[109]

In common with the broad protestant apocalyptic tradition, Robinson believed God began a gradual conquest of Antichrist on the Continent and in England when Luther, Zwingli, Calvin, Cranmer, Ridley, Latimer, and others separated

[105] John Robinson, *A justification of separation from the Church of England* (Amsterdam, 1610), 32. Like Calvin, Robinson accepted the idea that Antichrist was present even within the church of the apostles, but he believed its presence was invisible 'in the seed only, or as an embryo in the womb, not perfectly framed, much less visibly brought forth': ibid. 21, 279.

[106] Ibid. 34.

[107] Ibid. 277.

[108] Haller, *Foxe's Book of Martyrs*, 150–2.

[109] Robinson, *Justification*, 278; *Of religious communion private and publique* (Amsterdam, 1614), 64.

themselves from the 'whorish' Rome. While these pioneers of reform were, according to Robinson's 'wholesome counsel' to the departing pilgrims at Delftshaven, 'precious shining lights in their times, yet God had not revealed his whole will to them'.[110] Still, the effect of their confrontation with the Roman Antichrist was decisive; in England 'the many and main corruptions of the Romish church' were stripped from the established church through the efforts of the Henrician reformers until the popish reign of Queen Mary proved to be a shattering setback to the advances they had made.[111]

With Mary's accession there occurred a 'universal apostasy of all the bishops, ministers, students in the universities, yea, and of the whole church of England'.[112] When Elizabeth succeeded Mary and the English protestant exiles returned from the Continent, reform was once again revived among those of an emerging puritan persuasion who were 'painful and conscionable in their ministry and lives'.[113] Even so, the church under this godly ruler had not been sufficiently wrested from the grip of Antichrist to be entirely free of apostasy. Robinson rejected as preposterous and naïve the intriguing defence of the Elizabethan settlement marshalled by the puritan conformist, Richard Bernard of Worksop, who claimed that the English church had, in effect, become a true, albeit not perfect, church in the reformed tradition of Geneva through the faith and witness of the Marian underground churches, and through the 'covenant' (as Bernard called it) that was made in Elizabeth's first Parliament. From Robinson's perspective, however, the succession of the protestant Queen served only to dissolve the heretical Marian constitution, while the people continued to worship in the old parish churches that remained fundamentally tied by the cords of Antichrist; what Bernard called the

[110] Edward Winslow, *Hypocrisie vnmasked* (London, 1646), 97. Robinson's view of the early reformers was thus identical with that of other radical puritan churchmen. While the reformers had not received as much light as their successors concerning ecclesiology, this did not condemn them, as Joseph Hall said Robinson's position would logically do. Instead, Robinson said they were saved by ignorance: John Robinson, 'An answer to a censorious epistle', printed in Joseph Hall, *A common apologie of the church of England* (London, 1610), 34; Robinson, *Justification*, 98.

[111] Hall, *Apologie*, 63.

[112] Robinson, *Justification*, 54.

[113] Ibid. 81.

'solemn covenant' in Parliament was, according to Robinson, nothing more than 'a profane and presumptuous enterprise'.[114]

While he acknowledged the 'learning and godliness' of many puritans, Robinson suggested they were not so wise that they might not err, nor so godly that they might not 'reproach the truth'.[115] They were 'but men' and so, as Jacob had said about the Henrician reformers, he believed they were able 'to support Antichrist in a measure'. Puritan divines wore the 'mark of the beast' to the extent to which they submitted to the spiritual jurisdiction of the English hierarchy, 'some in their forehead and more professedly; and others as effectually, though more covertly, in their right hand'.[116] Consequently, they led many in the 'most deceivable ways, wherein the deepest mystery of iniquity, and the most effectual delusion of Satan that can be . . . as is by Mr. Barrow and others clearly discovered'.[117]

Robinson was persuaded that the effectiveness of the puritans as a reforming force within the old ecclesiastical order had ultimately collapsed because of their growing unwillingness to break with the security of the past and follow the further light God had revealed through the scriptures. The tap-root of the puritan failure could be seen in the way

> many of the most forward professors in the kingdom are well nigh as superstitiously addicted to the determinations of their guides and teachers, as the ignorant papists unto theirs, accounting it not only needless curiosity, but even intolerable arrogance to call into question the things received from them by tradition.[118]

Robinson perceived this deference to received tradition among many puritans to be 'a misery' that afflicted not only the godly in England, but contemporary Continental protestants as well; it was a malady that stifled their vulnerability to the

[114] Ibid. 460. [115] Ibid. 48–9.

[116] Ibid. 49; Robinson, *Of religious communion*, 31. Robinson cited the judgement of the fifteenth-century martyr, John Claydon (as found in *Foxe's Acts and Monuments*) who said that receiving the bishop's license to preach was 'the true character of the beast, i.e. Antichrist'. Robinson, *The Manvmission to a manvdvction* (Amsterdam, 1615), 4. While this may indicate Robinson's use of Foxe, he may also have been quoting from Francis Johnson, *Certayne reasons and arguments proving that it is not lawfull to heare the present ministerie of the Church of England* (Amsterdam, 1608), 59, where the Claydon passage from Foxe was cited in full for the same purpose.

[117] Robinson, *Justification*, 49. [118] Ibid.

living Word and their courage in the face of opposition, both characteristics of the earliest reformers, and it therefore represented the abandonment of the original protestant spirit, a situation that was 'much to be lamented'.[119]

As for himself, Robinson saw the Reformation as an event that was gradually being unfurled in history through the power of God's will. To that extent, he shared, along with other radical puritans and separatists, something of Thomas Brightman's optimistic and progressive understanding of the immediate historical situation in which, as Brightman wrote, 'the truth does get ground and strength every day more'.[120] Reminding the Plymouth-bound Leiden separatists of the 'further light' clause they had embraced years earlier in the separatist covenant at Gainsborough, Robinson expressed his conviction that because the church had 'so lately come out of such thick antichristian darkness' he was 'very confident the Lord had more truth and light yet to break forth out of his holy Word'. Although these words have become a celebrated symbol in modern literature of the adventurous spirit that inspired the perilous Atlantic crossing of the *Mayflower* separatists, the original context in which they would have been heard was charged with apocalyptic significance, and the implications would not have been lost on the godly pilgrims of Leiden. Their pastor had set the journey to a new world within the broad sweep of salvation history in which these pilgrim saints understood themselves to be playing a momentous part.[121]

Robinson believed that the true heirs of the reforming spirit that had motivated Luther and Calvin were the separatists; they alone in their day were willing to participate fully in the march of divine history to be, as P. H. Ballard has put it, the Lord's 'pioneers into the future pushing back the frontiers of

[119] Winslow, *Hypocrisie vnmasked*, 97.

[120] See above, n. 45.

[121] Winslow, *Hypcrisie vnmasked*, 97–8. Robinson's celebrated farewell speech to the departing pilgrims was recorded some 25 years after the event by Winslow. Timothy George has noted (and challenged) the tendency of historians to cast Robinson, on the basis of this famous passage, as a precursor of modern liberalism, individualism, religious toleration, and American democracy, rather than as the representative figure of seventeenth-century Calvinist separatism that he was: Timothy George, *John Robinson and the Separatist Tradition* (Macon, Ga., 1982), esp. 91–2.

God's historical will'.[122] But this willingness to follow the light they had received—by moving out of what they perceived to be an increasingly ossified puritan 'tradition' into the liberty of separatist practice—was also motivated by the pessimistic side of separatist eschatology. They were carrying out their ecclesiastical initiatives in 'the latter days', Robinson said, 'when Satan in his instruments [does] bend his force most directly against, and with might and main oppose, the sovereigny and crown of our Lord Jesus that he may not rule in his church by his own officers and laws'.[123] The Antichrist was alive and active in England because the old order remained so 'deeply drenched in apostacy' and continued to 'stoop to Antichrist in his offices and ordinances'; 'yet is there another King,' Robinson warned, 'one Jesus, Acts 17: 7, which shall return and pass a heavy doom upon the rebellious'.[124]

In these final days, the 'odious co-mixture' of the parish assemblies 'is that which advantages hell, in the final obduration and perdition'. Complete separation from the institutions of Antichrist was therefore necessary in order to avoid the judgement about to descend upon the English church, just as Lot finally 'forsook' the city of Zoar 'for fear of the same just judgement which had overtaken the rest of the cities'.[125] Recalling the warnings of the Apocalypse, Robinson advised faithful obedience in all matters doctrinal and ecclesiastical, 'knowing that he which worships the beast and his image, and receives his character in his forehead or in his head, shall drink of the wine of the wrath of God . . . and shall be tormented with fire and brimstone'.[126] Even the 'least ceremony or circumstance' of biblical church order should be conscientiously and visibly observed, 'knowing that if the Lord should let Satan loose upon us . . . the least sin would

[122] P. H. Ballard, 'The Dynamic of Independency', *Baptist Quarterly*, 23 (April 1970), 244. This should not be taken to mean, however, that Robinson or other separatists saw themselves blazing a new ecclesiastical trail. That had already been accomplished in the first century. They were merely clearing the old path originally cut by Christ and the apostles. See Robinson *Justification*, 40; and Geller's observation in Lawrence D. Geller and Peter J. Gomes, *The Books of the Pilgrims* (New York, 1975), 13.

[123] Robinson, *Justification*, 268.

[124] Robinson, 'Censorious epistle', 33, 37.

[125] Ibid. 141, 116.

[126] Robinson, *Justification*, 71.

prove a burden untolerable'.[127] The separatists were concerned to *practise* biblical ecclesiology in word and deed, he concluded, in order to avoid 'pulling down wrath from heaven upon our heads'.[128]

Robinson never explained exactly when he believed these 'latter days' in which they now found themselves would draw to a close. Nor did he ever indicate clearly that he envisioned a future period of glory for the saints when they would reign in triumph for a thousand years with Christ on earth. There is, however, one passage that, although admittedly vague, is laden with eschatological imagery and potential millenarian meaning. Using the biblical language of the harvest, which looms large as a figure of eschatological consummation in New Testament usage, Robinson explained:

> And the many that are already gathered by the mercy of God into the kingdom of his son Jesus, and the nearness of many more through the whole land (for the regions are white unto the harvest) do promise within less than a hundred years (if our sins and theirs [i.e., the godly in the church of England] make not us and them unworthy of this mercy) a very plenteous harvest.[129]

This conviction about the return of Christ in the near future, along with Robinson's sanguine expectation of the salvation of so many, laced the separatist's otherwise grim apocalyptic warnings with a theology of hope that looked forward to a blessed destiny for the separatists, as well as for many of the godly yet remaining in ecclesiastical Babylon.

It is clear that the apocalyptic visions which provided a substantial part of the conceptual backdrop of the Elizabethan and early Stuart era infused the puritan campaign, as well as the outlawed enterprise of the separatists, with a potent rationale for their radical activities. They understood human history to be a stage upon which a pre-ordained, cosmic conflict was being waged between Christ and Satan. In the prophetic passages of scripture they believed they had a window on particular divine patterns to be found in the vast and otherwise hidden movements of the centuries. What is

127 Robinson, *Justification*, 23.
128 Robinson, Preface to *Of religious communion*, not paginated.
129 Ibid. 62.

more important, they saw themselves in this vision not merely as observers but, by their openness to 'new light' and their unyielding opposition to the despised manifestations of the Antichrist in the world, as key participants in this monumental drama. A plain reading of the Old Testament prophets, the gospels and epistles—but especially the Apocalypse—promised dramatic changes in the near future, either by way of a cataclysmic end to history itself with the sudden return of Christ or, as a new vision began to emerge at the turn of the century, in a coming utopian era of spiritual prosperity and peace for the saints of Christ before the end of time. In either case, they saw themselves as conveyers of this future. It was a future in which their own participation would hinge, in part, upon their faithfulness to walk with the Lord's assistance in all his ways, in both doctrine and ordinances, as Christ had made them known or would make them known more fully.

3

CHURCH MEMBERSHIP AND SAVING FAITH

Elizabethan Radical Puritans

THAT Calvin placed a high value on church membership has already been observed; he considered it ordinarily 'necessary . . . to our salvation'.[1] This was a broadly held conviction in Continental reformed circles: as the *Helvetic Confession* put it, outside 'the true church . . . there can be no certain salvation'.[2] Neither Calvin nor his reformed contemporaries intended to suggest by this classical formula that church membership and salvation were necessarily correlated. Because of the mysterious and inscrutable character of predestination, true Christians could and very likely did exist outside the defined boundaries of the visible church; these were the hidden elect, known only to God, and should be accounted members of the invisible, universal church, although they had found no home within the institutional structures of a particular church. For precisely the same reason, reformed protestants believed there were in all probability also many reprobates, those destined by the will of God for eternal damnation who, nevertheless, possessed membership within the visible church on earth.[3] They were the deceiving hypocrites who, in their own will and strength, had manufactured a counterfeit faith; damned in the eyes of God for their inward wickedness, they yet appeared in the flesh to be true and faithful believers.[4] As a consequence, all visible churches were likely to be mixed assemblies of both

[1] See above, ch. 1, n. 37.

[2] *Harmony of confessions* (London, 1634), 208–9.

[3] John Calvin, *Institutes of the Christian Religion*, ed. J. T. McNeill, trans. F. L. Battles, (London, 1960), bk. 4, ch. 1, s. 7. *Harmony of confessions*, 217.

[4] Calvin, *Institutes*, bk. 4, ch. 1, s. 7.

kinds: like the parables of the fish and the wheat-field in Matthew 13, the church on earth included good fish and bad, both wheat and tares.[5] The invisible church was pure, comprised of God's elect alone, while the visible church was polluted by impostors.

But in the development of radical puritan ecclesiology, it is important to note that this crucial distinction between the true saints and the deceivers in Calvinist theology existed to a large extent only as a kind of theoretical hypothesis; for if, as puritans believed, the hypocrites within the church militant could not actually be discerned by the human eye, so masterful and subtle was their subterfuge, then their actual presence could only be a matter of speculation based on the doctrines of scripture. Therefore, the distinction between visible and invisible churches was, in practical terms, of little purpose, except in so far as it provided a theological apologetic against what they perceived to be the unorthodox perfectionist theories of the radical sectaries, the sixteenth-century 'Donatists' and 'Cathari' among the Continental anabaptists and, by some accounts, among the radical puritans and separatists of England. Indeed, when free of their anti-sectarian polemic, this distinction between the two churches in most late sixteenth-century Calvinist confessional formulations was not, as John New has noted, always so carefully guarded. In the *Belgic Confession*, for example, the section on the church begins with a discussion of the universal church of the elect, which exists in 'the mind and will' of God but in no particular place on earth. Yet without making a clear transition from one subject to the other, the *Belgic Confession* proceeds to discuss the nature of the visible, particular church in such a way that, unless the distinction is assumed, one is never sure if 'this holy company . . . of those that are to be saved' refers only to the invisible, or possibly to the visible church as well.[6]

This ambiguity provides the context for several passages in which reformed Confessions appear to describe the visible church in terms that sound very much like the invisible

[5] Ibid., s. 13; *Harmony of confessions*, 209–10.

[6] *Harmony of confessions*, 218–19. See also the observation of John F. H. New, *Anglican and Puritan: The Basis of Their Opposition, 1558–1640* (London, 1964), 33.

church of the elect, as when they identify the church militant with a select company of saints who are separated from the world by virtue of their faith and holy conduct. The *French Confession*, for example, defined the visible church as 'a company of the faithful, which agree together in following the Word of God, and in embracing pure religion'; in the *Belgic Confession*, true members were said to be recognizable by their godly conduct: they defied sin, crucified the flesh, and lived righteously, 'not as if no infirmity at all remained still within them, but because they do fight all their life long against the flesh by the power of the spirit'.[7] Members of a true, visible church were, in other words, active, visible saints.

As is well known, first generation 'magisterial' reformers insisted that a true church could be distinguished from its false competitors by the presence of two notes, or marks: (1) the faithful preaching of the Word, and (2) the correct administration of the sacraments. It was among second-generation reformers, however, that a third sign, discipline, was added to the original two, the earliest expressions of this three-mark doctrine being found in the writings of Martin Bucer.[8] While it is true that Calvin always formally adhered to the classical two marks of early protestantism, he did not disregard the importance of discipline and seems to have taken the necessity of such a discipline in the church for granted. While he believed that the presence of even openly profane members did not inevitably make a church a false one, he taught that, ideally, the church should never indiscriminately share its membership with the visibly unworthy.[9] Moreover, Calvin asserted that a level of pollution could be reached in which the abundance of openly wicked persons within a visible church would lead to the necessity of

[7] *Harmony of confessions*, 217, 219.

[8] P. D. L. Avis, '"The True Church" in Reformation Theology', *Scottish Journal of Theology*, 30 (1977), 319–45; Robert M. Kingdon, 'Peter Martyr Vermigli and the Marks of the True Church', in F. Forrester Church and Timothy George (eds.), *Continuity and Discontinuity in Church History* (Leiden, 1979), 198–214; V. Novskov Olsen, *John Foxe and the Elizabethan Church* (Berkeley and Los Angeles, 1973), ch. 3, esp. 141–8; and Kenneth R. Davis, 'No Discipline, No Church: An Anabaptist Contribution to the Reformed Tradition', *Sixteenth-Century Journal*, 12 (1982), 43–58, who points to anabaptist influence on Bucer in this matter.

[9] Calvin, *Institutes*, bk. 4, ch. 1, s. 15.

separation.[10] Calvin never defined just when this point would be reached, yet his concern here and elsewhere does testify to the considerable interest Calvin placed in the role of ecclesiastical discipline.[11]

Nevertheless, the elevation of discipline to the formal, technical status of a church 'mark' by most later Calvinists, especially after 1560, is a curious addition to the original protestant scheme. Second- and third-generation evangelicals never offered an explanation for this addition, nor, for that matter, did they ever acknowledge they had even made one. Consequently, any attempt to discover the motivation for this modification must necessarily be a matter of conjecture. P. D. L. Avis suggests the three-mark doctrine developed out of pastoral necessities of later reformers. A tightly disciplined community would be 'more practicable' than the dynamic, less coherent ecclesiology of the earliest reformers.[12] On the other hand, George Yule has argued that the shift toward what he calls the legalism among second-generation Calvinists, of which the inclusion of the third mark is symptomatic, may have been their response to the formidable theological barricades raised by the Roman Counter-Reformation at Trent.[13] While it is also easy to believe that discipline would naturally have come to play a more prominent role in second-generation protestant ecclesiology through the seemingly inevitable drift toward institutionalization of any ideological movement, the addition may reflect as well the subtle changes that were occurring in the theology of Calvin's spiritual

[10] Implied in Calvin's statement, 'we claim too much for ourselves if we dare withdraw at once from the communion of the church just because the morals of all do not meet our standard or even square with the profession of Christian faith': ibid., ch. 1, s. 19. The qualification, 'at once', implied that Calvin believed separation would eventually become necessary, an act that itself implies the church had grown utterly corrupt. Cf. also ibid., ch. 12, s. 11, for the same qualification with reference to private members separating because of vices among the elders.

[11] For a discussion of the significance of church discipline in Calvin's thought, see François Wendel, *Calvin: The Origin and Development of his Thought* (London, 1976), 298–301; Harvo Hopfl, *The Christian Polity of John Calvin* (Cambridge, 1982); 115–21, 211; and R. N. Caswell, 'Calvin's View of Ecclesiastical Discipline', in G. E. Duffield (ed.), *John Calvin*, 210–26.

[12] Avis, in '"The True Church"', 331; see also, Kingdon, 'Peter Martyr Vermigli', 200, who offers a similar rationale.

[13] George Yule, 'Continental Patterns and the Reformation in England and Scotland', *Scottish Journal of Theology* (1969), 321.

progeny concerning the issue of soteriological assurance.

As discussed above in Chapter 1, reformed theologians after Calvin made sanctification, or the visible 'effects' of grace, the foundation for assurance of salvation, while Calvin had taught that faith, not works, was itself assuring.[14] According to R. T. Kendall's analysis, the result of this small theological deviation is that reformed theology after Calvin became increasingly introspective and preoccupied with discerning evidence of personal obedience and good works as the visible signs of true faith.[15] In light of this, it seems likely that the Calvinist modifications in soteriology also made their way into reformed ecclesiology through the addition of discipline as a third mark of the church, developing therein an institutional framework that reflected the special interest of the 'experimental predestinarian tradition'; certainly, the three-mark doctrine would have been entirely compatible with the increasing value placed on sanctification by Calvin's successors on the Continent and in England.

The new soteriology would have also had implications not only for the formal definition of the church in terms of which marks denoted the boundaries of a true institution, but also for the meaning of church membership itself. This is especially clear in the ecclesiological writings of the Elizabethan radical puritans. Although the puritan precisionists accepted and worked from within the loose structure of the English parish system, they did not expect that every resident of every parish would be fit subjects for membership. To this end, they devised a predominantly exclusive—rather than inclusive—ecclesiastical policy, seeking to limit membership to a select company of the faithful, those whom they understood to have been called by God, separated from the ungodly, and dedicated to visible works of love in accordance with the

[14] See above, ch. 1.

[15] Kendall concluded that 'the origin of this departure is linked to Beza's doctrine of limited atonement; when Christ is not held forth as the ground of assurance, the result is not only introspection but a need for man to assure himself upon the very grounds Calvin warns against': R. T. Kendall, *Calvin and English Calvinism to 1649* (Oxford, 1979), 38. But note Collinson's criticism in 'England and International Calvinism, 1558–1640', in Menna Prestwich (ed.) *International Calvinism 1541–1715* (Oxford, 1985), 217.

commandments of Christ. According to Field and Wilcox, a true visible church was

a company or congregation of faithful people, whom God has chosen to himself, and gathered out of the world by the preaching of the Gospel, who following the same and embracing true religion, do in the unity of the spirit strengthen and comfort one another, daily, growing and increasing in true faith, framing their lives, government, orders and ceremonies, according to the Word of God.[16]

The church was to strive for visible purity from moral 'pollution', Travers explained, and membership should be restricted to 'lovers and professors of the truth'.[17] For this reason, Laurence Chaderton determined that 'the polluted should have no passage into the church . . . no noisome beast should be found there'.[18]

While always admitting that the visible church could never approach the perfection of the invisible church in this life, radical puritans, like the Continental reformers, did not always clearly regard the visible and invisible churches as two entirely distinct societies. The purity of the church triumphant should, they believed, be reflected in the church militant. Travers, for example, thought that the prophetic vision of Psalm 45, in which David looked forward to the day when Christ would sit 'in the midst of the church', did not refer merely to the church triumphant but had 'some relation to the beginning of [Christ's] kingdom in this life'. The deduction Travers drew from his exegesis of this Psalm was that the visible church should therefore be composed only of members who are doctrinally orthodox and who behave accordingly. Members 'ought not to be brutish and ignorant', and all 'men of vicious life and given to all sin and wickedness are to be cast out and banished from the church'. The visible church, he concluded, should be 'kept as near as is possible free and clean from all pollutions and profanations'.[19]

[16] *A Parte of a register countayning sundrie memorable matters, for the reformation of our Church* (n.p., 1593), 539.

[17] Albert Peel (ed.), *The Seconde Parte of a Register* (Cambridge, 1915), i, 171.

[18] Laurence Chaderton, *A fruitfull sermon vpon the 3. 4. 5. 6. 7. & 8. verses of the 12 chapters of . . . Romans* (London, 1584), 70.

[19] Walker Travers, *A full and plaine declaration of ecclesiastical discipline* (n.p., 1574), 10–11.

The two criteria of doctrinal orthodoxy and godly conduct listed by Travers seem to have been for the extremists the only requirements for church membership. Visible saintliness in religious and moral conduct of an individual was of primary concern. Udall, for example, explained that 'drunkards, papists, etc.' were 'not of the church, but without, 1 Cor. 5: 12, and therefore are not to meddle in any action [of the church]'.[20] But the radicals also placed a high priority on understanding: every member should offer an adequate account of his or her faith which accurately reflected the doctrinal teaching of the puritan clergy.[21] While, without further elaboration, these two requirements of godly conduct and biblical orthodoxy might appear innocuous enough, given the context of second-generation Calvinist doctrines regarding assurance the implications of the two criteria of orthodox faith and a godly life would have been for them rich with soteriological significance. As William Perkins put it with stark simplicity, 'knowledge of God's will joined with obedience' provided the saints with 'an *infallible* mark of one that is in communion with Christ'.[22]

Hence, the concern of radical puritans went beyond mere doctrinal orthodoxy to include *visible* evidence of true, saving faith by means of what they called an 'open' or 'outward' profession of faith that issued in a visibly active and obedient membership.[23] The 'rigid self-discipline and nervous, incessant activism of the puritan life', to use Michael Walzer's phrase,[24] found its theological basis in the commonplace puritan conviction that true faith was more than simply intellectual assent: it must also find expression in demonstrable obedience. That, from the human point of view, was the *sine qua non* for discerning evidence of saving faith among godly puritans. Hence, Chaderton's dictum: 'the Lord is more delighted with

[20] John Udall, *A demonstration of the trueth of that discipline which Christe hath prescribed in his worde for the gouernement of his Church* (n.p., 1588), 31.

[21] *Parte of a register*, 151.

[22] William Perkins, *The works of that famous and worthie minister of Christ . . . M. W. Perkins* (London, 1605), 374 (my italics).

[23] W. H. Frere and C. E. Douglas (eds.), *Puritan Manifestoes* (reprint. edn., London, 1954), 119; Travers, *Ecclesiastical discipline*, 166.

[24] Michael Walzer, *The Revolution of the Saints: A Study in the Origins of Radical Politics* (New York, 1976), 18.

obedience than with naked and bare knowledge'.[25] Thus, the activism of the radicals was more than a concerted effort for political or economic gain: there were from a sixteenth-century perspective higher stakes involved, for through active self-discipline in things of the faith, the radical puritan sought assurance and testimony of his or her eternal destiny. The will of Henry Hastings, the puritan Earl of Huntingdon, made precisely that point when he wrote, 'my days are not given me to be spent securely and carelessly . . . but religiously and soberly which must give assurance to myself and yield testimony to others that I am one of the number of those who are chosen to be children of so holy a Father who commands us to be as holy as He is holy'.[26] The import of this for the ecclesiological reforms desired by the more advanced Elizabethan puritans was that, by restricting membership to the 'visibly elect' and granting a significant participatory role to congregational life and discipline, membership in such an institution offered a controlled public arena in which the saints could actively exercise their gospel duties of mutual exhortation, edification, and of provoking one another to the doing of good works, providing thereby further testimony of their chosen status.

Left-wing puritan polity provided an unparalleled opportunity within the English church for the active involvement of all members in the affairs of church government. In the election of ministers, in the discipline of congregational members, and in 'every matter of great weight and importance', the people were to be involved in the decision-making process.[27] Moreover, each member was to be actively engaged in serving the whole: each 'must be one another's member,'

[25] Chaderton, *Fruitfull sermon*, 61.

[26] Quoted in Claire Cross, *The Puritan Earl: The Life of Henry Hastings* (London, 1966), 52. See also comments by A. S. P. Woodhouse in *Puritanism and Liberty* (London, 1966), 44–5; Owen C. Watkins in *The Puritan Experience* (London, 1972), 9; and William Haller, *The Rise of Puritanism* (Philadelphia, 1972), 299, and M. M. Knappen, *Tudor Puritanism: A Chapter in The History of Idealism* (Chicago, 1939), 394, concerning the puritan emphasis on visible godly activism for the assurance of election. Note also Charles Lloyd Cohen, *God's Caress: The Psychology of Puritan Religious Experience* (Oxford, 1986), 114, who recognizes the unidirectional nature of puritan views on the relationship between works and assurance: godly labour promotes assurance of salvation while the experience of assurance elicits good works.

[27] Dudley Fenner, *A counter-poyson* (London, 1584), 43.

wrote Chaderton, 'serving to the benefit of all . . . by diligence and love', a rule which not only required the 'diligent and continual service of every member', but also 'condemned all idleness and neglect of duty'.[28] Gifted private members were also encouraged to read the Word publicly and to pray and preach in private gatherings.[29]

In practice, this emphasis on lay, or congregational, involvement in the life of the church sometimes went even further. The activism of the untrained, non-professional godly element within certain 'puritan' parishes was recognized by the future Bishop of London, Richard Fletcher, in his own troublesome parish at Cranbrook in 1575, when he complained that 'it is a common thing now for every pragmatical prentice to have in his head and mouth the government and reformation of the church'. It was during a sermon Fletcher preached in Cranbrook on the necessity of conformity to church ceremonies that the more aggressive puritan lay members openly challenged his lawful ministry 'in the midst of [his] preaching in the congregation'. During the sermon, he observed that there were notes being taken ('pens walking') by several parishioners throughout the congregation, and after, numerous parishioners were arguing and even 'publishing' their own views'.[30]

The suggestion offered here is that it is very possible that puritan soteriology, with its stress on active good works for assurance, was the theological root for the drift toward 'congregationalism' among radical puritans. If the covenant relationship was considered more secure through evidence of visible obedience, then the congregational activism of advanced puritan churchmanship would have ensured that opportunities were available for each puritan soul within the church to make his or her calling and election more sure.

This, in part, also appears to be the purpose behind the concern of many radicals for a disciplined membership. Ecclesiastical discipline should focus on errors in both

[28] Chaderton, *Fruitfull sermon*, 46.

[29] Fenner, *A counter-poyson*, 68–71.

[30] Peel (ed.), *Seconde Parte*, i, 117–18. See also Patrick Collinson, 'Cranbrook and the Fletchers: Popular and Unpopular Religion in the Kentish Weald', in *Godly People: Essays on English Protestantism and Puritanism* (London, 1983), 417–20.

doctrine and conduct. Within the context of puritan soteriology, these two issues were, as Perkins said, the 'infallible' touchstone of true faith.[31] Through congregational discipline, then, church membership offered a controlled public setting in which individuals could learn to 'frame their wills and doings according to the law of God', since every member was responsible for 'instructing and admonishing one another' in faith and practice. The two formal procedures for the discipline of notorious sinners—suspension from the Lord's Supper and excommunication—were both used to identify those within the church who did not show evidence of true saving faith. In suspension, the spiritual health of a deviant member was called into question by the collective judgement of the congregation and not restored until the church became convinced by 'an outward profession' from the offender that he or she was one 'unto whom Christ himself belongs'. Similarly, excommunication indicated that, as far as the church could judge from the visible evidence, the excommunicant could not claim that Christ's 'promises and mercy belong to him'.[32] In these ways puritan churchmanship stressed the importance of a visibly disciplined community.

In the context of puritan soteriology, a disciplined, obedient life was the primary means for gaining personal assurance of everlasting life. From that perspective, then, membership within a puritan parish, modelled on the principles discussed in the writings of left-wing puritans, would carry with it definite soteriological implications, particularly with respect to the puritan search for the assurance of salvation. It was perhaps with this in mind that Field and Wilcox were led to the conviction that 'only' those who are members of a truly disciplined church, ordered according to the biblical pattern, could be considered to 'have their sins forgiven them'.[33]

[31] See above, n. 22.

[32] Travers, *Ecclesiastical discipline*, 165; Frere and Douglas (eds.), *Puritan Manifestoes*, 122.

[33] *Parte of a register*, 544.

Jacobean Radical Puritans

One of the many cases of conscience examined by William Ames in his treatment of puritan casuistry focused on the value that visible church membership held for puritan saints. The question was: is a believer 'bound to join himself to some certain particular church?' Ames answered with an unqualified, 'Yes, by all means,' and offered four reasons: first, because Christ commanded it in Matthew 18: 17; second, because if we wish to find God we must look for him where he is most present; third, because according to God's covenant promise, church members are 'directly under the blessings of God'; and fourth, because through their membership in the visible church 'believers are distinguished from unbelievers'.[34]

Among Jacobean radical puritans, church membership was thus one means of differentiating saints from sinners: they understood the church to be an exclusive society of visible saints alone. As Paul Baynes explained, 'the most holy God will not allow any in his family, openly unholy'. Rather than accepting the socially comprehensive institution of the English church as defined by the parish system, they narrowed the boundaries of the visible church more strictly: it should be a company of 'saints', segregated from the wicked of the world by the walls of godly faith and conduct.[35] Speaking from within this understanding of the church as a congregation of disciplined puritan disciples, William Ames claimed the visible church could justifiably be described as a 'congregation of the predestined'.[36]

While the intention of early Stuart radicals was thus to restrict membership to the visibly elect, they did not require prospective members to offer the congregation the narration of a personal inner experience of grace that Edmund S. Morgan has identified as a distinguishing feature of later New England

[34] William Ames, *Conscience with the power and cases thereof*, iv, 61–2, in *The workes of the reverend and faithfull minister of Christ William Ames* (London, 1643).

[35] Paul Baynes, *A commentarie upon the first chapter of the Epistle of Saint Paul, written to the Ephesians* (London, 1618), 9–10.

[36] *Bellarminus Eneruatus*, iii, 46, as quoted in Keith Sprunger, *The Learned Doctor William Ames* (Urbana, Ill., 1972), 184–5.

Congregationalism.[37] In what appears to be a typical description of admission procedures recommended by Jacobean non-separating congregationalists, Robert Parker made no mention of the necessity of relating an experience of interior transformation by grace, but emphasized instead the importance of a statement of faith by the candidate, learned through clerical instruction, along with a verbal commitment by the candidate to walk in Christian obedience. Parker explained that by following such a procedure, they intended to observe

> the solemn form of admitting into the fellowship of the church used in other reformed churches; wherein after time of instruction the party before his admitting to the communion makes confession of his faith, either in the presbytery or in the congregation, and promises to live thereafter and be subject to Christian discipline. The name of the party being published before, every man may inform the presbytery what he knows of him; that so he may be admitted with a common consent or deferred.[38]

Parker's description of admission procedures thereby centred upon evidence of doctrinal orthodoxy. But it is clear, from further comments, that he would not be satisfied with simply a recitation of what the English Calvinists called historical or general faith. Parker was in full agreement with a concern expressed by Bucer that membership rest upon 'such an effectual confession, as the church may well approve of, with such trial as . . . none may be admitted but upon good signs of regeneration'.[39]

Rather than demanding the relation of an inner experience on the part of a candidate for membership, Parker and other early seventeenth-century radical puritans intended to base church membership upon evidence of what they called 'actual' or 'effectual' faith. When Ames defined the church on earth as a community of the elect, he did not (in a crude, literal sense) mean that the visible church corresponded absolutely with the invisible church of those chosen in the secret councils of God, but rather that the visible church was made up of those who possessed an

[37] Edmund S. Morgan, *Visible Saints: The History of a Puritan Idea* (New York, 1963). For a critique of Morgan's thesis, see below, n. 68 ff.

[38] Parker MS, iii, 17.

[39] Ibid.

effectual calling, which is a kind of external election, as it were, made in time. Therefore the church has her name rather from this calling . . . , that by this means the company or community of actual believers is fitly designed, seeing that none are ordinarily called effectually, but such as by actual faith answer that call.[40]

By 'actual faith' Ames meant a faith that was visible or, as puritans generally understood it, a faith that manifested its inner reality 'in action'.[41] While admitting that true faith therefore ultimately depended upon the secret and invisible election of God, the radicals, steeped in the philosophical tradition of Peter Ramus who stressed experimental over abstract knowledge,[42] were inclined to identify saving faith by the manifestation of good works. The method of distinguishing true faith from general faith on this human level involved the use of the practical syllogism: one examined the evidence of visible good works in oneself or others and, if found, the 'infallible' conclusion followed, as William Perkins expressed it, that true faith was present.[43] Thus, sanctification, the visible expression of inner regeneration, provided an effective means—from a human perspective—for discerning those who were of the elect: 'So when God now has by faith and sanctification taken one out of this world, we may know that he was chosen forth of the world unto life.'[44] It was precisely on this basis that Jacobean non-separating congregationalists, much like the Elizabethan radical puritans, desired to construct congregations of the regenerate; as Parker explained the admission procedures, it was not 'inward virtues' that were to be examined by the presbyters and people, 'but sanctity is required'.[45]

In this way, admission into membership in an advanced puritan congregation carried with it the distinct implication

[40] William Ames, *The svbstance of Christian religion* (London, 1659), 143–4.

[41] M. van Beek, *An Enquiry Into Puritan Vocabulary* (Groningen, 1969), 77.

[42] For an informative discussion of the impact of theological Ramism on puritan theologians like Ames, see Sprunger, *William Ames*, ch. 7, and Hugh Kearney, *Scholars and Gentlemen: Universities and Society in Pre-industrial Britain 1500–1700* (London, 1970), 60–7.

[43] See, for example, Ames's discussion of 2 Peter 1: 10, *The marrow of sacred divinity*, 161–5, in *Workes*. For Perkins, see above, n. 22, and ch. 1, n. 60.

[44] Baynes, *Commentarie upon . . . Ephesians*, 71; see also William Bradshaw, *A treatise of justification* (London, 1615), 88–9.

[45] Parker MS, iii, 17.

that the newly received members also possessed true saving faith. By the same token, the formal disciplinary procedures of the gathered church, ensured that the soteriological affirmation, secured upon entrance, remained operative for those in active membership. Both Ames and Parker indicated that the purpose of church discipline was to shore up and maintain the sanctification of the congregation.[46] In the theological environs of radical puritan churchmen, then, church discipline was employed as a tool for the continued exercise of the practical syllogism, thus ensuring that one of the principal puritan mechanisms for ascertaining the assurance of salvation was continually available in the weekly life of a puritan congregation. By examining the conduct and beliefs of each member through the regular observance of congregational discipline, members were repeatedly reminded of their sanctification in Christ. In turn, sanctification provided the primary vehicle for personal assurance, for, as Baynes explained: 'If I be sanctified . . . I am justified; if justified, I have been called . . . ; if called, I was predestined . . . even to glory.'[47]

Thus, by focusing upon the 'manners and conversation of all the congregation',[48] the radical congregational disciplinary procedures of non-separating congregationalist polity offered the puritan soul a place where one's soteriological condition could be continually monitored and, in a sense, regulated. Without this public discipline, 'men do not safely enough content themselves,' Ames observed, 'unless that public defect be made up by a private care and watching one over another'.[49] While private discipline was always possible, participation within a church which was organized along the biblical pattern that included the disciplinary watch-care of the entire congregation made available a public, institutionalized, and therefore more dependable, source of soteriological assurance through its admission and disciplinary procedures.

[46] Ames, *Conscience*, iv, 86, in *Workes*; Parker MS, i, 41.

[47] Baynes, *Commentarie upon . . . Ephesians*, 72.

[48] William Bradshaw, *Several treatises of worship and ceremonies by the reverend Mr. William Bradshaw* (London, 1660), 43.

[49] Ames, *Marrow*, 157, in *Workes*.

Elizabethan and Jacobean Separatists

In his first book as a separatist, John Smyth made the assertion that visible saints alone were fit for fellowship in the visible church. He defined saints in the characteristic fashion of principled puritans and separatists as 'men separated from all known sin, practising the whole will of God known unto them . . . and . . . growing in grace and knowledge . . . continuing to the end.'[50] To the conforming puritan vicar of Worksop in Nottinghamshire, Richard Bernard, this requirement for membership was entirely too restrictive in the sense that he believed Smyth was attempting to do the impossible by limiting church membership to those of the invisible church, God's hidden elect. This criticism of Smyth's views was not, however, an entirely fair one, as Bernard should have known from the opening words of Smyth's book in which the separatist wrote

> A man may be a member of the visible church and no member of the catholic church . . . A man may be a member of the catholic church and no member of the visible church . . . The catholic church is the company of the elect . . . and it is invisible . . . The visible church is a visible communion of saints.[51]

Two years later, in response to Bernard's reservations, Smyth explained that the visible church could always be vulnerable to the presence of hypocrites because, as all strict Calvinists agreed, hypocrites were impossible to distinguish from genuine believers: they were capable of forsaking known sin, living in outward Christian obedience, growing in knowledge and grace, and even persevering in outward expression of the faith to the end.[52] Conversely, it was equally outside the grasp of human intelligence to know with divine certainty who was truly and inwardly of the elect. In fact, any attempt to identify either hypocrite or true believer in an absolute way would be to seek knowledge of what was for finite human creatures, strictly speaking, impossible to grasp:

[50] John Smyth, *The Works of John Smyth*, ed. W. T. Whitley (Cambridge, 1915), i, 253.

[51] Ibid. 251.

[52] Ibid. ii, 374.

'What have we to do with things invisible, hidden, and secret?' In any ultimate sense, Smyth concurred with the conventional Calvinist wisdom that knowledge of God's elect was reserved for the omniscient mind of God alone. As for Smyth, when it came to discerning the godly and the profane for the purpose of determining the qualifications of individuals for church membership, he did not, as he put it, 'dream of an invisible faith'.[53]

Nevertheless, having set to rest this frequently raised objection to separatist polity, there was a way in which Smyth believed earthbound, finite individuals could indeed know something of the mind of God concerning election through the signs God had revealed in scripture about what constitutes the visible marks of true saving faith. Of course, in the eyes of God, the manifestation of those marks could never be taken as the final criterion: ultimately, true faith depended upon the invisible work of God's free grace. All the same, as the puritan soul in search of assurance was often apparently only too eager to emphasize, good works provided credible guide-lines from which men and women could judge their probable destiny and, according to Smyth, they were to be taken by individuals as reliable evidence:

> When I define saints I must define them not as they are in show for the present, but as they are in deed and truth. Now truth is so either before men or before God, and before God that is true some time which is false before men. That is true before men which is proved by two or three witnesses. Matt. 18: 16, he therefore is a saint before men in show and appearance for the present, that for the present brings forth fruits worthy amendment of life. For a righteous man may forsake his righteousness: Ezek. 18:14. I am not therefore to define a saint as he is in show for the present, but as he is in deed for ever in the judgement of men: neither do I define a saint as he is in the Lord's knowledge which is not revealed to men, but as he is revealed to be judged by the Word of God.[54]

Smyth, along with other separatists, believed there were two distinctive visible marks of saving faith according to the Word of God: knowledge of doctrine and Christian obedience.[55]

[53] Ibid. 375.
[54] Ibid. 374–5.
[55] Ibid. 382; cf. also Robert Browne, *The Writings of Robert Harrison and Robert Browne*, ed. Albert Peel and Leland H. Carlson (London, 1953), 147, 227; Henry

Essentially, then, the separatists adopted the experimental approach to spiritual truth used by their radical puritan contemporaries: evidence of orthodox faith and good works was, in the words of Smyth, 'a proper note of life eternal'.[56] Only in this way did God allow men and women a glimpse of their destiny beyond the grave.

If visible Christianity was the basis for judging the reality of individual faith, it also became a test of the existence of a true church. This was one reason why the separatists rejected the moderate puritan argument that many parish churches were true because some of their members possessed true saving faith.[57] The separatists never doubted that, as Barrow explained to Whitgift, 'the Lord had many precious and elect vessels' in the Church of England, but they 'could not . . . count them faithful' because they were not visibly elect.[58] Essentially, this was also Ainsworth's response to the defence of puritan parish churches proposed by the Gloucestershire puritan, John Sprint, who maintained that 'true members of our best assemblies . . . are endued with true saving faith'. Ainsworth retorted, 'while you plead but for the true members of your best assemblies; yet neither tell you us which are your best assemblies, nor who be the true members of them; that how to follow or where to find you we cannot tell. You say', he continued, that true members

> are endued with true saving faith. I answer, faith is in the heart . . . The heart no man knows but God alone . . . So then I ask you how you know that your members have true faith? Your answer must needs be, (unless you will make yourself a God) you know it not but by their words and works.

Barrow, *The Writings of Henry Barrow, 1587–1590*, ed. Leland H. Carlson (London, 1962), 61; *The Writings of Henry Barrow, 1590–1591*, ed. Leland H. Carlson (London, 1966), 110–11; Henry Ainsworth, *The communion of Saints* (Amsterdam, 1607), 127; Fenner, *Counter-poyson*, 37.

[56] *Smyth*, ii, 382.

[57] The argument employed by puritans in their confrontation with separatists was similar to Calvin's defence of some Catholic assemblies: 'However, when we categorically deny to the papists the title of the church, we do not for this reason impugn the existence of churches among them . . . I call them churches to the extent that the Lord wonderfully preserves in them a remnant of his people.' Calvin, *Institutes*, bk. 4, ch. 3, s. 12.

[58] *Barrow, 1587–1590*, 197.

A church was true, therefore, only if it was exclusively made up of those who showed their faith in words and works; to define it simply in terms of 'inward graces' was, Ainsworth demurred, 'mere delusion'.[59]

In his recent study, *The Pauline Renaissance in England*, John S. Coolidge went to some lengths in order to discredit the conclusions of Perry Miller who had claimed the English separatists attempted to construct congregations of the elect. By contrast, Coolidge argued that the separatists 'never say they are trying to make the membership of the visible church coincide as closely as possible with that of the invisible . . . that is not a consideration that the apologists for the polity concern themselves with'.[60] But given the puritan understanding of assurance, it is clear that the separatists were very much concerned to restrict membership to the visibly elect. While never claiming to have established congregations with the purity of the invisible church, separatists nevertheless considered their churches to be communities of the visibly elect because of what they believed sanctified living (or visible faith) proved about inner faith. Those who were received into church membership were to be examined, Smyth said, for 'faith testified by obedience', and upon that basis accounted 'holy, faithful, and elect'.[61] Entrance into church fellowship commenced in the act of covenanting which included for each individual an 'open and voluntary profession of their own faith and obedience',[62] the purpose of which was to manifest to the church that candidates were filled with the spirit and so qualified for membership. Barrow explained in some detail the theology and purpose of the profession of faith used for entrance into church membership:

But now while we acknowledge the whole work of our salvation, from the beginning to the end, to be of God and not of ourselves, to

[59] Fenner, *Counter-poyson*, 36–7, 18.

[60] John S. Coolidge, *The Pauline Renaissance In England* (Oxford, 1970), 72–3, n. 53; see also, 71–5, 89. It should be noted in Miller's defence that he never said the separatists believed their churches were exact replicas of the invisible church, but rather that this was their 'ideal', and that they were 'practically certain' their members were elect. Miller also acknowledged the separatists' conviction that ultimately God alone knew the identity of the elect: Benjamin Miller *Orthodoxy on Massachusetts 1630–1650* (New York, 1970), 54–7.

[61] *Smyth*, ii, 382.

[62] *Barrow, 1587–1590*, 159.

proceed from and to be established upon his free grace . . . yet make we not thereby the grace of God and his Holy Spirit which he has given to all his elect to be idle, vain, or fruitless in any of them, but to regenerate, change, enlighten and sanctify them, to bring all their affections into, and to keep them in the love and obedience of the truth. By the profession of which truth they are known and received as members of the visible church, made partakers of the communal comforts and covenant of the saints.[63]

The profession of a prospective member therefore manifested much more than a mere intellectual assent to sound doctrine, important as that might be; it also had to convince the congregation that the life of the one professing squared with his or her confession. Johnson explained, a 'verbal profession helps little when men in practice and particulars deny that which in word in general they seem to hold, and thereby deceive the world, as if they held the truth, when in deed they fight against it'.[64] Those who could thus testify to their faith in word and deed were then admitted into that select company of those whom, in the words of Browne, 'Christ has redeemed . . . unto holiness and happiness forever, from which they were fallen by the sin of Adam'.[65] They entered into 'the secret and congregation of the righteous which looks forth as the morning, fair as the moon, pure as the sun . . . the house of the living God, the gate of heaven, the pillar and ground of truth'.[66] They became members of that divine society where, as Barrow said, 'all the people that enter and are received there are chosen, redeemed, called out of the world from amongst the heathen, saints by calling, partakers of the same precious faith and glorious hope, humble, obedient loving sheep . . . clean and holy, as bowls before the altar, etc.'.[67]

It is clear, then, that the separatists' understanding of a profession of faith for church membership was soteriologically far more significant than Edmund S. Morgan thought. As Morgan understood it, 'the faith implied in a [separatist] confession of faith was not saving faith but simply an

[63] *Barrow, 1587–1590*, 163.

[64] Francis Johnson, *A treatise of the ministery of the Church of England* (Amsterdam, 1595), 21.

[65] *Browne*, 253.

[66] Ainsworth, *Communion*, 228.

[67] *Barrow, 1587–1590*, 300.

intellectual understanding of, and consent to, a set of doctrines; it was the product, not of grace but of instruction'.[68] Morgan's conclusion arose out of his conviction that separatists were concerned only with evidence of doctrinal knowledge and Christian conduct, but not evidence of an inward experience of grace. Yet within the context of Elizabethan and early Stuart puritan soteriology, doctrinal knowledge and Christian conduct were understood to comprise, as we have seen, the *visible* touchstone of true, saving faith; a person accepted into membership on this basis would therefore have been received as one who bore the marks of election.

The problem, then, with Morgan's thesis in *Visible Saints* is located in his analysis of the English puritan notions of soteriological assurance that informed separatists' views. Morgan rightly said that Elizabethan and Jacobean radical puritans, like the separatists, believed true faith 'cannot be attained by human effort but comes from God's free grace', but he then mistakenly concluded that in left-wing puritan and separatist thinking, true saints were, therefore, defined *only* as those 'who had felt the stirrings of grace in their soul'.[69] Two factors seemed to be at work in Morgan's conclusion. First, by focusing solely on the puritan affirmation of unmerited grace, he missed the soteriological importance they attached to good works. Second, by saying that puritans required a testimony of religious experience as the criterion of true faith, Morgan seems to have projected the 'experiential' soteriology of John Cotton in New England after 1634 back on to Elizabethan and early Stuart English radical puritan views of church membership. But Cotton was the first major figure to depart from the prevailing puritan soteriology, making assurance dependent not upon sanctification but an inner experience of grace.[70] This is probably the reason Morgan could find no evidence that New England churches required a testimony of a personal experience of grace until after Cotton arrived. Morgan's observation that Thomas Hooker rejected the new admissions requirement of Cotton is also significant.[71] Hooker never warmed to the new soteriology of Cotton, but

68 Morgan, *Visible Saints*, 43.

69 Ibid. 34, 113.

70 See Kendall, *Calvin and English Calvinism*, 167–83.

71 Morgan, *Visible Saints*, 82–98, 106.

instead maintained the 'experimental predestinarian' theology of the Elizabethan and Jacobean puritans.[72] The additional requirement of a personal relation of an experience of grace in New England churches after 1634 more likely reflects the modifications of Cotton's soteriology rather than, as Morgan believed, a new concern to limit the church only to those with saving faith.[73]

While the experiential component was never a part of English separatist requirements for a profession of faith, the twin criterion of an orthodox creed and godly conduct served, as we have observed, the same purpose as the personal relation of faith did in the later New England Congregational Way. Thus, for the troubled puritan conscience in Elizabethan and Jacobean England, entrance into a separatist enclave would have undoubtedly proved to be a powerful source of spiritual help and comfort; in essence, church membership provided communal confirmation of his or her election.

While entrance into the church thus provided public assurance of salvation, the active Christian life within the radically disciplined separatist congregations would have sustained that conviction. The focus of church life for each member was on fulfilling the demands of God's covenant relationship. In taking the church covenant, 'they set up the Lord in that day to be their God, and to walk in his ways, and to keep his ordinances and his commandments and his laws, and to hearken unto his voice: and they promise to walk in the paths of God as he shall teach them'.[74]

The 'congregational' polity of the separatists, which stressed the active role of 'private' or lay members in the affairs of each gathered church, also appears to have been tailor-made to fit the prevailing soteriological context of English puritanism; if, as they believed, assurance could be derived through active godly living, then the activism of separatist churchmanship

[72] Kendall, *Calvin and English Calvinism*, 170–3.

[73] See also Baird Tipson, 'Invisible Saints: The "Judgement of Charity" in Early New England Churches', *Church History*, 44 (1975), 46; and Raymond Stearns and David Brawner, 'New England Church "Relations" and Continuity in Early Congregational History', *Proceedings of the American Antiquarian Society*, 75 (1965), 29, 36, who claim Morgan erred in saying the early English radicals were not concerned with the requirement of saving faith for church membership.

[74] Ainsworth, *Communion*, 218.

in which the 'chief care of every member' was to minister to the needs of their brothers and sisters in the faith would have provided a consoling source of spiritual security.[75] As Ainsworth put it, 'the faithful have fellowship together in all Christian offices spiritual and human . . . for the helping forward and assurance of their salvation'.[76] The separatists' emphasis in ecclesiology on mutual concern and care for the social needs of the brethren was one means of fulfilling this ecclesiological principle.

Patrick Collinson has noted the impressive extent to which 'puritan saints appear to have proved their calling by the faithful performances of social virtues' towards members of the family and religious group.[77] This is equally characteristic of the separatists. Barrow, for example, believed that acts of Christian charity were themselves signs of election, as much as the practice of a biblical ecclesiology, because Christ did not 'exempt the consciences of men from the second table, and bound them with, and unto the first table only'.[78] Voluntary contributions to the church treasury and the distribution of alms, explained Ainsworth, were ways in which the saints could 'lay up in store for themselves, a good foundation, against the time to come, that they may obtain eternal life'.[79]

Much more, of course, was required from separatist church members than practising these social virtues; there were also the more spiritual concerns which included:

> the mutual exhorting and building up one of another in the faith labouring together unto the truth, admonishing the unruly, comforting the feeble minded, bearing with the weak, considering one another to provoke unto love and good works, rebuking for sin and trespass, confessing of faults one to another, and praying one for another, bearing one another's burden, etc.[80]

[75] *Smyth*, i, 261.

[76] Ainsworth, *Communion*, 229.

[77] Patrick Collinson, 'Toward a Broader Understanding of the Early Dissenting Tradition', in C. Robert Cole and Michael E. Moody (eds.), *The Dissenting Tradition: Essays for Leland H. Carlson* (Athens, OH, 1975), 23.

[78] *Barrow, 1587–1590*, 412. Note J. Sears McGee's comment that while puritans tended to emphasize the first table more than the second, it did not mean they were disinclined 'to obey the commands of the Second Table . . . Both anglican and puritan saints obeyed all ten of God's commandments to the best of their ability': *The Godly Man in Stuart England* (New Haven and London, 1976), 92.

[79] Ainsworth, *Communion*, 249.

[80] Ibid. 212–13.

Church discipline provided the formal procedure which ensured that this high ideal would be carried out.

While the attention of separatist congregational discipline focused in this way on doctrinal and behavioural deviancy from the laws of God, the soteriological import of these two emphases appears to have been the overriding concern of their interest in maintaining disciplined congregations of believers. Barrow said that discipline was essential for the church because God's covenant relationship depended upon a watchful and continual obedience.[81] Church discipline helped guarantee that this relationship would remain inviolable because all members, not only the bishop or presbyters, were to monitor the conduct and beliefs of their brothers and sisters.[82] For the individual puritan wrestling in the soul's dark night with the immense question of his or her eternal destiny, the 'congregational' structure of separatism offered an institutionalized means of continuing in 'the obedience of faith', so that

> after we have ended this warfare in the flesh and have so fought as we win the victory and none other get our crown, when our souls shall flit out of these earthly tabernacles, our bodies may sleep and rest in their beds, till our charge come and our souls not sent to the spirits in prison but received among the spirits of just and perfect men, we may so rest from our labours.[83]

Henry Jacob

Writing from Leiden near the end of 1610, Jacob set down what appears now to have been his most precise definition of a true church:

> The true visible and ministerial church of Christ is a number of faithful people joined by their willing consent in a spiritual outward society or body politic, ordinarily coming together into one place, instituted by Christ in his New Testament, and having the power to exercise ecclesiastical government and all God's other spiritual ordi-

[81] *Barrow, 1587–1590*, 305–7.
[82] Ibid. 456–7; Ainsworth, *Communion*, 213.
[83] Ainsworth, *Communion*, 297.

nances (the means of salvation) in and for itself immediately from Christ.[84]

In this compact statement Jacob provides a glimpse into his thoughts about qualifications for membership and how candidates were to be united into church fellowship: they should be 'faithful people joined by their willing consent'. While he never discussed either of these matters at length in any of his writings, enough evidence has survived to demonstrate that he intended membership to be limited to those who (1) showed visible signs of saving faith, and (2) were willing to join together in a covenant relationship.

Jacob nowhere discussed the need of a personal profession of faith for entrance into church membership, but he did offer, in one instance, what seems to have been his criteria for membership: Christ's church should consist 'only of such people as are not ignorant in religion, nor scandalous in their life'. Elsewhere, he said it should be 'a free congregation of visible Christians'.[85] As with other left-wing puritans and separatists of the period, there is no evidence that Jacob required anything like a testimony of an 'experience' of grace for membership; but this should not be taken to mean, as Edmund Morgan has argued, that Jacob was not interested in drawing a link between church membership and true saving faith. Morgan supported his assessment by citing Jacob's statement that 'the profession of saving faith is not the true and proper form of Christ's visible church'.[86] While this is the only occasion on which Jacob referred to a 'profession of saving faith', it appears that Morgan entirely misapprehended Jacob's intent. Jacob was not talking here about the profession of faith required for church membership, as Morgan alleged, but rather about what did, or did not, constitute the true polity or form of a church. By arguing against the opinion of some puritans that 'true . . . faith is the very form and essence of the church', Jacob was taking the same position that separatists adopted against puritans like John Sprint who

[84] Henry Jacob, *The divine beginning and institution of Christs true or visible Ministeriall church* (Leiden, 1610), Sig. A1.

[85] Henry Jacob, *An attestation of many learned, godly and famous divines* (Middelburg, 1613), 17; *A collection of sundry matters* (Middelburg, 1616), Sig. A2.

[86] Jacob, *Divine beginning* (not paginated). See also, Morgan, *Visible Saints*, 79.

had claimed that inner faith, not church structures, was the mark of a true church.[87] But that is an altogether different issue from the one Morgan was addressing. From the standpoint of the conditions for church membership (and not the proper form of the church's constitution), Jacob set his discussion about membership requirements within the context of puritan notions about the assuring nature of preserving doctrinal orthodoxy and persevering in good works. As we have already noted, this is significant since it was understood that right belief and conduct provided the saints with conclusive signs of the Spirits's saving work. Thus, as in the case of other radical churchmen, there were clear soteriological implications operative in Jacob's conviction that membership should be limited to those two requirements.

While it is not entirely accurate, one recent study has suggested that Jacob *never* mentioned the idea of a covenant as the basis for gathering local Christians into church fellowship.[88] There is, admittedly, very little discussion of the subject in his writings, in spite of the conviction held by other modern authorities that the church covenant idea formed a focal point of his ecclesiology.[89] Although Jacob more than likely had an ecclesial covenant in mind when, in 1610, he defined a true church as a 'faithful people joined by their willing consent',[90] he referred specifically to the church covenant only once, in his catechism of 1605. In answer to the question, 'How is a visible church constituted and gathered?' Jacob replied: 'By a free mutual consent of believers joining and covenanting to live as members of a holy society together in all religious and virtuous duties as Christ and his apostles did institute and practise in the Gospel.'[91] Beyond this,

[87] See above, n. 59.

[88] von Rohr, 'The Congregationalism of Henry Jacob', *Transactions of the Congregational Historical Society* (1962), 112.

[89] Raymond Stearns, quoting Perry Miller, identified it as an 'essential' element of Jacob's churchmanship: R. P. Stearns, *Congregationalism in the Dutch Netherlands* (Chicago, 1940), 4. See also Sprunger, *William Ames*, 221.

[90] As quoted above, n. 84.

[91] Champlin Burrage, 'Lost Prison Papers of Henry Jacob', *Review and Expositor*, 5 (1908), 506, believed a good model for church covenants could be found in civil contracts: 'By such a free mutual consent also all civil perfect corporations did first begin': ibid. He was not the first to employ this kind of analogy; cf. *The humble and unfaned confesion of the belefe of certain poore banished men* (Wittenberg, 1554), as quoted in

however, Jacob apparently published no other explicit word about church covenants. The reason for this, as well as his failure to discuss the need for a personal profession of faith, may possibly be related to the fact that, by rejecting complete separation, Jacob never seriously had to face the problem of organizing a new church until 1616, by which time he had also evidently written his last treatise.

When Jacob eventually did become involved in founding the Southwark church, the covenant formed its basis. The decision by Jacob and others to plant a new, independent church body on English soil was not made quickly or taken lightly. It occurred only after years of personal rumination[92] that included 'much conference' first in England, then in 'the Low Countries . . . with Mr. John Robinson . . . and with others about them', and finally back in England where he 'held many several meetings with the most famous men for godliness and learning (viz.) Mr. Throgmorton, Mr. Travers, Mr. Wing, Mr. Richard Mansell, Mr. John Dodd . . . and some others', the latter probably referring to Arthur Hildersam who opposed him in this action.[93] Once they had determined to proceed, Jacob along with a small party of lay men and women prayed and fasted together until 'at last it was concluded' to establish the new church. The seriousness of the decision was underlined not only by the extraordinary caution exercised in preparation for the event, but by the expectation of certain 'troubles', presumably from the authorities in London, that might ensue. Jacob, the record says, 'was

Burrage, *The Early English Dissenters* (Cambridge, 1912), i, 77. For church covenants in English dissent, see Champlin Burrage, *The Church Covenant Idea* (Philadelphia, 1904).

[92] See Stephen Brachlow, 'Puritan Theology and Radical Churchmen in Pre-Revolutionary England' (Oxford University D.Phil. Thesis, 1979), 248.

[93] I have not been able to identify Throgmorton. Walter Travers had returned to England from Ireland in 1598, but there is no evidence of his residence or occupation at this time. S. J. Knox, *Walter Tavers: Paragon of Elizabethan Puritanism* (London, 1962), 141–7. Wing was possibly John Wing, pastor in the 1630s of an English congregation in the Netherlands. Burrage, *Early English Dissenters*, ii, 293. Richard Mansell had been deprived and imprisoned as a puritan a decade earlier. While apparently at first approving Jacob's intentions, he later came to reject the entire enterprise: Stuart Barton Babbage, *Puritanism and Richard Bancroft* (London, 1981), 273; Sabine Staresmore, *The unlawfulness of reading in prayer* (n.p., 1619), 6. For the participation of Hildersam in these conferences, see Samuel Clarke, *Lives of two and twenty* (London, 1660), 151.

willing to adventure himself', and so the others 'encouraged him'.[94]

A day was set on which those who were to found the church would 'seek the face of the Lord in fasting and prayer' in order to commend the proposed union of persons 'to the Lord'. And then, in a vivid display of solidarity:

> [those] who minded this present union and so joining together joined both hands each with another brother and stood in a ringwise: their intent being declared, Henry Jacob and each of the rest made some confession or profession of their faith and repentance, some were longer, some were briefer; then they covenanted together to walk in all God's ways as he had revealed or should make known to them.

And so, the church at Southwark was gathered. Within a few days they notified 'the brethren here of the Ancient [separatist] Church' in Amsterdam and then chose and ordained Jacob as their first pastor.[95]

While it appears that Jacob, in harmony with the proposals of other radicals, was inclined to limit membership to those who gave visible evidence of saving faith, his concern for an active involved membership continued to support the soteriological orientation of radical puritan churchmanship. Using the language of an earlier catechism written by William Perkins, Jacob affirmed the soteriological significance of performing good works when he said 'Our sanctification, our obedience to the Word, or our good works have two uses. 1. They are the fruits and sure witnesses of true faith justifying us. 2. They are the highway necessary for all men to walk in unto salvation'.[96] Put more succinctly and less theologically, Jacob said some years later: 'we must do . . . that we may be accepted'.[97]

Church membership committed each member to a life of active *doing* within the church community. This was the essential thrust of the covenant idea. The members covenanted together 'to walk in all God's ways', as the Southwark covenant said, or, as Jacob had put it a decade earlier, 'to live

[94] Stinton MSS, 'A repository', 1–2 (Angus Library, Regent's Park College, Oxford).

[95] Ibid., 2.

[96] Burrage, *Early English Dissenters*, ii, 156.

[97] Henry Jacob, *A confession and protestation of the faith of certaine Christians in England* (Amsterdam, 1616), Sig. D3–4.

as members of a holy society together in all religious and virtuous duties as Christ and his apostles did institute and practise in the Gospel'.[98] The overriding concern to seek a membership of active, faithful people in whom resided 'the power to exercise ecclesiastical government'[99] was probably derived in part from the soteriological concerns of puritan theology; at least Jacob was convinced that 'our uniform constitution of the church and administration thereof, cuts off all occasion of . . . doubting, and leaves our consciences safely resting on Christ alone'.[100]

John Robinson

There is no evidence to suggest that, like Jacob and other puritan contemporaries, John Robinson would have required prospective church members to relate an experience of grace in their profession of faith; similarly, there is every indication that he believed all members should none the less be accounted true saints possessing saving faith. In a brief definition of the New Testament term *ecclesia*, Robinson explained that a true church 'denotes an assemblage of persons called out of the state of corrupt nature into that of supernatural grace'.[101] In other passages be described members variously as 'saints by calling', those 'spiritually hewn and lively stones . . . purchased with the blood of Christ', who were to be judged as 'members of the invisible church . . . in truth . . . *elect, redeemed, justified, sanctified*'.[102] Understandably, in view of sweeping statements such as these, critics of Robinson's ecclesiology in his own day claimed he naïvely failed to discriminate clearly the invisible church of the elect from the visible church, and instead made them all one.[103] But this criticism, which was often levelled against separatist

[98] Stinton MSS, 'A repository', 2; Burrage, 'Lost Prison Papers', 506.

[99] Jacob, *Divine beginning*, Sig. A1.

[100] Jacob, *Attestation*, 156.

[101] John Robinson, *A just and necessarie apologie* (Amsterdam, 1625), 30.

[102] John Robinson, *Of religious communion private and publique* (Amsterdam, 1614), 17; 'An answer to a censorious epistle', printed in Joseph Hall, *A common apologie of the church of England* (London, 1610), 16; *A justification of separation from the church of England* (Amsterdam, 1610), 34, 51.

[103] Champlin Burrage (ed.), *An Answer to John Robinson of Leiden* (London, 1920), 75.

polity, did not take into account a crucial distinction that Robinson, like other separatists, employed whenever he discussed the relationship between true faith and church membership.

In Robinson's mind, true saving faith was to be considered from either one of two different perspectives:

> The scriptures do speak of a justification before God, which is by faith alone; and of a justification before men, which is by works: the former of which we may truly call invisible justification, as known to none but God, and the conscience of the party justified: the other visible justification, as being manifest and made visible unto men, by works . . . the same from the scriptures compared together may be affirmed of visible, and invisible election, redemption, sanctification.[104]

While he admitted that true faith ultimately depended upon an interior spiritual relationship between the individual and God, proof of one's faith rested entirely upon good works:

> A man has in truth so much religion as he has between the Lord and himself in secret, and no more; what shows soever he makes before men and makes sound proof of his religion both before God and men, so far as he is forward and ready to every good work.[105]

The criterion for discerning true faith in others was visible faith, that is, faith recognizable through 'soundness of knowledge' and the 'holy practice of their duty'.[106] While theologically speaking, Robinson understood faith and holiness as gifts graciously conferred by God in election, epistemologically he understood that one's election was verified through human endeavour. Thus, 'the putting on of Christ by faith and obedience, is our work by God's grace and not God's'. Through the strenuous life of godly obedience, others were able to recognize that one had indeed 'put on' Christ and that one was, therefore, of the elect.[107]

This did not, of course, imply that Robinson necessarily posited an unqualified correlation between visible godliness

[104] Robinson, *Justification*, 312–13.
[105] John Robinson, *Observations divine and morall* (Amsterdam, 1625), 41.
[106] John Robinson,
[107] John Robinson, *A defence of the doctrine propounded by the synode at Dort* (Amsterdam, 1624), 52, 48, 55.

and true faith; only God, who alone could see the inner life, possessed that higher level of infallible knowledge of election, while human knowledge, based on visible observation, should properly be considered only probable.[108] Robinson was painfully aware of the inadequacies of judging 'according to outward *appearance* . . . because we often err in our judgements . . . through ignorance, negligence, or partiality'. Nevertheless, after all of these Calvinist disclaimers had been duly rehearsed, Robinson averred that visible evidence was, in actuality, the only firm basis upon which finite human beings could make determinations. So, he concluded, it is 'a certain rule that we must never proceed, either in judgement or practice, against appearances which we approve; if it *appear* good, and yet we condemn it'.[109]

If the manifestations of sound doctrine and Christian conduct were the only requirements for membership, they were also the basis upon which members were to be considered elect. Admission was based upon a 'personal profession of faith, and confession of sin' followed by voluntarily joining in the church covenant. Robinson considered this profession of faith to be 'the ordinary means by which . . . hidden and invisible graces are manifested, and made visible unto men'.[110] Robinson's emphasis here was not merely on the presence of orthodox content, but also—and especially—on evidence of visible obedience to the laws of God. Robinson agreed with Smyth that mere knowledge, however sound, was not enough: that is what the Leiden separatist understood to be 'general' faith. The crucial factor in recognizing 'saving' faith was to find that a person's knowledge was joined with obedience.[111] So it was not 'just the prattling of a verbal profession' that he demanded, but also evidence of active godliness, or 'actual' faith.[112] Thus, a church would not accept a member 'for the profession of faith, *ex opere operato*', but only if the congregation was persuaded by both 'his profession and other outward appearances'.[113]

[108] Robinson, *Justification*, 312.
[109] Robinson, *Observations*, 232 (my italics).
[110] Robinson, *Justification*, 91; Burrage, *Answer to John Robinson*, 21.
[111] Robinson, *Of religious communion*, 85.
[112] Robinson, *Justification*, 272; *Apologie*, 157; Burrage, *Answer to John Robinson*, 17.
[113] Robinson, *Justification*, 271.

While Robinson admitted that he was 'not so fond, or rather frantic, as to require, in respect of others, other holiness in the members thereof than that which is visible and external',[114] the expectation that one could require more was never a real possibility, simply because externals were the sole criteria on which human beings could judge one another. Any attempt to probe deeper would be useless; faith could only be validated empirically through the senses.[115] And so a profession of faith without corresponding visible works indicated to Robinson that the professor was, as far as men and women could perceive, 'a natural child of the devil'.[116] But when the professing one convincingly manifested saintliness through outward obedience to the moral laws of God, that individual was to be, 'in the judgement of charity,' considered 'within the gracious covenant of God's mercy and love and under the promises of the gospel, and so by us to be reputed holy'.[117]

It was over the pressing question of infant baptism, however, that Robinson, like other separatists, momentarily stepped back from his concern that churches restrict membership to the visibly elect. Those separatists who departed from the separatist mainstream by adopting believer's baptism as the form of the church refused to baptize infants primarily because, as they pointed out, infants were incapable of manifesting their faith.[118] This contention by the new baptists that infants are not to be considered regenerate because they do not have 'actual' faith appeared preposterous to Robinson, 'as if some idiot would affirm that infants are not born, nor to be reputed reasonable creatures, nor endued with the faculties of understanding and reason, because they make no manifestation thereof, no more than brutes do'.[119]

Robinson's rather brutal assessment of early English baptists in this regard was, in fact, a distortion of the baptist

[114] Robinson, *Apologie*, 60.

[115] The 'nominalist' nature of his approach to knowing is evident in Robinson's discussion of the idea of the visible catholic church. He accepted the idea of an invisible catholic church on the basis of faith, but he rejected the concept of a visible catholic church on the basis that only things which 'have their existence in nature, that is in the individuals', can be 'intelligible'. Universals exist 'only in the understanding': Robinson, *Apologie*, 12.

[116] Robinson, *Justification*, 62.

[117] Ibid. 271, 316. See also, Tipson 'Invisible Saints', 467.

[118] See below, ch. 4, n. 7.

[119] Robinson, *Defence of the doctrine*, 152.

position, for they did not intend to say that because the visible signs were lacking therefore infants could not be regenerate. On the contrary, as we shall see, English anabaptists argued that infants could experience inward grace, even if they could not show it.[120] In this sense, they were merely being consistent with the puritan criterion for the recognition of true faith by unflinchingly applying it to their children.

In order to avoid the logic of the anabaptists, Robinson was forced to depart from the usual two-fold criterion of orthodox faith and godly conduct as church admission requirements and say that the faith of infants could be ascertained on a basis other than an empirical one. The 'want of faith' in infants 'by which men of years are justified or of works by which they are judged' should not, he argued, prejudice the judgement of infants. Rather than being judged by their fruits, infants were to be assessed according to evidence of their parents' 'actual' faith. The conditional aspects of the covenant applied only 'to men of riper years', so it did not follow that 'because the infants of the faithful now cannot for the present observe the conditions of the covenant of grace . . . that therefore they are excluded from the covenant of grace'.[121]

While this was not exactly what the English baptists had argued, the implication for Robinson's ecclesiology is that by being willing to admit children into membership on the basis of faith without empirical evidence, he was, in effect, to some extent undermining the separatists' virtual obsession with visible saintliness, at least until infants came of age; at that point they became subject to the same requirements for visible obedience as their parents. If in coming of age their faith did not become actual, they were to be 'cut off from God's covenant'.[122]

Children aside, then, membership for Robinson was determined by external tests. On this basis, he could consider the visible church a replica of the invisible church, while realizing, at the same time, that from a divine perspective the two were not necessarily exactly correlated. Christ, said Robinson, purchased with his blood 'not two', but a single church, 'and

[120] See below, ch. 4.
[121] Robinson, *Of religious communion*, 71, 89.
[122] Robinson, *Defence of the doctrine*, 157.

accordingly to this purchase of Christ and ordinance of God, all that are of the visible church are also of the invisible, and all of the invisible of the visible church, which are indeed not two, but one church in two sundry respects, as I have formerly shown'.[123] Timothy George has argued that this statement by Robinson should not be taken to imply that Robinson envisioned a direct correspondence between the visible and the invisible church. According to George, Robinson always carefully distinguished between the two.[124] While it is clear, as discussed above, that such a distinction was invariably assumed by Robinson and other separatists in their pronouncements concerning the relationship between church membership and election, George's own discussion of the matter errs by ignoring the perspective from which Robinson was very often willing to posit a correlation between the visible and the invisible church. As Robinson said, the two churches must be understood 'in two sundry respects'. In God's eyes they were clearly distinct, while from the human vantage point (but in that respect only), the two *appeared* to be one in a biblically ordered church. Thus, in this matter, as in so many others, puritan and separatist ideology was often dialectical and, therefore, open to manipulation, depending upon which side of that dialectic they chose to speak from.

Precisely because the church could be considered from either the divine or the human perspective, Robinson was willing to admit that in the eyes of God there was every likelihood that each true church, while visibly pure, nevertheless embraced 'painted and deceitful hypocrites' within her walls.[125] But while theologically significant, this was at most only a statement of faith, since hypocrites in a visibly pure church were impossible to discern because they did not manifest any of the visible marks of reprobation. Once they did, they were cut off from the body:

And for hypocrites, as they may perform all the conditions here required (visible or to us) so do we take knowledge of none such in

[123] Robinson, *Justification*, 313.

[124] Timothy George, *John Robinson and the Separatist Tradition* (Macon, Ga., 1982), 102, n. 40.

[125] John Robinson, 'An appendix to M. Perkins his six principles of Christian religion' in *A just and necessary apology* (London, 1644), not paginated.

the church; in the particular, till they be known in their day by the outbreaking of sin, and being so discovered, they are no longer to be retained in the church, but to bear their sin, except they repent and then who can repute them hypocrites?[126]

So the visible church could be conceived, in this sense, as being entirely free of hypocrites.

This did not mean, however, that the church was a community of visibly perfect saints.[127] The godly were also subject to infirmities of the flesh: 'A rebel lurking in a kingdom may, by some advantage watched and taken, prevail against the lawful King in a conflict or two, and yet, for all that, not reign in the Kingdom: so may the treacherous flesh, lurking in a spiritual man, get the mastery in some combat; and yet not, therefore, drive the Lord quite out of his Kingdom, there.'[128] With respect to church membership, it was, then, not visible perfection that Robinson demanded, but a willingness on the part of every member to submit his or her 'treacherous flesh' to the corrective hand of Christ. This was possible primarily through the displinary procedures prescribed by Christ in Matthew 18: 15–17, and exemplified in 1 Corinthians 5.

If, for various economic reasons, the discipline of the puritan sectaries in early Jacobean society had been attractive to the hard-working yeomen and merchants who have been the concern of Christopher Hill,[129] it would have appealed also to the spiritually industrious yet anxious souls in the ranks of those who were most 'painful and conscionable' in their lives by offering them the security of a corporate spiritual conscience. Robinson's understanding of congregational discipline provides an example of the strong religious society that radical puritan polity tended to foster: church discipline was designed in such a way that the judgement of the community always held priority over that of the individual. Even if a member of the congregation was aware of 'some great wickedness by a brother', he or she was expected to remain in communion with that person until the church 'discover him'. Conversely, members were expected to refrain from communion with an

[126] Robinson, *Justification*, 106. [127] Ibid.

[128] Robinson, *Observations*, 33.

[129] Christopher Hill, *Society and Puritanism in Pre-Revolutionary England* (London, 1969), 130–5; 344–8.

innocent excommunicant as long as that one remained under the censure of the church.[130] Individual judgement, at least within the visible church fellowship, was buried while the communal conscience prevailed.[131]

It was this intense conviction about the priority of the community over the individual that lay behind Robinson's advice to the pilgrims on their way to New England: 'Let every man repress in himself and the whole body in each person, as so many rebels against the common good, all private respects of men's selves, not sorting with the general convenience.'[132] All members of the congregation were responsible for the spiritual vitality of the others, not just their own: 'they are not priests only for themselves,' Robinson explained to Bernard, 'but for their brethren . . . neither are they kings for themselves alone, but for their brethren also, having the power of Christ whereby to judge them, the keys of the kingdom to bind and loose them, in the order by him prescribed'.[133] The sense of spiritual security that this arrangement created in the life of a serious puritan soul is indicated in a rare but telling autobiographical passage where Robinson discussed the personal comfort he found as one who, while being 'subject to sin, yea, and to forwardness in sin, as much as the brethren are', was still subject to 'that blessed ordinance of the church's censures':

> In the very writing of these things, my soul is filled with spiritual joy, that I am under this easy yoke of Christ the censures of the church, whereof I am, and how much I am comforted in this very consideration, against my vile and corrupt nature, which notwithstanding, I am persuaded the Lord will never so far suffer to rebel, as that it shall not be tamed and subdued by this strong hand of God, without which it might every day and however so hazard my salvation.[134]

Robinson believed communal discipline was an effective means of securing oneself from the spiritual wilderness of the

[130] Christopher Lawne, *The prophane schisme of the Brownists, discovered* (London, 1612), 50.

[131] Note Larzer Ziff's discussion of this in New England congregationalism: 'The Social Bond of the Church Covenant', *American Quarterly*, 10 (1958), 452–4.

[132] John Robinson, 'Certain useful advertisements', in H. M. Dexter (ed.), *Mourts Relation* (Boston, 1865), xiv.

[133] Robinson, *Justification*, 226.

[134] Ibid. 216.

world that surrounded the covenanted community of saints. God had established communities, he once wrote, to 'fence' those within them 'the better, on every side, against evil'. The gathered congregations of the separatist churches provided, Robinson believed, just such a 'walled orchard'.[135]

[135] Robinson, *Observations*, 210; *Of religious communion*, 4.

4

VISIBLE SAINTS AND THE LOGIC OF ENGLISH ANABAPTISM

Elizabethan Radical Puritans

THE rise of the English General Baptists out of the exiled separatist congregation of the Ancient Church in Amsterdam, which occurred with John Smyth's self-baptism in 1608, has generated considerable discussion among historians concerning the source of this novel twist in the history of early English dissent.[1] One of the central questions has been whether the Dutch Anabaptists or the English separatists provided the seed for Smyth's antipaedobaptist convictions.[2] Indeed, one of the frequent criticisms the separatists themselves encountered from English traditionalists and conforming puritans in their own day was that the radical ecclesiology of separatism inevitably led to the practice of believer's baptism. By rejecting the ministry and constitution of the established church, their opponents argued, it was only reasonable that separatists discard its baptism as well. However convincing

[1] As early as the autumn of 1607, Smyth indicated his uneasiness about the baptism he had received in the false English church: B. R. White, *The English Separatist Tradition* (Oxford, 1971), 131. The traditional date for Smyth's self-baptism is 1609. E.g., see Michael R. Watts, *The Dissenters* (Oxford, 1978), 45. What appears to be the ealiest reference to Smyth's rebaptism, however, is that made by Henoch Clapham, the separatist turncoat, in *Error on the left hand* (London, 1608), 22, evidence which would indicate the event had already occurred in that year.

[2] Recent discussions of the matter include Ian Sellers 'Edwardians, Anabaptists and the Problem of Baptist Origins', *Baptist Quarterly*, 27 (1981), 97–112; James Coggins, 'Theological Positions of John Smyth', *Baptist Quarterly*, 30 (1984), 247–64; Douglas Shantz, 'The Place of the Resurrected Christ in the Writings of John Smyth', *Baptist Quarterly*, 30, (1984), 199–203; Stephen Brachlow, 'John Smyth and the Ghost of Anabaptism: A Rejoinder', *Baptist Quarterly*, 30 (1984), 296–300; B. R. White, 'The English Separatists and John Smyth Revisited', *Baptist Quarterly*, 30 (1984), 344–7. See also, Stephen Brachlow, 'Puritan Theology and General Baptist Origins', *Baptist Quarterly*, 31 (1985), 179–94, much of which is reproduced by permission of the Baptist Historical Society, 4 Southampton Row, London WC1B 4AB.

the argument may have sounded to some, especially in the aftermath of Smyth's notorious descent into this forbidden ecclesiastical territory, Keith Sprunger has observed that—Smyth and his followers aside—there is little historical evidence to support the claim that antipaedobaptism inevitably followed from radical puritanism or separatism. The reason for this, Sprunger suggests, is that while their congregational ideology would seem to lead in that direction, 'non-separating Congregationalists, and all Brownists, preached something very close to the believer's church' ideal of the anabaptists, thus making the revolutionary and, for most Calvinists, highly offensive plunge into anabaptism unnecessary for them.[3] While this is very likely true, it should not cloud the fact that, given the puritan preoccupation with sanctification, or 'actual', visible faith and the emphasis, by separatists and radical puritans alike, on the necessity of visible churchmanship, there was an inherent logic in these concerns driving separatists toward the practice of believer's baptism.

As in the reformed tradition generally, the separatists defended infant baptism on the basis of the Old Testament rite of circumcision. Baptism was the sign or seal of God's promise and 'everlasting covenant of grace made with the faithful and their seed, and of the righteousness which is by faith in Jesus Christ'.[4] While the weight of this argument rested heavily on the unconditional covenant of grace, radical puritan and separatist soteriology and ecclesiology, as we have seen, laid considerable stress on the conditional covenant relationship and the importance of visible obedience. When, for example, the separatist Richard Clifton argued on the basis of Genesis 17, that children of believing parents were to be included in church membership through the rite of infant baptism because 'the promise is made to you and to your children, and to all that are afar off, as many as the Lord our God shall call',[5] he was, in effect, undercutting the principle of visible churchmanship upon which the separatist cause had been constructed.

[3] Keith Sprunger, 'English Puritans and Anabaptists', *Mennonite Quarterly Review*, 46 (1972), 128.

[4] Henry Ainsworth and Francis Johnson, *An apologie or defence of svch trve Christians as are commonly (but vniustly) called Brownists)* (Amsterdam, 1604), 71.

[5] John Smyth, *The Works of John Smyth*, ed. W. T. Whitley (Cambridge, 1915), ii, 578.

It was Smyth, among the separatists, who first challenged and rejected the practice of infant baptism for this very reason. The seal or sign of a true covenant relationship with God, he said, was not baptism, but the Holy Spirit, who became manifest through visible obedience.[6] His difficulty with infant baptism was not that children were incapable of receiving God's grace, but rather that they could not exhibit evidence of saving faith: 'Infants are not to be esteemed actually under the possession of the New Testament, which New Testament is visible in the visible ordinances thereof.'[7] They were capable of inward faith, but not 'actual faith'.[8] True baptism only appertained 'to them that are of Abraham's faith, that is actually believing to justification, and showing the faith of Abraham by the works of Abraham'.[9] Since church membership, for English radicals in general, belonged only to the visibly elect, Smyth's rejection of infant baptism on this basis was no doubt a logically compelling one.

The same could be said about the theological shift made by Smyth and his followers to theological 'Arminianism'. For example, John Murton's 'Arminian' convictions were essentially of one mind with the soteriology expressed in the Calvinist 'experimental predestinarian tradition' of English puritanism and separatism. His declaration that 'the promise of God's election is free, without any desert in us originally, yet upon condition of faith and obedience to Christ's Gospel' and that, although God loves men and women first, 'yet after they must love him and continue in his love, by keeping his commandments' or be subject to the wrath of God, both accurately reflect the puritan concern for visible saving faith.[10] From this perspective, then, it appears that what has often been described as a transition from 'Calvinism' to 'Arminianism' in the theology of the first English baptists did not necessitate a radical readjustment of their original puritan theology.[11] Puritan soteriology, apart from the question of

[6] Smyth, ii, 581, 586. [7] Ibid. 638. [8] Ibid. 589. [9] Ibid. 678.

[10] John Murton, *A description of what God hath predestinated concerning man* (London, 1620), 78, 87–8.

[11] Lonnie Kliever has argued that Smyth and his followers most likely modified their Calvinism through the influence of Peter Baro: 'General Baptist Origins', *Mennonite Quarterly Review*, 36 (1962), 316–17. While possible, it is highly unlikely; the arguments for Waterlander influence, as Watts has pointed out, are too strong:

whether or not God's grace could be resisted, was highly compatible with Arminianism, a point recognized by Jacob Arminius himself in his own critique of the theology of William Perkins.[12]

The compatibility of early English baptists with the soteriology and ecclesiology of separatism is underscored—if indeed not betrayed—by observing the peculiar separatist response to the threat posed by the defection of their co-religionists to antipaedobaptism. While separatist propagandists invariably invoked a 'mutualist' covenant theology to justify separatism when confronting puritans and conformists, they now shifted ground and turned to the unconditional covenant concept when disputing with the new baptists in their midst, much as in Chapter I we observed radical puritans to have adopted an unconditional covenant defence of the parish churches in light of the separatist crisis. Johnson, for example, responded to Smyth's first publication as a baptist, *The Character of the Beast*, by arguing that Smyth did 'highly . . . derogate from the grace of God, the fullness of Christ and his Gospel' by rejecting infant church membership.[13] In defending paedobaptism, Johnson was, in fact, driven further than any other separatist to justify a baptism received in Rome or England as being a true baptism. But in order to do that, he was again forced to rely on an unconditional gracious rendering of the covenant relationship. Baptism once received in the churches of either Rome or England was not to be repeated, he said,

> because the covenant of God's grace in Christ is an everlasting covenant: into which it pleased God to take us with Abraham our father, when he made that covenant with him and his seed forever. And as the Lord himself, who knows his works from the beginning, has regard unto it in his merciful dealing concerning his people, even when they are as yet in apostatical churches.[14]

Watts, *Dissenters*, 45–6. The subject of early baptist 'Arminianism' is not considered in Nicholas Tyacke, *Anti-Calvinists: The Rise of English Arminianism c.1590–1640* (Oxford, 1987).

[12] George Yule, 'Continental Patterns and the Reformation in England and Scotland', *Scottish Journal of Theology*, 22 (1969), 317; R. T. Kendall, *Calvin and English Calvinism to 1649* (Oxford, 1979), 141–50.

[13] Francis Johnson, *A brief treatise . . . against two errours of the Anabaptists* (Amsterdam, 1609), 14.

[14] Ibid. 17–18.

In 1617, Johnson outlined his position even more sharply. By then he not only justified infant baptism on the basis of the Abrahamic covenant of grace, but also made baptism, and not sanctification, the sole foundation of soteriological assurance:

For the seal of God (in circumcision and baptism) confirms a perfect sure and firm covenant, even the Lord's everlasting covenant of grace . . . whereas our faith and observation of the Lord's commandments, like as theirs in Israel, is infirm and imperfect . . . And it is our comfort in temptations, that although we are weak and sinful, yet the Lord's covenant of grace, confirmed unto us in baptism, as it was to them in circumcision, is firm and holy, even an everlasting covenant.[15]

There was, however, a way in which most separatists tried to bridge this yawning gap between their mutualist ecclesiology and this unconditional doctrine of baptism. While they had traditionally taught that the baptism of Rome and England was not of itself a true baptism, they nevertheless would not say it was utterly false either, because it held the potential of a true, effective baptism upon the repentance and visible obedience of the one baptized. But in so saying, the separatists shifted their understanding of baptism, like Smyth and Murton, to a conditional rather than an unconditional covenant interpretation. Johnson alone, it seems, realized this incongruity. Some separatist arguments justifying baptism received in the church of Rome and Canterbury, he said, were 'plain anabaptistry and covert popery and Arminianism whereby they debase God's grace and exalt man's works'.[16] The only way to justify a baptism from either church, he now argued, would be to acknowledge both Rome and the church in England to be true churches, not because of their obedience, since he believed they were both yet drenched in apostasy, but because God's grace was larger than their apostasy. Yet to do this, Johnson was compelled to give up the greater part of the conditional covenant theology of separatism and cast his ecclesiology on, as he was now inclined to say, the Lord's 'free grace'.[17]

Yet this was not the end of their waffling. Neither Johnson

[15] Francis Johnson, *A Christian plea conteyning three treatises* (Leiden, 1617), 13. 23.
[16] Ibid. 32.
[17] Ibid. 58–64.

nor the other separatists, it appears, were entirely consistent in their use of unconditional and conditional covenant theology even in this manner. Johnson, who came to emphasize the unconditional covenant in his defence of Rome, nevertheless remained a strict separatist in practice; but in order to defend this practice he returned to a 'mutualist' emphasis, now saying that one should separate because God 'has promised to show mercy graciously to them that love him and keep his commandments'.[18] The same inconsistency appears in Ainsworth's treatment of the matter. When writing against Johnson's new views on baptism, he stressed the conditional nature of the covenant, saying, 'there is no covenant between God and men, but conditional: for without faith and holiness no man shall see the Lord'.[19] Yet when writing against John Murton (the baptist), Ainsworth—like Johnson and John Robinson—emphasized the covenant of grace. Baptism is 'God's work in grace', he reminded Murton, and is therefore known only through faith and not by outward signs such as visible obedience. Thus, the saints 'are to believe that our infants are sanctified creatures, and are born believers not infidels, though outwardly they can manifest no faith or sanctification unto us'. The effect was, of course, to undermine the whole principle of visible churchmanship upon which separatist polity was built. Ironically, it was this same Ainsworth who had said to John Sprint some years earlier that to define faith wholly in terms of 'inward graces' was 'mere delusion'.[20]

Whether the first appearance of a baptist ecclesiology within English dissent arose primarily as the result of dynamics inherent to left-wing puritanism and separatism or from the cross-fertilization of separatist and Dutch anabaptist ideals is a problem likely never to be solved to every historian's satisfaction. None the less, when one views the issue from within the broader context of radical protestantism in England, it is evident that there is a kinship of ideals

[18] Ibid. 215–17. Although Johnson now argued that the church of England was true, he nevertheless believed that because of its corruptions it was still necessary to, as he said 'leave' it.

[19] Henry Ainsworth, *A reply to a pretended christian plea* (Amsterdam, 1620), 133.

[20] See above, ch. 3, n. 59.

between the first English baptists and the theology and ecclesiology of early English dissent. The compatibility of Smyth's antipaedobaptist persuasion and his modified Calvinism within the puritan and separatist theological environment indicates that he may, indeed, not have travelled as far on his religious odyssey as historians are sometimes inclined to say. Smyth himself, at least, indicated that there was something of a direct line between the two ends of his irregular career that began in puritan Cambridge and ended with his rebaptism as an exile in Amsterdam, when he explained in *The Character of the Beast* that he had arrived at this surprising destination after having progressed 'from the profession of puritanism to Brownism, and from Brownism to true Christian baptism'.[21] Nowhere does Smyth indicate that ideas he may have received from the Continental anabaptists played a formative part in this celebrated pilgrimage. Even if he had, there is sufficient evidence of a shared perspective concerning theology and ecclesiology between Smyth and his co-religionists within the radical puritan and separatist context in which his religious ideals had first been fostered. The evidence warrants the conclusion that the logic of Smyth's baptist convictions was rooted in the visible churchmanship of English nonconformity, a logic which, once recognized by those who remained wedded to the broad stream of puritan dissent, caused an obvious reassessment of their mutualist ecclesiological convictions that formed such a substantial component of their biblical enterprise.

[21] *Smyth*, ii, 564.

5

GOVERNMENT OF THE GATHERED CHURCH: DEMOCRACY AND ARISTOCRACY

Elizabethan Radical Puritans

THE structure of government for the gathered church in the thinking of Elizabethan radical churchmen revolved around the question of the use of power and its distribution between the officers of the church and private members of the congregation. An examination of the carefully nuanced imagery, rhetoric, and doctrinal formulations in the writings of advanced puritan ideologues concerning the role and place of the ministry in a particular congregation reveals that, while wanting to grant real power to the laity, they yet strove to preserve an elevated level of authority for the ministry. Ideally, the Elizabethan radicals envisaged a form of government that allowed a mixed and balanced use of power by both the people and the elders, thus guarding against the arbitrary rule of either. The result of this attempt to preserve two centres of power for the direction of a gathered congregation, each working in harmony with the other under the absolute reign of Christ through scripture, provides a complex theoretical model which eludes straightforward definition and has therefore been amenable to diverse interpretations by historians, as it often was by left-wing puritans themselves.

Despite the challenge of Continental protestant reformers to the authority of the hierarchy at Rome, they never doubted that the church required the guidance of a separate, ordained ministry. 'Fanatical men' might think a formal ministerial order superfluous, Calvin said, but it was his settled opinion that the prophets and godly teachers of the visible church were 'necessary and highly approved' by the Word.[1] While vehemently denouncing the proud titles and lordly practices of the worldly Roman episcopate,[2] Calvin always firmly maintained that the church 'can never go without' its pastors and teachers.[3] Indeed, the ordained officers of the church were considered by Calvin to be the representatives of Christ, or 'ambassadors', who, as they opened the Word of God to the people from the pulpit, were to be heard as 'the mouthpiece of God'.[4] Thus, the preaching ministry was to receive the 'highest honour and esteem' from the people and be regarded by them as 'the most excellent of all things'.[5] Ordination, particularly in the solemn rite of laying on of hands by the elders, was itself a sign of the special dignity accorded to the office.[6] The duty of the people toward their ministers, according to the Genevan reformer, should be fulfilled primarily through obedience to and reverence for their governors.[7]

While these pronouncements placed the ministry above the people, there were other dynamics at work within the Calvanist understanding of the ministry that provided a counterbalance to the autocratic tendencies implicit in Calvin's discussions of ministerial honour and power, and contributed to the radicalization of congregational authority in late sixteenth-century English protestantism. For example, the pastor was often described by Calvin in the biblical imagery of a servant, who was under the ownership of the congregation as one 'bound' to his charge, 'not . . . as it were to the glebe . . . so that he cannot move his foot from it', but that he 'ought not to think of leaving or to seek release'.[8] Ownership of the church's pastoral offices lay in the hands of the people, who possessed a 'common right and freedom' from Christ to appoint the officers of the church by the 'consent and approval' of the gathered congregation.[9] While laying on of

[1] John Calvin, *Institutes of the Christian Religion*, ed. J. T. McNeill, trans. F. L. Battles (London, 1960), bk. 4, ch. 1, s. 5.

[2] Calvin, *Institutes*, bk. 4, ch. 7, s. 3; and ch. 10, s. 7.

[3] Ibid., ch. 3, s. 4; *Harmony of confessions* (London, 1634), 253.

[4] Calvin, *Institutes*, bk. 4, ch. 3, s. 1; Hopfl, *The Christian Polity of John Calvin* (Cambridge, 1982), 60.

[5] Calvin, *Institutes*, bk. 4, ch. 3, s. 3.

[6] Ibid., s. 16.

[7] *Harmony of confessions*, 249.

[8] Calvin, *Institutes*, bk. 4, ch. 3, s. 7.

[9] Ibids., s. 15, though Calvin advised 'that other pastors ought to preside over the election in order that the multitude may not go wrong'.

hands by the elders in the solemn rite of ordination symbolized the 'dignity' of this divine office, Calvin indicated that the rite should also be received as a warning to 'the one ordained that he is no longer a law unto himself, but bound in servitude to God and the church'.[10] Ordained officers of the church should thus accept their high calling as a stewardship granted by the people, not a private possession, and they must therefore shepherd the flock not as having 'dominion' over their charge, but, as the reformed *Harmony of Confessions* expressed it, with a deep sense of 'humility' as a servant of the congregation.[11] In contrast with the display and spendid ritual of the ordination service in the Roman liturgy, Calvin emphasized the simplicity of the apostolic rite for the church at Geneva, in which 'no other ceremony than the laying on of hands' was used. While he appears to have held the rite of hands 'virtually obligatory', to use his own words, because of the apostles' practice, he nevertheless further divested the ceremony of its divine mystique when he noted that scripture actually gave 'no set precept' for its use.[12] Some reformed churches, notably those of Zurich and Bohemia, went a step further and considered the imposition of hands optional, a ceremony that ministers 'may use . . . or else they may omit'.[13]

Finally, just as the congregation possessed power to elect officers, so the power of 'the keys' and of 'binding and loosing' were, according to the reformed understanding of Matthew 18: 17, committed by Christ 'to the church'.[14] While the discipline of the congregation was to be administered by the elders, Calvin agreed with Cyprian that nothing was to be

[10] Ibid., s. 16.

[11] *Harmony of confessions*, 238–9. [11] Calvin, *Institutes*, bk. 4, ch. 3, s. 16.

[12] John T. McNeill, 'The Doctrine of the Ministry in Reformed Theology', *Church History*, 12 (1943), 81; Hopfl, *The Christian Polity of John Calvin*, 92, has emphasized the elevating function of the imposition of hands in Calvin's treatment, arguing that while troubled by the superstitious associations it had with Roman ceremoies, 'what Calvin found to approve in imposition of hands was clearly its effect in signalling the distinction between ministers and laymen'. While this may be true, Calvin's guardedness on the subject also provides an important dimension of the reformed context for radical puritan and separatist conceptions.

[13] *Harmony of confessions*, 251; see also 246, where the Helvetic Confession said church officers 'may' be ordained by the rite of hands. Seventeenth-century puritans understood this to mean that 'we neither have any commandment touching that matter, neither can it everywhere be performed'. See ibid., 'Observations', Sig. 14.

[14] Calvin, *Institutes*, bk. 4, ch. 11, s. 1–2; cf. also *Harmony of confessions*, 250–2.

done 'without . . . the consent of the people'.[15] The Calvinist conceptualization of the rule for excommunication expressed, perhaps as well as any, the balance that reformers in the Calvinist tradition were attempting to strike between the two poles of what they called an 'aristocratic', elder-dominated polity on the one hand, and a 'democratic' or 'popular' form of government on the other: 'the elders do not do it [excommunicate] by themselves alone, but with the knowledge and approval of the church; in this way the multitude of the people does not decide the action but observes as witness and guardian so that nothing may be done according to the whim of a few'.[16]

The mixed model of reformed polity was a complex paradigm of three forms of government. 'It is not simple,' Peter Martyr Vermigli explained in his *Common Places*, 'but it is compounded of monarchy, aristocracy, and democracy.' In respect of Christ, it was called a monarchy, for Christ ruled the church by the spirit and word of the holy scriptures. As an aristocracy, the presbyters, bishops, and teachers rule the church by executing the office of Christ. Finally, it was a democracy in the sense that serious matters of discipline and the election of officers must not be accomplished 'without the consent of the church'.[17]

Radical Elizabethan puritans, who incorporated many of these same dynamics into their own conception of ministerial power, embraced the fundamental conviction of the Continental reformed tradition that an ordained ministry, formally set apart, was crucial to the well-being of the church, though unlike Calvin, they did not believe that its presence was necessary to the church's existence. Travers, at least, said that while an ordained ministry would be requisite for 'a perfect and well-established church', a true church could nevertheless stand without it.[18] At the same time, it must be said that left-

[15] Calvin, *Institutes*, bk. 4, ch. 11, s. 6.

[16] Ibid., ch. 12, s. 7.

[17] Peter Martyr Vermigli, *Loci Communes* (London, 1583), iv, 5, 9, as translated and quoted by Robert M. Kingdon, 'Peter Martyr Vermigli and The Marks of the True Church' in F. Forrester Church and Timothy George (eds.), *Continuity and Discontinuity in Church History* (Leiden, 1979), 210.

[18] Walter Travers, *A full and plaine declaration of ecclesiastical discipline* (n.p., 1574), 75. Udall appears more traditional, however, by agreeing with Ignatius who said

wing Elizabethan puritans attributed a high role to the ordained ministry in their programmes for reform. Travers may have thought a true church could survive without an ordained ministry, but paradoxically, he did not believe that the sacraments (which, of course, comprised an essential mark of a true church) could be administered without an ordained ministry.[19] The officers of the church were, according to Chaderton, to be considered as God's 'gifts' to the people who were to receive them 'as the angels of God, even as Christ Jesus himself'.[20] The ceremony of hands in ordination, which many radical puritans understood to be obligatory,[21] was viewed as a means of setting the minister apart from the people. The rite expressed their conviction that the ministry possessed its authority directly from God and encouraged the people 'to be obedient unto them'.[22] Ministers were characterized as the 'eyes' of the congregation, set apart to 'lead and direct' the people who, through ignorance or blind desire, might otherwise 'slide . . . in the way'.[23] For the people's part, they were expected 'to suffer themselves willingly to be ruled and governed by those whom God hath set over them'.[24] In this way, radical puritans, as much as Elizabethan formalists, Patrick Collinson has recently remarked, 'breathed a neo-clerical ideology'.[25]

But like Calvin's own many-sided model of the ministry, the reformed matrix of advanced puritan thinking about ministerial

that 'no church . . . can stand without her eldership or council': John Udall, *A Demonstration of the trueth of that discipline which Christe hath prescribed in his Worde for the governement of his Church* (n.p., 1588), 55–6.

[19] Travers, *Ecclesiastical discipline*, 24; 'There can be no sacrament without a minister.'

[20] Laurence Chaderton, *A fruitfull sermon, vpon the 3. 4. 5. 6. 7. & 8. verses of the 12 chapters of . . . Romans* (London, 1584), 53; *A parte of a register contayning sundrie memorable matters, for the reformation of our church* (n.p., 1593), 210.

[21] Travers, *Ecclesiastical discipline*, 68; Udall, *Demonstration*, 41, 45; though Nicholas Crane seems to have viewed it as optional: *Parte of a register*, 120–1.

[22] Travers, *Ecclesiastical discipline*, 68.

[23] Ibid. 56. Chaderton, *Fruitfull sermon*, 48. The imagery of the eyes was generally, though not always, reserved for the officers. While in the appended 'addition' to the 'Lamentable complaint of the Comonaltie', ministers were referred to as the eyes of the congregation, the 'complaint' itself attributed the imagery to the congregation. *Parte of a register*, 287, 208–9.

[24] Travers, *Ecclesiastical discipline*, 185; Chaderton, *Fruitfull sermon*, 35.

[25] Patrick Collinson, *The Religion of Protestants: The Church in English Society 1559–1625* (Oxford, 1982), 111.

power provided other dynamics in contention with this exalted estimation of ministerial authority and function, especially in the repeated warnings by the radicals against the distressing temptation to lordly domination, worldly vanity, and ambition that had, they believed, so thoroughly corrupted the hierarchy of the established church. The famous godly preacher Edward Dering was happy to admit that ministers were 'worthy of double honour . . . singular love . . . [and] great reverence', but he also added, 'yet I dare by no means make them lords in the ministry'.[26] Citing passages from Calvin and other Continental reformers, Richard Gawton, a puritan firebrand from Norwich, openly repudiated before the Consistory Court all the titles of lordship attributed to the hierarchy.[27] If anything, explained Throkmorton in offering a protestant commonplace, ministers were to consider themselves simply as 'servants'.[28]

The puritan tendency thus to sap the sacerdotal thrust of the ministry as it was perceived to function within the English episcopal structure was aided by a conviction they shared with the reformed tradition that ordination was always tied to a specific congregation. Officers were 'inseparably joined with the rest of the body', wrote Travers, and, according to the New Testament, always linked with a local church.[29] They were an organic extension of the people, described by Chaderton as a 'branch' of the congregation.[30] The rite of ordination was in part a recognition that the one being ordained had been set aside by God specifically for the ordaining church.[31] Thus, an ordained ministry with all its benefits and honour dispensed in ordination was not at liberty

[26] *Parte of a register*, 76. For Dering's views on the ministry see also Patrick Collinson, *A Mirror of Elizabethan Puritanism: The Life and Letters of 'Godly Master Dering'* (London, 1964), 10–12, 25–7.

[27] *Parte of a register*, 396.

[28] W. H. Frere and C. E. Douglas (eds.), *Puritan Manifestoes* (reprint. edn., London, 1954), 106–7, 126.

[29] Travers, *Ecclesiastical discipline*, 38, 75.

[30] Chaderton, *Fruitfull sermon*, 60.

[31] Travers, *Ecclesiastical discipline*, 37: 'the apostles did at no time appoint ministers or deacons that afterwards should provide themselves churches where they should teach . . . but they ordained deacons, pastors and elders as the necessity of the church did require'. See also Udall, *Demonstration*, 16; Albert Peel (ed.), *The Seconde Parte of a Register* (Cambridge, 1915), ii. 70.

to 'wander . . . freely where it lists', but was necessarily joined only to 'some certain place and church'.[32] Finally, it was believed that ordination was ineffectual unless the candidate had been called with congregational consent.[33]

The congregational bent of left-wing puritan views on the ministry was magnified further by their prescriptions concerning pastoral duties, which were directed almost entirely to the edifying of the saints within the fellowship rather than evangelizing those outside the church. Ministers were encouraged to preach and teach solely within their own charge for the purpose of 'the feeding of Christ's flock'.[34] Laurence Chaderton summed up the puritan concept of ministerial dependency upon the gathered congregation with the scriptural image of the pastor who 'must continually abide with his flock' and 'by cords . . . be tied to [his] own people'.[35]

In the ecclesiological treatises of the radicals, considerable emphasis was also given to the role of the people in the demanding process of examining, electing, and ordaining their own ministers. Before election and ordination, it was deemed necessary for the congregation to know that a candidate was indeed 'gifted' by the Holy Spirit for the specific ministry needs in their particular church.[36] According to *A Second Admonition*, it was envisaged that a church in need of pastoral care would apply to a local conference of ministers for an appropriate candidate, often from the universities, who was 'learned and of good report'. After a trial period within

[32] Travers, *Ecclesiastical discipline*, 60: laying on of hands was a recognition 'that the Lord had laid on his hands before and given them worthy gifts for the places they were called unto'. Peel (ed.), *Seconde Parte*, i. 165: ordination was 'to the place whereunto a man is chosen'.

[33] Travers, *Ecclesiastical discipline*, 36.

[34] Frere and Douglas (eds.), *Puritan Manifestoes*, 99. See also *Parte of a register*, 407: 'Pastors can preach nowhere save in their own charge': Chaderton, *Fruitfull sermon*, 56, 59; Dudley Fenner, *A counter-poyson* (London, 1584), 186–877. The idea was reflected in the *Helvetic Confession*, as well: *Harmony of confessions*, 237, 240. The answer to 'Certaine Articles', appended to the *Second Admonition* in Frere and Douglas (eds.),*Puritan Manifestoes*, 146, was, however, ambivalent on the subject. Edward Dering was less categorical when he allowed officers to preach outside their own cures 'upon occasion' if 'requested'. *Parte of a register*, 77.

[35] Chaderton, *Fruitfull sermon*, 63.

[36] Travers, *Ecclesiastical discipline*, 59; Thomas Cartwright, *The second replie of Thomas Cartwright* (n.p., 1575), 125; Udall, *Demonstration*, 32, 34: though Udall specified that the examination was to be guided 'by the eldership.'

the conference, he would be presented to the congregation for a period in which the people themselves could become 'acquainted with his gifts and behaviour'.[37] At that juncture the congregation was granted the authority to examine the candidate for evidence of sound doctrine and a godly life, along with an exceptional knowledge of scripture and the ability 'fruitfully . . . [to] communicate with the church'.[38] After this examination, the people proceeded to their election, 'that old and true election, which was accustomed to be made by the congregation' according to the example of the apostles in Acts 1, 6, and 14.[39] It is clear in the literature of the radicals that the election of a minister was the preserve of the congregation: it 'belongs to the church' as a donation from Christ.[40]

But while the congregation possessed the right to elect its own ministers, radical puritans were not thereby advocating a simple democracy. In response to the accusation by the bishops that the *Admonition* 'will have the ministers to be called, allowed, and placed by the people', Throkmorton explained that the admonitioners did not propose an election by the congregation alone, but '*by* elders *with* the common consent of the whole church'.[41] This equation, 'by the elders/with the people', however useful as a rebuttal to the rather facile allegations of 'popularity' and 'anarchy' repeatedly made by the prelates, ultimately left the question unresolved in the writings of the more advanced puritans as to which of the two seats of authority in the gathered church—the people or the officers—weighed most heavily in determining ministerial elections.

This uncertainty in the formulations of the puritan left is most clearly evident in the lengthy and intriguingly elusive

[37] Frere and Douglas (eds.), *Puritan Manifestoes*, 96–7. While expressing preference for a university trained man, Cartwright made it clear that the authority to minister was not derived from an academic degree, but rather from spiritual gifts and the call from a congregation. Ibid., 99.

[38] Travers, *Ecclesiastical discipline*, 91.

[39] Frere and Douglas (eds.), *Puritan Manifestoes*, 12; Travers, *Ecclesiastical discipline*, 46.

[40] Udall, *Demonstration*, 29–30; Travers, *Ecclesiastical discipline*, 46.

[41] Frere and Douglas (eds.), *Puritan Manifestoes*, 137–8 (italics mine): cf. also Travers, *Ecclesiastical discipline*, 44: election was 'by elders' with the rest of the church 'allowing'.

answer Walter Travers gave to the question posed by traditionalists—a perfectly sensible one, given the mixed messages within the puritan paradigm—about whether the extremists intended to grant the power for elections 'unto all or only unto certain chosen men'. Travers began by stressing the executive authority of the eldership, noting that the Apostle Paul called them 'leaders and overseers and exhorted the church to obey them and suffer itself to be ruled by them'. While exercising their authority in all ecclesiastical affairs, the elders 'should also have most ado' in elections 'to govern . . . guide and direct the judgement of the rest'.

While at the outset Travers thus placed the authority firmly in control of the eldership, this was not the conclusion of matter. He went on to add that he had no intention of allowing 'the rule of a few' to diminish 'the majesty of the whole church', and argued forcefully that after having heard the 'sentence and decree' of the elders, the people 'may either by some outward token or else by their silence allow it if it be to be liked of, or gainsay it if it be not just and upright; and not only gainsay it, but, if just cause of their disliking may be brought, make it altogether void and of none effect'. Thus, as the argument progressed, ecclesial elections, in the event of dissension between the two branches of power, appeared to hinge ultimately upon the will of the people since they held the power of veto.[42]

Yet whether that is actually where Travers would have wished the pendulum to rest is not clear either; for, having placed the veto democratically, he pressed the matter further by exploring the situation (which the Reformation first made relevant) in which a church was being established anew, using the apostolic proceedings outlined in Acts 6 and 14 as his model. In that event, Travers quite naturally surmised that the power to govern should reside entirely with the people until such time as elders were elected: 'so that when as yet there were none set over them, all the authority was in all men's hands'. After the first election, however, this power was transferred 'only to those who were chosen by them to steer and govern the church of God'. Having thereby reaffirmed the

[42] Cartwright also attributed the power of 'approval' and 'refusal' to the people: *Second replie*, 125.

unique governing role of the eldership, Travers then proceeded to propose what amounts to a virtual contradiction of his earlier conviction about the power of veto residing in the people. From the examples in Acts he gathered that, once established, the apostles of the fledgling church reserved the right of 'allowing or disallowing the judgements and voices of the people, which power and authority . . . was translated to the ecclesiastical counsel and the elders'.

While this appears to place the final authority for church elections back in the lap of the eldership, Travers was still unwilling to allow such an imbalance and, in the end, utterly failed to commit himself to either side of the equation. Instead, he summed up his position with the decidedly equivocal pronouncement that

> nothing be done not only against the good will [of the people] or unknowingly to the same, but also not without the consent and approbation of it. But we must keep also the just authority of the elders, that they go before the people in the election, that they try and examine those that are to be chosen, that they judge of their worthiness and publish unto the church.[43]

While his ambiguity over the matter suggests that Travers was hardly an 'unashamed aristocrat', as Professor Collinson styled him,[44] a similar ambivalence over the locus of authority also appears when Travers discussed procedures for discipline. As with the election of officers, he considered disciplinary procedures to be an amalgam of three forms of government: monarchy, aristocracy, and democracy. The 'heavenly order' of the church, explained Travers, was realized when

> all these three met in one kind of government . . . wherein all the citizens obediently submit themselves to God which commands, as king and monarch, and the assembly which decrees by his will and authority, where also the assembly and approbation of the rest of the church and people.[45]

Congregational discipline should thus flow out of the same integrated channels of authority that radical puritans envisaged for the election of officers. The ideal was neither one nor

[43] Travers, *Ecclesiastical discipline*, 54–6.
[44] Patrick Collinson, *The Elizabethan Puritan Movement* (London, 1967), 108.
[45] Travers, *Ecclesiastical discipline*, 178.

another form of government, but a fusion of three, in which matters were determined 'by the elders/with the people', both of whom willingly subjected their convictions to the rule of Christ through his Word.

The ambiguity of the position taken by the radicals on the authority of the ministry in the gathered church is evident in a variety of other ways, but perhaps most clearly in their interpretation of Matthew 18: 17, the classic text for their discussions of authority in the church. At times, they took Christ's instructions that first-century believers should 'tell it to the church', if an erring member of the fellowship refuses to repent before two or more witnesses, to mean 'tell the elders'; while at other times they understood Christ to mean 'the whole church'. In addition, there are occasions, remarkable for their apparent inconsistency, when these two distinct renderings appear within the same writing.[46] Cartwright exemplifies this ambiguity in radical puritan thought when he argued in his controversy with Whitgift that, while on the one hand, the 'charge of excommunication belongs . . . chiefly to the eldership and pastor', on the other, the elders could 'do nothing without the advice of the whole church'.[47] Moreover, he refused to accept Whitgift's reading of Matthew 18: 17, which Cartwright believed made the congregation essentially passive in disciplinary proceedings. They were not just 'lookers on', the radical insisted, but 'doers'. Then turning Whitgift's attention to 1 Corinthians 5: 4, Cartwright explained that the apostle gave the active 'judgement of this matter' to the whole congregation: 'Now to judge or to give sentence of malfactors is more (I think) than to look on or to be witness.' The participation of the people in this congregational action was to be construed as the voice of God's judgement, equal in every respect (according to 1 Corinthians 5: 13) to the activity of God's own self in judging those outside the church.[48]

Cartwright, like other Elizabethan left-wing puritans, was convinced that the elders could never act without the consent

[46] e.g. Frere and Douglas (eds.), *Puritan Manifestoes*, 18, 111, 119, 124; Travers, *Ecclesiastical discipline*, 168, 179–80; Thomas Cartwright, *A reply to an answere made of M. Doctor Whitgifte* (n.p., 1574), 146; Thomas Cartwright, *The rest of a second replie* (n.p., 1577), 82–3; Fenner, *Counter-poyson*, 112; Udall, *Demonstration*, 67.

[47] Cartwright, *A reply*, 146; *Rest of a second replie*, 77.

[48] Cartwright, *Rest of a second replie*, 81.

of the people in either 'weighty' or 'light matters'.[49] They were often at pains to check the levelling tendency of this inchoate congregationalism by insisting on the dignity and importance of the ministry in a reformed church, especially through the guiding function of the eldership in ecclesiastical matters. Nevertheless, the theoretical proposals of puritan radicals had the unquestionable impact of elevating the status of the English laity to a new, more prominent level in church affairs: always unwilling to grant the people *carte blanche* in ecclesial decisions, they were, at the same time, discovering democratic meanings in the scriptures. Commenting on a passage from Isaiah, Cartwright went so far as to say 'in the days of the gospel, the people shall not stand in the outward courts but he [God] will bring them into the sanctuary, that is to say that they should be all, for their knowledge as learned as the Levites and priests, which only had entrance into it'.[50] From the perspective of Travers, at least, a pure, thoroughgoing democracy was, in fact, the ideal they desired:

> surely if all men were so taught of God that they could know and judge of these things, then indeed we should need no certain men, who by their spiritual wisdom and discretion should govern and direct the judgements of the people . . . There would be no danger of confusion and uproars.

But because of the reality of human corruption and ignorance even among the saints in this life, such an achievement, Travers lamented, was 'rather to be wished than hoped or looked for'.[51] A true democracy under the lordship of Christ was the form of the church triumphant; until that day dawned, the church on earth would have to be content with the blend of democratic and executive forms of government that Elizabethan radical puritans so cautiously delineated in their many proposals for reform.

Jacobean Radical Puritans

In the writings of the early Stuart 'non-separating congregationalists', the issue of organizational patterns for particular

[49] Cartwright, *Rest of a second replie*, 77; *Second replie*, 125.
[50] Cartwright, *A reply*, 21.
[51] Travers, *Ecclesiastical discipline*, 57–8.

churches was cast in the same complex and conceptually ambiguous formulas issued by their Elizabethan radical predecessors: the Jacobean proponents of radical ecclesial reform desired to establish a balance of power between people and pastor in the churches that would maintain the prestige and authority of the saints, along with a genuine respect for the dignity and rule of the elders. Although they did not all give identical expression to their views, none of the radicals, despite playing a formative role in the prehistory of the 'Congregational Way', stood clearly to one side or the other of the line that ran between aristocratic and democratic forms of church governments.

Among this new generation of puritan radicals, Paul Baynes and William Bradshaw—the only two of Perry Miller's five non-separating congregationalists who did not migrate to the Netherlands—appear to lean more heavily on the side of an aristocratically directed government for the gathered church. Bradshaw, for example, argued that, according to Matthew 16: 19, the spiritual keys of the kingdom were committed by Christ to the 'officers and governors, and unto none other'.[52] In a similarly 'aristocratic' vein, Paul Baynes submitted his settled judgement that the possession of ecclesiastical authority belonged to the officers alone, who, significantly, derived their power directly from Christ, not via the congregation. Baynes was, in fact, distressed by what he perceived to be the excessive radical proclivities of Luther and Melanchthon who, he said, had erroneously asserted that ecclesiastical power flowed from Christ to the officers through the body of the church:

> Ordinary power thereof was not given to the community of the church or to the whole multitude of the faithful, so that they were the immediate and first receptacle, receiving it from Christ, and virtually deriving it to others. This I set down against . . . Luther and Melanchthon . . . Yea, this seems to have been Tertullian's error; for in his book, *de pudicitia*, he makes Christ to have left all Christians with like power.

In opposition to the more democratically oriented model of

[52] William Bradshaw, *Several treatises of worship and ceremonies by the reverend Mr. William Bradshaw* (London, 1660), 43.

civil power advocated by some, in which the power of government resided first in the commoners and only subsequently in the Crown, Baynes explained that ecclesiastical power belonged primarily to Christ the King who then commits the power 'immediately' to 'some person, and not to the whole community which are the queen of Christ. For it is not fit a king should commit power to his queen to serve herself properly, but to have persons who in regard of his relation should stand distinguished.'[53] On this basis, Baynes reasoned in a remarkably 'non-congregational' fashion that the power of censure pertained to the 'representative church' and that Christ in Matthew 18: 17, did not intend 'all the congregation. For then Christ should give not some, but all the members of the church to be governors of it.'[54]

While these remarks reveal a decisively conservative inclination to set the presbyters apart from and above the laity, there are other indications that Bradshaw and Baynes were, all the same, concerned to check this 'aristocratic' force of their doctrine of the ministry, indications that lend some justification to the place they have come to occupy historiographically as progenitors of mid-seventeenth-century Congregationalism. Like others in the Calvinist stream, they insisted that ordination tied a minister directly and only to the ordaining congregation.[55] Furthermore, Bradshaw was careful to point out that with respect to excommunication the elders could act only with 'the free consent of the whole congregation itself'.[56] Moreover, the congregation not only possessed the power 'freely' to choose their guides, but they also held the 'free power to depose them, and to place others in their room'.[57] While Baynes consistently declined to say that the people possessed *ministerial* power, he yet admitted that in practice the congregation owned the 'power . . . of choosing

[53] Paul Baynes, *The diocesans tryall* (London, 1621), 83. The 'congregational' dimension of Luther's ecclesiology, which Baynes calls attention to in this passage, has been a subject of considerable interest and debate for Luther scholars. See G. H. Williams, 'Congregationalist Luther and the Free Churches', *Lutheran Quarterly*, 19 (1967), 283–95; and Gert Haendler, *Luther on Ministerial Office and Congregational Function*, trans. Ruth C. Gritsch (Philadelphia, 1982).

[54] Baynes, *Diocesans tryall*, 77, 80.

[55] Ibid. 10.

[56] Bradshaw, *Several treatises*, 46.

[57] Ibid. 85–6, though he added that this was possible only when 'all' the elders acted 'scandalously'.

worthy, so of refusing unworthy' officers. Finally, Baynes attempted to redress the imbalance between the congregation and the ministry of his otherwise 'aristocratic' views by pointing out the paradoxical role of the presbyters in a gathered congregation who, while shepherds of Christ's flock, were yet sheep in the same pasture. And although they functioned as 'spiritual fathers' of the congregation, the elders were nevertheless 'in some respect . . . children of the whole church'.[58]

In contrast to the views of Baynes, the exiled non-separating congregationalists William Ames and Robert Parker placed possession of the ministerial power of the church unambiguously in the hands of the people. Using the Pauline metaphor of the body, Ames implied that the power of Christ was communicated immediately to every member of the gathered church: 'For as all sense and motion of a sensitive creature is derived from the head into every particular member, so also all spiritual virtue is derived by influence from Christ into his church.'[59] Robert Parker, citing the opinions of Cartwright, explained that according to Matthew 16: 19, Christ 'gave the keys to the whole church'.[60] While he argued that the ministers eventually assumed the administration of the keys, it was 'but mediately by the church of the faithful'.[61] It was Parker's conviction that the Apostle Peter symbolized 'the person of the church not of bishops but of all the faithful'.[62] Correspondingly, he interpreted Matthew 18: 17 to refer to 'the congregation of the faithful'.[63] In this respect, Parker considered the people 'superior' to the presbyters;[64] they were styled 'kings', while the ministers fulfilled the role of 'servants'.[65] For Parker, the 'eye' metaphor—employed by most reformed churchmen to designate the special role of the ministry—was an expression of ministerial subordination:

[58] Baynes, *Diocesans tryall*, 89.

[59] William Ames, *The substance of Christian religion* (London, 1659), 144. See also 147; and *Conscience with the power and cases thereof*, iv, 68, in *The workes of the reverend and faithfull minister of Christ William Ames* (London, 1643).

[60] Parker MS, iii. 1.

[61] Ibid. 3.

[62] Ibid. 2.

[63] Ibid. 4.

[64] Ibid. 13. See also 9: 'the church is above her rectors; all authority flowing from and to her'.

[65] Ibid. 13.

'Peter in respect of ecclesiastical government was subject to the church as the eye to the man.'[66]

Yet, looking at this same congregational paradigm from a different angle, Ames and Parker appear to soften the radical edge of these convictions in several ways. While having implied, as we have seen, that ministerial power was given directly to the people, Ames wrote elsewhere that 'the authority of administering divine things is immediately communicated from God to all lawful ministers.'[67] Parker would have entirely agreed, arguing that 'the pastors as other officers have authority immediately from Christ, and in that respect are superior to men and angels, Gal. 1: 8, as being in Christ's stead as long as they use their authority lawfully'.[68] While in an earlier chapter of his *De politeia*, Parker had averred that ministerial power was 'founded more principally in the church' than with the elders,[69] he appeared to make something of an about-face when, much later, he explained that 'the full power to govern' the church resided 'more principally' in the rectors and 'less principally' in the people.[70] In much the same way, both Ames and Parker at times modified their otherwise congregational exegesis of Matthew 18: 17 to say that Christ therein placed the disciplinary actions of the church with the presbyters, not the people. To quote one example from Parker: 'We say, "church" here [in] Matthew 18, precisely signifies the presbytery.'[71]

The key to unlock these apparently contradictory claims is to be discovered in the tightly drawn distinction they often made between *possession* and *use* of power. Like the puritan left of the Elizabethan generation, Ames and Parker set out to establish a mixed government, partly democratic and partly aristocratic. By democratic government they meant that the power of Christ belonged to the people, though inactively. This power became active only after it passed to the elders, who alone were granted the responsibility of exercising the power of government, in which respect the church was said to be governed aristocratically. Explained in a variety of ways, Parker defined the outline of this complex configuration in a

[66] Parker, MS, iii. 13. [67] Ames, *Conscience* in *Workes*, i. 154.
[68] Parker MS, ii. 13. [69] Ibid. 9. [70] Ibid. 13.
[71] Ibid. 16; Ames, *Conscience*, iv, 88, in *Workes*.

typical passage when he said that the congregation held power 'only virtual, not actual . . . The authority of rectors which is given to the church by Christ rests not in the whole church, but conditionally to be communicated to rectors to the edification of the whole.'[72]

Yet this distinction was not, they agreed, always a valid one since the non-separating congregationalists maintained that the power of the people was not entirely passive, either. Ames, for example, stipulated that while the elders were to 'exercise' the power of discipline possessed by the church, the elders needed more than 'the church permitting' for their administration of this crucial function. They also needed the people to exercise their right of approval and appointment.[73] Similarly, Parker insisted that those who said the church entrusted all her power to the presbyters for administration were deceived, 'for she passes to the presbytery not all her power but so much as Christ ordained for an aristocratical presbytery, retaining a democratical power which the Lord committed to her exercise'.[74]

Jacobean radicals, like their Elizabethan forerunners, were in this way equally as ambiguous about where to draw the line between aristocratic and democratic forms of government in the gathered church. This was true not only among non-separating congregationalists, but also among those commonly placed ecclesiologically further to the right of them. For example, William Stoughton, labelled a thoroughgoing presbyterian,[75] urged not only that ministerial elections proceed only by the people's consent, but also that the discipline of parish churches be guided by the pastor with the consent of the more serious (i.e., puritan) members of each parish.[76] In much the same way, the 'presbyterian' John Paget of Amsterdam tempered the aristocratic side of his ecclesiology when criticized by the separatists for setting up an oligarchic rule of the presbytery. While Paget admitted that his eldership met apart from the congregation to consider disciplinary

[72] Parker MS, iii. 9; see also Ames, *Conscience*, i. 145, in *Workes*.

[73] Ames, *Conscience*, i. 169–70, in *Workes*.

[74] Parker MS, iii. 9.

[75] Stuart Barton Babbage, *Puritanism and Richard Bancroft* (London, 1981), 139.

[76] William Stoughton, *An assertion for true and christian church-policie* (Middelburg, 1604), 201, 385.

cases, he explained that the consistory was always an open meeting which any church member could attend. In the event that excommunication proved necessary, Paget insisted that the elders could never act without first bringing the matter to the people for their 'advice and consent'.[77] From this it appears that Thomas Hooker, whose congregationalism is often contrasted with Paget's presbyterianism, was not far from Paget's own position on the role of the elders. While Hooker said that a sinner deserving to be cut off from the fellowship ought to be brought before the congregation,[78] he nevertheless believed that the consistory could determine certain matters of discipline 'without the public cognition of the church'.[79]

In later generations of English Independents, for whom the likes of Ames and Hooker were taken as ideological forerunners, the problem of precisely how this aggregate of members and officers should function in the decision-making procedures of the institution remained as elusive and unresolvable as ever. As Robert Baillie, the Scottish presbyterian critic of English nonconformity during the Civil War, observed about the views of the Independents on ministerial power: 'So far as we can learn, there is yet no full agreement among them, either in New or Old England in setting the march-stones of power betwixt the eldership and the brotherhood . . . they cannot come to concord.'[80]

Elizabethan and Jacobean Separatists

Separatist thinking about the place of ministerial authority in the gathered church, formed as it had been within the radical puritan ideological milieu, provides yet another example of the fluid, often ambivalent nature of separatist ecclesiological convictions; like the radical puritans, the English separatists

[77] John Paget, *An arrow against the separation of Brownists* (Amsterdam, 1618), 32.

[78] From the Preface to Ames, *A fresh suit against human ceremonies* (Rotterdam, 1633), not paginated. For Hooker's authorship of the Preface, see Frank Shuffelton, *Thomas Hooker, 1586–1647* (Princeton, NJ, 1977), 155–6.

[79] From the *Boswell Papers*, i, 67–72, as printed in R. P. Stearns, *Congregationalism in the Dutch Netherlands* (Chicago, 1940), 108.

[80] Robert Baillie, *A dissuasive from the errours of the time* (London, 1645), 109–10.

attempted to parcel out the locus of authority in the gathered church evenly between three centres of power with Christ as monarchic head, the officers exercising an aristocratic rule, and the people democratically possessing the power of governance. When taken together, it is evident that separatist views on ministerial power were not necessarily more congregationally dominated than mainstream radical puritan formulations of the issue; they certainly did not advocate, as Peter Lake claimed, a 'populist revolt against any sort of ministerial élite'.[81] Indeed, far from being democratic extremists, as they are often portrayed, separatist propaganda reveals that, while enhancing the prestige of the laity, they were also concerned to give equal expression to the more conservative instincts of the English puritans. Despite their often truculent opposition to episcopal tyranny, separatist ideologies nevertheless maintained a 'profound veneration for order and a strong disposition towards obedience' similar to that which Professor Collinson has detected in puritan writings, through the executive role that separatists granted to the ordained ministry.[82]

Robert Browne has often been cited as the one separatist who most unambiguously subordinated the ministry to the gathered congregation, thus constructing a thoroughgoing ecclesiastical democracy within the separatist tradition.[83] Even though he did not, as B. R. White has pointed out, define the doctrine of ministry as thoroughly as did some later separatists, Browne appears to have developed his understanding of ministerial authority far more precisely than Dr White has given him credit for, particularly in his treatise, *A booke which sheweth*, 1582.[84] In that lengthy work, Browne's first and only attempt at a systematic treatment of ecclesiology, the separatist apologist devoted an impressive fifty-seven

[81] Peter Lake, *Moderate puritans and the Elizabethan church* (Cambridge, 1982), 89.

[82] Collinson, *Religion of Protestants*, 153.

[83] H. M. Dexter, *The Congregationalism of the Last Three Hundred Years* (Oxford, 1880), 106–7, 239; W. T. Whitley, 'Records of the Jacob–Lathrop–Jessey Church 1616–1641', *Transactions of the Baptist Historical Society*, i (1908–9), 207; Champlin Burrage, *The Early English Dissenters* (Cambridge, 1912), i, 130; and Perry Miller, *Orthodoxy in Massachusetts 1630–1650* (New York, 1970), 173.

[84] While White criticized Dexter's view of Browne, he nevertheless believed that Browne's concept of ministerial authority in *A booke which sheweth* was 'underdeveloped': B. R. White, *The English Separatist Tradition* (Oxford, 1971), 73, 53.

pages to discussing separatist views on the government of the gathered congregation. If it could be said that Browne moved the discussion toward one or the other side of the puritan aristocratic/democratic equation, he very often appears to emphasize the place and role of the ministry over that of the people.

He began by explaining that ordained church officers should be received by the congregation as those who had been given their office and authority 'of God' for the purpose of guiding the people in worship, determining controversies in the church, commanding the people to do their Christian duties, and monitoring their obedience. Conversely, the duty of the people towards their guides included being

> moved at their [the ministers'] presence, and . . . stricken with their worthiness . . . humbling ourselves in an honouring of them by abasing ourselves according to our unworthiness and their excellency above us . . . despising our right and welfare as unworthy to have or to seek it at their hands when they wittingly withhold it [and] . . . gladly to suffer their correction as being meet for us.

Moreover, Browne insisted that the people should 'yield and stand to their judgements' and follow their 'superiors' by being willing to 'put in practice any duty by their particular appointing'.[85]

While this appears to place the centre of church authority squarely in the hands of the eldership, there was, all the same, a strong democratic strain running throughout Browne's writings that counterbalanced these otherwise aristocratic inclinations. According to Browne, the people held the power of government immediately under Christ, and were therefore elevated to the status of prophets, priests, and kings with authority 'to execute the Lord's government'. When his separatist congregation was first founded in Norwich, it was agreed that the people ought to have the right to 'protest, appeal, complain, exhort, dispute, reprove,' as the occasion arose—'but yet', he added significantly, 'in due order'.[86] Nevertheless, as things developed between Browne and his

[85] Robert Browne, *The Writings of Robert Harrison and Robert Browne*, ed. Albert Peel and Leland H. Carlson (London, 1953), 335–61.

[86] Ibid. 428–9

congregation, the democratic side of his ecclesiology apparently proved a more virile force in the minds of his people than did the convictions about ministerial supremacy; at least, he did not manage to survive the quarrels that broke out between himself and a faction led by Harrison. In the end, Browne was ejected by his own congregation.[87] While Browne's removal was for him, no doubt, a tragic rejection by the small flock of Christ he truly desired to shepherd, the unfortunate event should not be taken to imply that separatist ideologues like Browne had thereby fashioned a polity that encouraged clerical subjugation any more than their left-wing puritan progenitors. It is simply not true, as Dr Zaret maintains in his recent study of popular dissent and puritan ideology, that 'Separatists argued that lay interest in godly religion required congregational *control over* membership and choice of pastors.'[88]

After Browne passed from the separatist scene, the ambivalence about the nature of ministerial authority in separatist ideology remained. There was, of course, a proclivity toward egalitarian participation in their congregational polity that favoured an increasingly assertive and independent puritan laity. Barrow, for example, insisted that power for 'excommunication, election, ordination, etc. is not committed into the hands of one particular person . . . nor yet into the hands of the eldership only, or of the pastors of many particular congregations . . . so much as it is given and committed to the whole church'.[89] Similarly, the exercise of prophecy was viewed as the lawful property of every member 'and none of them ought to be shut out', a conviction reiterated by Ainsworth some years later.[90] Like Browne, Barrow said every member was a prophet, priest, and king, with the power to cast out church officers for either apostasy or disability caused by 'old age . . . frenzy, madness, melancholy, or by maiming as loss of the tongue'.[91] In the separatist *Apologie* of

[87] Ibid. 428–9.

[88] David Zaret, *Heavenly Contract: Ideology and Organization in the Pre-Revolutionary Puritanism* (Chicago, 1985), 91.

[89] Henry Barrow, *The Writings of Henry Barrow, 1587–1590*, ed. Leland H. Carlson (London, 1962), 638.

[90] Ibid. 530; Henry Ainsworth, The *communion* of saincts (Amsterdam, 1607), 233–4.

[91] *Barrow, 1587–1590*, 509; see also John Smyth, *The Works of John Smyth*, ed. W. T. Whitley (Cambridge, 1915), i, 264.

1604, it was determined that all public actions of the church must be administered with the 'brethren's knowledge, presence, approbation, and consent'.[92] While the scriptural basis for this was, more often than not, Matthew 18: 17, it was Henry Ainsworth, the Hebrew scholar, who found an Old Testament precedent for the saints' 'right and interest in the covenant of God and seals of the same'. He noted that 'in the primitive church established by Moses', all public actions such as building the temple, ordaining the priests and Levites, making of the covenant, and repetition of the laws and ordinances were carried out in the presence of 'the whole congregation'.[93]

The separatists drew a line on the ecclesial practice of participatory democracy, however, at the administration of the sacraments. All separatists agreed that the saints possessed the power of the seals, but most would say the people did not thereby have the use of that power.[94] It was the first English baptists, in the process of planting their church on the basis of believer's baptism, who understandably first broke this particular barrier. As early as 1608, Smyth was reasoning that if the whole congregation could preach, pray, sing psalms, admonish, and take part in 'all other actions' of the church, then 'by necessary consequence' the church has the power 'to administer the seals of the covenant'.[95] Murton, who noted that even paedobaptist separatists were not of one mind on the subject, went a step further, claiming that 'baptizing is *no* part of the pastor's office', though he could baptize as an ordinary member. When criticized by the separatists, however, Murton quickly tempered the levelling effect of these sentiments by admitting that baptism ought only to be administered by a 'gifted' male from the congregation who, therefore, already possessed a semi-ministerial status of leadership.[96]

Of all the separatists and radical puritans, Smyth appears

[92] Henry Ainsworth and Francis Johnson, *An apologie or defence of svch trve Christains as are commonly (but vnjustly called Brownists* (Amsterdam, 1604), 64.

[93] Ainsworth, *Communion*, 236–7.

[94] e.g. Francis Johnson, *A trve confession of the faith* (Amsterdam, 1596), art. 34.

[95] *Smyth*, i, 315.

[96] John Murton, *A description of what God hath predestined concerning man* (London, 1620), 162–3, 172–3. Murton cited the separatist, John Wilkinson, as evidence that at least some separatists believed it lawful for members out of office to baptize. If this is true of the Colchester separatist leader, there is no evidence in Wilkinson's single extant writing to either confirm or deny it.

at times to give more than usual authority to the gathered congregation, especially in the way he described the flow of power from Christ to the elders via the people and placed the power of veto firmly in the hands of the congregation. Smyth compared the flow of power in the church to the power structure of civil corporations where the charter was given by the king directly to the corporate owners who, in turn, passed the governing authority on to officers of the corporation: 'so the church which is Christ's body, has power from Christ, and the eldership a part of the body has power from the body'.[97] Like Walter Travers,[98] Smyth invested the elders with the power to govern and the people with the 'negative voice', but he was less ambiguous than Travers about where the tension between the two was to be resolved:

> We say that the definitive sentence, the determining power, the negative voice is in the body of the church, not in the elders: yet we say the elders are to lead and govern all persons and causes of the church, but to lead and govern contrary to the definition and voice of the body that we deny, and that we say is antichristian.[99]

While this adds some support to David Hall's contention that, among the separatists, it was Smyth (as well as John Robinson) who 'most radically subordinated the office of the ministry to the gathered church',[100] this should not entirely obscure the extent to which even Smyth sometimes exercised the kind of reformed rhetoric that tended to elevate the ministry above the people. Smyth not only adhered to the reformed, Pauline dictum about the 'double honour' that should be reserved for the ordained officers of the church, he also explained,

> that the power of the church is, for order's sake, committed into some particular person's hands who, in the church's name and for the church's good and in the church's presence, are to handle all church matters and therefore . . . you are to remember that Christ's

[97] *Smyth*, ii, 391.
[98] See above, n. 42.
[99] *Smyth*, ii, 417.
[100] David Hall, *The Faithful shepherd: A History of the New England Ministry in the Seventeenth century* (rev. edn. New York, 1974), 38–40. While this seems to be a more accurate assessment of Smyth's position among radical churchmen, it is not true of Robinson. For a detailed discussion of Robinson's doctrine of the ministry, see below, nn. 163–208.

church in several respects is a monarchy, an aristocracy, a democracy.[101]

Smyth's analogy with the civil corporation would certainly have leaned toward the subordination of the ministry by making the flow of power between Christ and the elders indirect; it should be noted that he also employed the imagery of a 'channel' or 'pipe', commonly used by other radical puritans to imply that Christ appointed his ministers directly. Smyth envisioned the people as providing the conduit of ministerial power. 'Some members of the church have special gifts given them of God, but the power of using those gifts they have from the head Christ by the means of the body, which is the *pipe* that from the fountain conveys all power ecclesiastical to every officer.'[102] Yet, like most radical puritans, Smyth maintained that 'all the saints shall yield obedience to the elders in things commanded by God', a conviction by which Smyth, according to Ainsworth, attempted to 'sweeten the ill favour' of his otherwise extreme notions.[103]

In numerous ways, separatists strengthened their concept of a separated ministerial order and curbed the democratic force of their more radical doctrines. For example, they emphasized that only spiritually gifted men could be lawfully elected to office, a separatist concept which Johnson used to support the substantial modification he made late in his career as a separatist in his exegesis of Matthew 18: 17, which he changed from 'tell the congregation' to 'tell the elders'.[105] While, by the same token, most separatists were willing to allow for the practice of lay ordination, they indicated that this highly unusual procedure could be used only in the rare event that a church was entirely bereft of its own or neighbouring elders, a view which would have found wide support in the reformed tradition generally; otherwise, ordination was to be administered by the elders alone. When lay

[101] *Smyth*, i, 319; ii, 416. [102] Ibid. ii, 424.

[103] Henry Ainsworth, *A defence of the holy scriptures and ministery* (Amsterdam, 1609), 129.

[104] Henry Barrow, *The Writings of Henry Barrow, 1590–1591, ed. Leland H. Carlson (London, 1966), 146; Ainsworth and Johnson, Apologie*, 45.

[105] Francis Johnson, *A short treatise concerning the words of Christ. tell the church* (Amsterdam, 1611), Sig. A4.

ordination was lawful, there were, in addition, further limitations to be observed, for even in that situation the separatists were concerned to emphasize that not just any member could ordain, but only the 'men of best gifts' appointed by the congregation.[106] This semi-ministerial status of giftedness was necessary for lay prophets as well. Lay prophecy, in fact, seemed to be viewed by the 1596 *Confession* not so much as something that enhanced the role of the people, as it is often understood by modern historians, but rather either as a temporary measure to be used in infant churches where a preaching ministry had not yet been appointed,[107] or as an exercise through which a particular lay member could display his homiletic talents and thus move with the knowledge and approval of the congregation toward full ordination.[108]

Similarly, although the separatists made provisions for the administration of discipline by private members when an ordained man was not available, they added the common puritan proviso that this should be carried out only by recognized lay leaders from the congregation.[109] In short, all church actions were to be done 'in order' with due respect for a ministerial or social hierarchy. Thus, it was not only among the 'mainstream Calvinists' of a moderate puritan persuasion that a fear of religious and social anarchy prevailed, as Professor Collinson suggests, but even among the 'less privileged' enclaves of the outlawed separatists that Collinson does not include in his discussion of the conservative tendencies in puritan thought.[110] As Ainsworth explained,

[106] *Browne*, 337; *Barrow, 1590–1591, 233; Smyth*, i, 258.

[107] This, of course, was the situation of the separatist congregation in Amsterdam when the *Confession* was written. Johnson, their minister, was imprisoned in London and did not join the exiled congregation in Amsterdam until 1597. F. J. Powicke, *Henry Barrow, Separatist (1550?–1593) and the Exiled Church of Amsterdam 1593–1622* (London, 1900), 228.

[108] Johnson, *Trve confession*, art. 34. See also *Barrow, 1587–1590*, 532. For the practice of lay prophecy in the reformed tradition, see G. F. Nuttall, *The Holy Spirit in Puritan Faith and Experience* (Oxford, 1946), 77; Collinson, *Elizabethan Puritan Movement*, 169.

[109] Johnson, *Trve confession*, art. 24; *Smyth*, i, 266.

[110] See Collinson's disparaging critique of the way Christopher Hill and Michael Walzer have portrayed Elizabethan and early Stuart puritans as harbingers of revolutionary social and political ideology, in *Religion of Protestants*, 141–88; especially 181, where Collinson says: 'We speak, of course, as Michael Walzer does, of

we hold it necessary that all church actions be orderly carried, either by the officers if there be any, or by the magistrates as in Israel, or by the fathers of families, or the most excellent in gifts requested thereunto by the congregation: this we firmly maintain, against all popular confusion and disorder whatsoever.[111]

It is worth noting in this context the story about Henry Barrow's denunciation of the action of one 'T. L. and others', who, in a private separatist conventicle, excommunicated two of their members without an ordained minister being present.[112] While the story may be apocryphal, it is certainly not out of character with the separatist emphasis on the importance of ordained officers in all church actions. Like Browne before him, Barrow had a deep respect for the authority of the elders. There may be communion in the church, he once said in a statement that is laden with traditional clerical values,

yet there is no equality. The church knows how to give honour and reverence unto their elders, especially to them that labour in the Word and doctrine. The church of Christ is taught to obey and submit unto their leaders, to acknowledge them that labour amongst them and that are set over them in the Lord, and to admonish them, and to hold those in superabundant love for their work's sake.[113]

The duty of admonishing the elders mentioned by Barrow raises the critical question surrounding the issue of ministerial authority: could the congregation, through the power of Christ invested in them, effectively overrule their guides, or did the aristocratic side of separatist polity ensure that the really crucial power lay in the hands of the elders by virtue of their governing capacity? The question is difficult to answer, primarily because, while separatists advocated the concept of congregational dissent, they often qualified this liberty with the important stipulation that it be done 'in due order',[114] a puritan idiom indicating the need to yield to the judgement of

mainstream Calvinism and not of the more radical religious tendencies which doubtless articulated the "unsettledness" of the less privileged.' Collinson does not identify these 'less privileged' ones, but given the period of his study (1559–1625), one must assume he had in mind some of the more radical puritans and separatists as being those of a more 'unsettled' disposition.

[111] Henry Ainsworth, *An animadversion to Mr. Richard Clyftons advertisement* (Amsterdam, 1613), 58.

[112] Cited by Carlson in *Barrow, 1587–1590*, 585, n. 1.

[113] Ibid. 610.

[114] e.g. *Browne*, 422.

the Word as determined by those trained and entrusted with the responsibility of teaching and preaching scripture. Moreover, even Smyth taught that in any potential church disciplinary case, it was advisable to involve the elders long before the matter ever reached the church meeting, thereby following the advice of Barrow who maintained that 'the trial and censuring of elders ought chiefly to be done by the elders of that church', though this did not mean, Barrow added, that 'the reproof of elders only belongs to elders'.[115] Ainsworth said the people could dissent, but, significantly, warned that 'if in matter or manner they [the people] transgress, they are to bear their [the elders'] rebuke, all things in the public judgements of the church being carried holily, peaceably and by the government of the elders'.[116]

Uncertainty between upholding the power of the people or maintaining the rule of the elders, therefore, generally marks separatist thinking about the locus of authority in the church, much as it did in the writings of the radical puritans. This ambiguity has found its way into the treatment of the issue in the separatist tradition by modern historians, who have variously cast the separatists as advocates either of ministerial subordination or of the rule of the eldership. For example, Perry Miller was inclined to accentuate what he recognized to be the aristocratic bent of separatist polity, while David Hall has more recently emphasized its radically congregational orientation.[117] Henry Powicke observed that Barrow held the office of the ministry in high esteem, but perhaps overstated the case in the other direction when he said that Barrow nevertheless saw the minister as a mere 'layman', without 'any peculiar grace which severed him from the rest of the brethren'.[118] Barrow did, in fact, say that ministers had been granted a greater measure of spiritual gifts than non-ordained members.[119] More recently, B. R. White stressed the idea that the 'mainstream' of the separatist tradition firmly subordinated the elected ministry to the power and authority held by the congregation.[120] However, when comparing the 1644 Baptist

[115] *Smyth*, i, 262; *Barrow, 1587–1590*, 619–20.
[116] Ainsworth, *Animadversion*, 35.
[117] Miller, *Orthodoxy in Massachusetts*, 173; Hall, *Faithful Shepherd*, 30–48.
[118] Powicke, *Henry Barrow, Separatist*, 119.
[119] *Barrow, 1590–1591*, 146.
[120] White, *English Separatist Tradition*, 62.

Confession with the 1596 *Confession* of the separatists, White noted the frequent stress in the separatist *Confession* 'on the importance of the ministry' and, in this context, now concluded that it was not until the Baptist *Confession* of 1644 that 'the ministry was more firmly subordinated to the immediate authority of the covenanted community'.[121]

The issue of authority and its division between the people and the ministry in the gathered congregations of the separatists proved to be fraught with ambiguities that, as R. W. Dale concluded, 'are too delicate, too subtle, too variable, to be fixed by a rigid rule'.[122] Separatist convictions tipped conclusively neither toward the rule of an élite nor toward that of the people. Rather, at varying times and in the context of differing controversies, they reveal a complex amalgam of competing tendencies in which a balance of power between executive and popular rule was sought. At the same time, because of the equivocal nature of such a paradigm, emphasis on one side or the other, or on the balance of both, varied within separatist literature itself, depending largely, it seems, upon the practical demands of a given situation. Radically minded when attacking the 'tyranny' of episcopacy, separatists none the less appear relatively conservative when countering the allegations that separatism fomented social anarchy and 'popularity'. Richard Bernard's remark that investing the people with the power to preach, administer the sacraments, and exercise censures was 'the A. B. C. of Brownism',[123] sparked off an ecclesiastical skirmish between Ainsworth, Smyth, Johnson, and Robinson which provides a good, if rather tangled, illustration of the fluidity of their positions.[124] At one point in his controversy with Smyth over the issue, after a series of charges and counter-charges, Ainsworth threw up his hands in dismay and declared: 'that which I have

[121] B. R. White, 'The Doctrine of the Church in the Particular Baptist Confession of 1644', *Journal of Theological Studies*, 19 (1968), 581.

[122] R. W. Dale, *History of English Congregationalism* (London, 1908), 107–9, 209.

[123] Richard Bernard, *Christian advertisements and counsels of peace* (London, 1608), quoted in *Smyth*, ii, 393.

[124] See especially, *Smyth*, ii, 393–436 *passim*; Henry Ainsworth, *Counterpoyson* (Amsterdam, 1608), 103; *Defence of the holy scriptures*, 102–29; *Animadversion*, 4–50, 111–17 *passim*; Johnson, *Tell the church*, *passim*; and *A Christian plea conteyning three treatises* (Leiden, 1617), 307–8, cf. also 252–3.

written is further confirmed by Mr. Smyth himself'.[125] At times, it seems, they argued in circles, until the business became so involved that some found it altogether impossible to sort out the sides being taken in the controversy. As one unidentified friend of Ainsworth observed, 'Those that come over of Master Johnson his side, say they held no more concerning the eldership than Master Ainsworth has written against Master Smyth: others say the contrary.'[126]

It is this uncertainty and confusion even within their own ranks which indicates most clearly that the separatists were stumbling over the same unsettled conclusions which plagued the radical puritans of Elizabethan and Jacobean England about the place of authority in the gathered church. Like their advanced puritan contemporaries, the separatists were not always able to determine decisively where to draw the line between ministerial and lay authority in the church.

Henry Jacob

In the opening words of *An attestation of many learned, godly and famous divines*, Henry Jacob noted that 'many things at diverse and sundry times heretofore' had been written about the necessity of purging the church in England of its insufferable antichristian practices. While not everyone entirely agreed about the finer points of such a reform, there was, he believed, one common feature shared by the many voices of dissent, which he summed up as a demand that 'church government ought to be exercised always with the people's free consent'.[127] This, he felt, was the central issue 'which makes the matter and puts the difference indeed between the ecclesiastical reformation which in all dutifulness we seek and that church government which the lord bishops in England do exercise'.[128] The intent of Jacob's *Attestation* was, therefore, to prove to the Jacobean prelates that the most reputable theologians through-

[125] Ainsworth, *Defence of the holy scriptures*, 120.
[126] Ainsworth, *Animadversion*, 1.
[127] Henry Jacob, *An attestation of many learned, godly and famous divines* (Middelburg, 1613), 9–10.
[128] Ibid. 16.

out Christian history unanimously concurred that the government of the church could lawfully be executed only with the willing consent of the people. To support this contention, Jacob amassed an impressive list of quotations to that effect, ranging widely from pronouncements of the earliest church fathers to the confessions and revered writings of more recent protestants in England and abroad. From Ignatius and Cyprian to Luther, Calvin, and Thomas Cartwright, Jacob teased out corroborative hints and uncovered bold, clear statements to reinforce his thesis that all the most discriminating Christian commentators in history agreed that a true ecclesiastical government flows from 'the people's free consent'.[129]

By government 'with a people's free consent', Jacob intended to promote the kind of mixed policy advocated by other radical puritans and separatists who sought a composite form of church government which balanced democratic and aristocratic sources of authority. The extent to which it may be understood as either one or the other, in Jacob's writings, largely depends upon two factors: the perspective from which he was viewing the issue and the historical circumstances about which he wrote at any given time. In the first instance, Jacob's views reflect alternate emphases, depending upon whether he was looking at the issue of power in the gathered church from the perspective of who *possessed* the power or of who *exercised* it. But even this formula could be complicated by a second variable of historical circumstance: one must determine whether Jacob was discussing the issue under the assumption that a church was with or without an ordained ministry; according to that variable, as we shall see, the puritan distinction between *possession* and *use* would be brought into play or set aside.

From the perspective of possession, Jacob wrote with a thoroughly democratic bent. According to the example of Matthew 18: 17, the power of Christ for the government of each church resided 'in the body of the congregation substantially, essentially, and fundamentally'.[130] When individual lay believers joined together into a church estate, the power of Christ for 'all the holy things of God, all God's

[129] Jacob, *Attestation*, 52.

[130] Ibid. 80.

ordinances spiritual' flowed directly into their hands. United in fellowship, the people became the 'sacred body [of Christ] . . . from whence by a necessary and undeniable consequence it follows that Christ has given the power of imposing hands, of censures, of sacraments, of preaching the Word and all, unto the congregation'.[131] In language so characteristic of the Elizabethan radicals and separatists, Jacob believed the congregation held the power of government 'immediately under Christ' as a 'right and privilege'.[132]

While conceptually Jacob identified the congregation as trustees of the church's authority, functionally his polity leaned toward the aristocratic side of the puritan equation by the way that he posited the effective use of that authority in the hands of the church officers. Even though he believed the 'keys of the kingdom' belonged to the laity, Jacob consciously attentuated the revolutionary force of this idea with the following circumscription:

yet consider secondly that the people thus have received all these spiritual things, and so can give them only potestatively (as I may say) that is, they have the power of them. But active, actually they only can administer them who are the church's instruments for that purpose by them assigned [namely, the officers].[133]

This was true for virtually every area of the church's life; the people possessed the power but only the officers could exercise it. While he campaigned tirelessly for 'elections and excommunications by the people', Jacob was quick to add the typical puritan gloss that his programme for reform should not be confused with 'any popularity which can be either prejudicious to princes, or tumultuous in itself'. Strictly speaking, the polity he advocated was not a democracy because 'the ecclesiastical guides there (apart from the people) do first by themselves prepare and determine the whole matter [in either elections or excommunications] namely in such sort that the people may not need to do ought

[131] Ibid. 298.

[132] Henry Jacob, *A Christian and modest offer of a most indifferent conference* (Middelburg, 1606), 2; *A humble supplication for toleration, and libertie* (Middelburg, 1609), 14.

[133] Jacob, *Attestation*, 298; *A declaration & plainer opening of certaine points in the divine beginning* (Middelburg, 1611), 9.

afterward but only consent with them and freely signify their consent to it'.[134] In this respect, Jacob's congregationalism was on the face of it no more radical than Calvin's, whose requirement that church actions be approved by the 'common consent' of the people meant, as Harro Hopfl has recently claimed, that 'the congregation's part in all this was that of a cypher', and little more.[135]

So for Jacob, power for elections and discipline belonged theoretically to the people, but operatively with the ministry. Even the matter of ministerial nominations potentially belonged to the eldership alone: 'Letting the people to nominate their ministers' was, Jacob believed, an ecclesiastical action 'in some sort indifferent'.[136] Presumably, since there was no scriptural warrant, nominations were to be controlled by either ministers or magistrates. Ordination, usually administered by the imposition of hands, also belonged functionally to the officers, even though conceptually, ministerial power flowed from the people.[137] Similarly, only officers were allowed to administer the sacraments.[138] Cases of discipline were apparently not only to be judged by the eldership before reaching the congregation, but, at the discretion of the elders, some cases could be determined not worthy of congregational attention. Failure to distinguish between light and weighty matters of discipline, Jacob observed soberly, was the grievous error of the French radical Calvinist, Jean Morély, who 'sought in churches perfectly established to bring all things in particular, and ordinarily to the people's hearing, examining, judging, and voice-giving'.[139] This, he rather uncritically believed, was also the peculiar heresy of the English separatists, who took Matthew 18: 17 'more popularly than there is need . . . That is, they will examine all scandals . . . whatsoever

[134] Henry Jacob, *Reasons taken out of Gods Word* (Middelburg, 1604), 27–8.

[135] Hopfl, *Christian Polity of John Calvin*, 92.

[136] Jacob, *Reasons*, 12.

[137] Jacob, *Attestation*, 299.

[138] Ibid. 298.

[139] Ibid. 24. Morély's advocacy of congregationalism in *Traicté de la discipline & police chrestienne* (Lyon, 1562), drew vigorous criticism from Geneva, but was perhaps not so democratically oriented as Jacob here implies. Indeed, Morély qualified the 'popularity' of his ecclesiology in much the same way as many of the English radicals did. While there are similarities between Morély's ecclesiology and that of his English counterparts, there is no evidence of any direct influence in puritan circles. On Morély, see Robert M. Kingdon, *Geneva and the Consolidation of the French Protestant Movement 1564–1572* (Madison, Wis., 1967), 46–62, 127–35.

in the presence and under the judgement of the whole multitude.'[140]

With the use of power thus residing in the officers, the question about congregational dissent deserves some attention. Could private members effectively oppose the rule of the elders? In some respects, it appears they could. Like all radicals, Jacob despised what he judged to be the lofty protocol of the English prelatical system, which tempted clerics to act as 'lords over the people'.[141] He therefore declared that nothing should ever be imposed on the people by the pastor 'against their will'.[142] Nevertheless, it does appear that, whether consciously or not, Jacob's polity maintained a kind of traditional differential between minister and people which made congregational dissent conceivably impossible. Theoretically, Jacob granted the congregation power to discipline their own officers,[143] yet within the structure of his polity, the officers were potentially immune to discipline if they were unwilling to co-operate, since they controlled the entire disciplinary process and, as he said, 'determined' the matter before (and if) it ever reached the people for their consent.[144] It is easy to see how this could be used to executive advantage, especially when Jacob underscored the point that while all 'matters of weight' should be carried out by the officers in the presence of 'the whole congregation', it was equally important 'that they (the said congregation) do not manifestly dissent there from'.[145] The primary duty of the people, and one that affected the status of their salvation, was to respond with obedience to their minister:

But it is necessary ordinarily to salvation for all Christians to have some approved, trusty, and faithful pastor and guide of their souls. To which end we are commanded to obey them that have oversight

[140] Jacob, *Attestation*, 249. He did not say who they were, but he may have been thinking of Ainsworth's party in the controversy which had recently split the Amsterdam separatist church. Nevertheless, considering the manner in which separatists also curbed the democratic side of their ecclesiology, the accuracy of Jacob's remark must be called into question.

[141] Ibid. 250.

[142] Ibid. 24.

[143] Henry Jacob, *A confession and protestation of the faith of certaine Chritians in England* (Amsterdam, 1616), Sig. B7.

[144] Jacob, *Reasons*, 28.

[145] Jacob, *Confession*, Sig. B7.

of us . . . So that now it concerns every man's life and peace to receive Levi, the approved pastors and teachers of the Word of God.[146]

With this in mind, the weightier side of his equivocation, that 'the church may compel pastors . . . and yet properly he [the pastor] cannot be compelled', becomes more evident. He was, in fact, convinced that the minister's 'own will carries him . . . so that howsoever the church (when they see need) may enjoin him, yet his own will is it which he shall answer for. Pastors therefore shall indeed give account to God for their administering the Word and sacraments', and, presumably, not the congregation.[147]

The 'free consent' of the people was potentially, then, in his thought not much more than a rubber stamp, a guaranteed public affirmation of judgements enacted by the ruling elders in the name of the congregation. Congregational opposition, by the structure of things, was, at the least, perilous for the eternal security of private souls, if not potentially impossible. In the end, the congregation's hold on the church's purse-strings was possibly the one effective leverage they possessed. Jacob approved a system of maintenance by voluntary contributions from the people, 'according as the Lord has prospered'.[148] Yet even in this matter, final control of the proceeds rested in the hands of the ruling group: contributions were to be collected every Lord's Day by the deacons and then 'committed into the hands of the elders, and with their direction to be disposed of by the deacons'.[149] Thus, looking at Jacob's polity from the perspective of who could actually use the power theoretically held by the congregation, it was certainly not a pure democracy and carried the potential of government by the few.

There was, however, one variable that could alter this, namely, historical circumstance. Only if a congregation found itself deprived of all officers could the people themselves

[146] Henry Jacob, *A collection of sundry matters* (Middelburg, 1616), Sig. A8.

[147] Jacob, *Attestation*, 301.

[148] Jacob, *Confession*, Sig. C7. Jacob did not categorically reject the practice of state support by tithes. He believed tithes lawful so long as the congregation gave their consent, though this would be less than ideal.

[149] Ibid.

execute the government of the church: 'When a church is destitute of guides (as it has fallen out, and may again fall out on occasion) then the people themselves have full power to accomplish any ecclesiastical action in the best order they can, and particularly church censures.'[150] The history of the church at Southwark, founded by Jacob, provides an instructive example. In the absence of a pastor following Jacob's departure in 1624, the Stinton MSS record that 'the congregation remained a year or two edifying one another in the best manner they could according to their gifts received from above'.[151] It is difficult to say how far this privilege extended. As we have already observed, most separatists manifestly refused to allow anyone to administer the sacraments except an ordained pastor.[152] While it is likely that Jacob concurred, the peculiar way in which he finally chose to interpret Tertullian's dictum, 'a layman may baptize', seems to indicate that Jacob, like John Smyth and possibly John Murton, was open to the lay administration of baptism in the event that a church was bereft of officers: 'Tertullian may mean well . . . namely, if the church assign him [the layman] in a case of necessity, when an ordinary minister cannot be had. Otherwise, I cannot justify his speech.'[153]

Yet ordinarily, as we have seen, the congregation was to submit itself to the discretionary powers of the ruling elders. As Jacob answered in his catechism the question about whether or not the entire church could elect their ministers and correct offenders, 'They are to do no more of necessity and in their ordinary carriage, but freely to consent to their guides preparing and directing every matter.'[154] The Baptist historian, W. T. Whitley, was in this respect entirely fair when, early in this century, he determined that Jacob's views on ministerial authority came very near Calvin's original ideal

[150] Jacob, *Attestation*, 278.

[151] Stinton MSS, 3.

[152] See above, n. 94, and Johnson, *Trve confession*. art. 34. The most notorious example was John Robinson's refusal to allow even his ruling elder, William Brewster, to administer the sacraments to the pastorless congregation of Pilgrims at Plymouth colony in New England. See below, n. 170.

[153] Jacob, *Attestation*, 298–9. For Smyth and Murton, see above, nn. 95–6.

[154] Champlin Burrage, 'Lost Prison Papers of Henry Jacob', *Review and Expositor*, 5 (1908), 509.

of a congregation governed by its officers.[155] As Jacob himself quoted Calvin, 'nothing indeed may be done without the consent and allowance of the people, and yet the pastors should moderate them'.[156]

Finally, it should be noted that the differential between people and ministry in the use of power also existed to a degree within the ranks of the church officers themselves. While Jacob rejected the national and diocesan structure of episcopacy, he nevertheless supported something of a hierarchy of authority among the officers of a local church. There were, Jacob explained, basically three, and sometimes four, kinds of ministers: 'A pastor or bishop, with elders, and deacons', and elsewhere he added the office of 'teacher'.[157] Contrary to those who believed that he advocated equality between the officers of a gathered church, Jacob replied,

> as for a general parity we mislike and detest it also. Yea, in short we say that the church's state is monarchical. For we affirm that in every several true church there ought to be a disparity of church ministers: viz. the pastor above the elders, and the elders above the deacons, as Ignatius saith.[158]

The same hierarchy applied to the fourfold ministry, with the office of teacher resting somewhere between the pastor and elders. This seems to be the intention of his rather novel interpretation of the Pauline metaphor of the church as a human body 'in which all members are not eyes or heads or hands, but one is a head, another is a hand, etc., so in the body of Christ one is pastor, another teacher, others elders, others deacons, etc.'.[159] This is something of an unorthodox use of the metaphor. Puritans and separatists usually employed the image of the 'head' to represent Christ alone, whereas the parallel Jacob appears to draw here is between the 'head' and

[155] Whitley, 'Jacob–Lathrop–Jessey Church', 207.

[156] Jacob, *Attestation*, 27.

[157] Burrage, 'Lost Prison Papers', 510; Jacob, *Humble supplication*, 16; *A plaine and cleere exposition of the 2d. commandement* (Leiden, 1610), Sig. E6. Burrage noted that Jacob's ideas about the categorization of church officers fluctuated between 1605–16. In 1605, Jacob listed a threefold order, which he expanded to fourfold in 1610, only to revert to his earlier trichotomous division in 1616; Burrage, *Early English Dissenters*, i, 315–16.

[158] Jacob, *Reasons*, 37.

[159] Jacob, *Humble supplication*, 18.

the pastor. Whether this was his intention or not, Jacob did acknowledge that each particular church should be governed by one man; as he once explained, 'in every church we acknowledge a superior'.[160] This was the reason why, for example, Jacob maintained that elders, deacons, and other laymen could ordinarily only preach by the 'special appointment' of the pastor.[161] Given this understanding of ministerial authority, it is understandable why Jacob felt confident that the church polity he advocated would never be subject to the 'chaos' of a mere democracy. Like other radicals, he, too, spoke with more than one voice: with respect to who possessed the power for government, he constructed a thorough-going democracy; but with respect to its effective use, he maintained that power should remain firmly in the hands of the eldership under the supervision of a single, 'superior' pastor.[162]

John Robinson

'The Lord Jesus is the king of his church alone, upon whose shoulders the government is, and unto whom all power is given in heaven and earth,' John Robinson wrote in *A justification of separation*, 'yet has he not received this power for himself alone, but does communicate the same with his church.' This power, he explained further, was communicated like anointing oil which,

> being poured by the Father upon [Christ], the head, runs down to the skirts of the clothing, perfuming with the sweetness of the Saviour every member of the body and so makes every one of them severally kings and priests and all jointly a kingly priesthood or communion of kings, priests, and prophets.[163]

With this vivid biblical imagery, Robinson described how the power for church government lawfully resided not in the

[160] Jacob, *Reasons*, 38–9.

[161] Ibid. 70.

[162] *Contra* Carr's assessment of Jacob's views on the issue in Frank Benjamin Carr, 'The Thought of Robert Parker (1564?–1614) and His Influence on Puritanism Before 1650' (London University Ph.D. thesis, 1964), 176–7.

[163] John Robinson, *A justification of separation from the church of England* (Amsterdam, 1610), 133.

officers alone, but with the entire congregation, even down to 'the meanest member of the body'.[164]

Robinson's understanding of ministerial power in the gathered church has led David Hall to conclude that more than any separatist or puritan before him, Robinson—like John Smyth—radically subordinated the ordained ministry to the authority of the gathered church.[165] But a careful examination of Robinson's writings suggests that he, too, struggled to establish, much like other left-wing puritans and separatists, something of an Aristotelian point of equilibrium between popular consent and executive rule in the distribution and use of power between minister and people. He never entirely resolved the inherent tensions between these two: the people, he said, were 'sheep, yet not unreasonable beasts' while the officers were 'shepherds, as they are also themselves sheep'.[166]

As with Jacob and other radicals and separatists, Robinson distinguished between the possession and use of ministerial power, believing that the two could properly be fused only in the highly irregular event that a church was bereft of all ordained officers as, for example, at the time of planting an entirely new congregation.

The distinction between possession and use was most clear over the issue of the possession and administration of the sacraments. He explained that 'every true visible church of Christ [has] direct and immediate interest in and title to Christ himself and the whole New Testament and every ordinance of it'.[167] But this did not mean 'that because the church hath the power of Christ for all things, therefore it can enjoy all things without officers. The power is one thing which is inseparable from the body, the use of the power another thing, which in many cases it may want.'[168] Robinson agreed with article 34 of the separatist *Confession*, which said that the sacraments were ordinances of Christ which the congregation possessed but could not use.[169] Only an ordained, preaching

[164] Robinson, *Justification*, 133.
[165] Hall, *Faithful shepherd*, 38–40.
[166] Robinson, *Justification*, 219–20.
[167] Ibid. 131–2.
[168] Ibid. 223–4.
[169] Ibid. 123–4; John Robinson, *A defence of the doctrine propounded by the synode at Dort* (Amsterdam, 1624), 103–4.

minister with Oxbridge credentials had authority to administer them. Thus, he flatly denied William Brewster's request from New Plymouth that, as the elected ruling elder of the Plymouth separatist church, Brewster be allowed to administer the Lord's Supper to the pastorless pilgrim congregation in the New World; instead, Robinson advised they seek the services of 'any learned man' who might come to them.[170] This constriction seems only to have applied to the administration of the Lord's Supper, however, because Robinson, like Jacob and others, appears not to have denied the possibility of lay baptism in a church without ministers.[171]

The same distinction between possession and use applied to other areas of the church's life, though not always as sharply. Prophecy, for example, was primarily the domain of the preaching elders, yet private members had the 'liberty to move and propound their questions and doubts for satisfaction, as also having received a gift to administer the same unto edification, exhortation, and comfort'.[172] While this offered the people a practical role in the ministry of the church, it did not elevate the congregation as a whole to the level of the ordained ministry. Rather than raising the status of the body, Robinson seems to have understood lay prophecy primarily as an exercise set aside for a few gifted members in preparation for possible ordination, insisting, along with the 1596 separatist *Confession*, that lay prophets should possess a 'calling' from the church.[173] This in itself reduced the number of lay prophets to a small minority, 'happily two or three in each of our churches',[174] and provided a significant formal difference between lay prophets, who possessed a 'call', and ordinary members, who did not. The close association of lay preaching with eventual ordination was underscored by Robinson's remark that he viewed the practice in much the same way as

[170] William Bradford, *History of Plymouth Plantation, 1606–1646* (Boston, 1912), i, 371. While Brewster is known to have mariculated at Peterhouse, Cambridge, in 1580, he evidently never received a degree and so either did not seek ordination or, because he did not hold a divinity degree, failed in Robinson's estimation to meet the qualifications necessary to exercise this ecclesiastical rite. H. M. Dexter and M. Dexter, *England and Holland of the Pilgrims* (London, 1905), 256, 283–4.

[171] Robinson, *Defence of the doctrine*, 179. See above, n. 153.

[172] John Robinson, *Of religious communion private and publique* (Amsterdam, 1614), 23.

[173] John Robinson, *The peoples plea* (n.p., 1641), 32; *Defence of the doctrine*, 102.

[174] John Robinson, *A just and necessarie apologie* (Amsterdam, 1625), 50.

the Dutch Reformed Church, where 'such as have bent their thoughts towards the ministry, should beforehand use their gifts publicly in the church'.[175] Lay prophecy was thereby not intended to undermine the place of the ordained ministry, but to strengthen it, the entire procedure being tightly monitored by the officers themselves. Robinson agreed, for example, with the words of the *Confession of Emden*, 1571, that gifted members could prophesy 'but so as they first be allowed by the judgement of the ministers and others'.[176] Moreover, the elders were to preside over the affair 'and so order, moderate, and determine the whole exercise by the Word of God'. They could thus 'refuse' anything 'unsound'. 'And in this', Robinson added dryly, 'I suppose it appears to all men that the officers govern.'[177]

The power of Christ was also given to the people for the election and ordination of church officers,[178] so that, as one puritan adversary quipped, Robinson believed 'the path of popular election' was 'so right on'.[179] However, while Robinson did advocate 'the free voluntary choice and election of ministers' by the congregation in which they would serve, Robinson's position on the issue was no more 'popular' than the views of other advanced puritans and separatists. As in all church matters, Robinson's dictum, 'where there are officers in the churches . . . things are not to be attempted without them',[180] applied to church elections as well. A church with officers should submit the electoral proceedings to their direction so that even 'though the calling did chiefly depend upon the multitude, yet did the government of the whole action lie upon the officers'.[181] As he understood the practice of the apostolic church recorded in Acts 6, the people chose those whom the elders throught fit.[182] Only in the remote event that a church would be without officers, as for example,

[175] Robinson, *Peoples plea*, 71.

[176] Robinson, *Apologie*, 143.

[177] Robinson, *Of religious communion*, 23; 'An appendix to M. Perkins his six principles of Christian religion', in *A just and necessary apologie* (London, 1644), not paginated.

[178] Robinson, *Justification*, 420.

[179] Champlin Burrage, *An answer to John Robinson Of Leyden* (London, 1920), 73.

[180] Robinson, *Justification*, 137.

[181] Robinson, *Of religious communion*, 24; Justification, 372.

[182] Robinson, *Apologie*, 34.

when a new church sprang up in foreign parts by the preaching of private Christians, or (as in his own experience) when an assembly of Christians separated 'from idolatry, whether heathenish or antichristian', could the people alone choose their ministers 'within themselves.' But this was hardly a novel doctrine in reformed circles, as he noted similar views expressed in the writings of Perkins, Melanchthon, Vermigli, Zanchy, and others.[183]

While it is true that, like Smyth, Robinson at times pictured the flow of ministerial power between Christ and his officers as being mediated through the people,[184] he nevertheless moderated the radical force of that image by retaining the reformed ideal that ministers were spiritually set apart from the people by God himself. Only those who manifested the gifts of the spirit for ministry were to be considered eligible for election by the people; they possessed those gifts, Robinson explained, 'from Christ, and not from or by the church at all'.[185] Neither did congregational elections divest ministerial appointments of their sacerdotal nature: elections were the way in which God himself directly appointed his ministers without impinging the liberty of the people at the same time.[186] As Robinson understood the spiritual dynamics of congregational elections in the primitive church, the officers of the church 'were made bishops or overseers of the same church by the Holy Ghost'.[187]

Concerning the matter of ordination, David Hall asserted that, unlike other puritan churchmen, Robinson accorded formal ordination little value because he had renounced his orders in the established church and allowed himself to be reordained by the Leiden congregation.[188] But Robinson's rejection of the orders he received in the national church proves nothing consequential about his estimation of ordination, especially since Jacob, whom Hall contrasts with Robinson in this respect, did exactly the same.[189] Robinson himself viewed his renunciation of the orders he had received from the bishops as compatible with the action taken by numerous puritan ministers who 'renounce and disclaim their

[183] Robinson, *Justification*, 420–1.

[184] *Contra* Hall, *Faithful shepherd*, 40.

[185] Robinson. *Justification*, 160.

[186] Robinson, *Apologie*, 34.

[187] Ibid. 26.

[188] Hall, *Faithful shepherd*, 39.

[189] Stinton MSS, 2.

ordination by the prelates and hold their ministry by the peoples' acceptation'. More positively, rather than attaching so little value to ordination, Robinson described the rite as 'absolutely necessary' for a church ministry. And while he was willing to admit that a number of reformed churches considered the ceremony of hands to be indifferent, Robinson (like Calvin) preferred to uphold the rite.[190] Although he allowed private members the privilege of ordaining their own officers, this was again possible only under the unusual circumsance that a church was entirely destitute of other officers; and even in that case, for order's sake, the ceremony was to be administered by the 'fittest instruments' in the church. Otherwise, 'no ministers are to be ordained but by ministers'.[191]

On the vital issue of church discipline, Robinson concurred with his separatist predecessors and other left-wing puritan reformists who interpreted Matthew 18: 17, to mean the congregation rather than bishop or presbyters.[192] In the event of excommunication, 'the sin must be told to the church and they, upon knowledge of it, must admonish the sinner, and so the excommunication is publicly to be prepared with the foreknowledge and fore-consent of the body'.[193] While in this way he ensured that discipline would only be administered with the people's consent, his vision of disciplinary procedures indicated that he expected the people to play a relatively passive role. Scandalous sins were to be brought before the church 'at the officers' appointment', who were then to admonish the erring party. The congregation's judgement would thereupon rest with the decision of the elders, 'the men manifesting their assent thereunto by some convenient word, or sign, and the women by silence'. In this way, 'the admonition which before was Christ's, and the officers', becomes the church's'.[194] So for church censures, the rule was: 'officers going before, the brethren following in their order', by which Robinson signified that the officers should first deter-

[190] Robinson, *Justification*, 414–16. [191] Ibid. 420, 406.

[192] Ibid. 208–10, where, with less detail, Robinson compiled the comments of Continental and English reformists on the subject in much the same manner as Jacob would do three years later in an *Attestation of many learned and godly divines*.

[193] Robinson, *Justification*, 234. [194] Robinson, *Of religious communion*, 24.

mine the issue so that the congregation would, in turn, know how to vote. As he quoted Peter Martyr on 1 Corinthians 5: 'In judging, [the apostle] goes before others, as it is meet the chief in the church should do, that so the less skilful multitude might be directed in judging by their voting before them.'[195]

The duty of the elders, according to the Leiden separatist pastor, was 'publicly [to] propound and order all things in the church'. The main duty of the people was to 'give their assent to their elders holy and lawful administration; that so the ecclesiastical elections and censures may be ratified and put into solemn execution by the elders'.[196] Desiring to dispel the 'odious clamours' of 'popularity and the like' that Richard Bernard had raised against the separatists, Robinson stressed the rather servile role of the multitude who 'are most straightly bound to obey [the elders] without disturbance, intrusion, or opposition, under pain of God's wrath for their rebellion against him and them'.[197]

The high esteem in which Robinson held ordination is further confirmed by his insistence—this time, he acknowledged, contrary to the practice of the Dutch Reformed Church—that the tenure of an ordained ministry should be 'perpetual' and not 'annual or triennial or temporary'.[198] While he ostensibly rejected the representative church government of the Dutch presbyteries, he nevertheless believed the elders should

> meet apart at times from the body of the church to deliberate of such things as concern her welfare, as for the preventing of things unnecessary, so for the preparing (according to just order) of things necessary, so as publicly and before the people, they may be prosecuted with most convenience and least trouble that may be.[199]

[195] Robinson, *Apologie*, 33. [196] Ibid. 38.

[197] Robinson, *Justification*, 169–70.

[198] Ibid. 25–6. His model was, significantly, the great priestly tribe of the Levites who, as Roland de Vaux has written, were 'set apart to perform sacred functions' in the temple. One branch of the tribe received the promise of 'perpetual priesthood': *Ancient Israel, its Life and Institutions* (London, 1961), 360. Robinson's association of the ministry with the Levitical tribe was compatible with reformed puritan and separatist thinking and must be viewed as another indication of the respect in which he held the ordained ministry.

[199] Robinson, *Apologie*, 25–39. He was referring here to presbyteries of particular churches, not synods.

While this could prove an effective means of avoiding unpleasant, as well as inconsequential, business in the church, it is also important to remember that Robinson's interpretation of Matthew 18: 17 did not entirely rule out the possibility of private admonition by an elder without the consent of the church; he was careful, however, to distinguish this private practice from a 'church' admonition.[200]

Finally, however, the factor which, theoretically at least, raised the ordained ministry well above the ordinary membership, was his consideration of its role as ambassador of Christ's Word. As preachers and teachers of the Word, Robinson wrote in 1610, the elders 'are infinitely above and superior unto all men and angels'. Like Calvin, he said that they stood in the pulpit before the congregation 'in the very stead of Christ, and of God himself', and therefore 'are absolutely and simply to be obeyed'.[201] While, as we have seen, Robinson allowed lay preaching in the restricted sense used by other reformed churchmen, it seems fairly clear that he believed it was the ministers who possessed the lion's share of this powerful commodity, a fact which seems to be supported by his appeal to Malachi 2: 7. In a letter of 5 April 1624, to the Southwark church, Robinson said he had been reluctant to read to his own congregation their letter asking for advice because he believed that interchurch advice should be handled by the elders alone. They, after all, had been appointed 'in every particular church . . . for ordinary counsellors, to direct it and the members thereof in all difficulties'. Then he added the passage from Malachi: 'The priest's lips should preserve knowledge and they should seek the law at his mouth: for he is the messenger of the Lord of hosts.'[202]

The assumption underlying all of these claims by Robinson for the sacerdotal role of the ordained ministry was that the elders functioned in ministry according to 'the laws by [Christ] prescribed'.[203] Nevertheless, while called by God, ministers were only human, and so subject to error and

200 Robinson, *Justification*, 235. 201 Ibid. 218–19.
202 As appended to John Robinson, *The lawfulnesse of the hearing of the ministers of the church of England* (Leiden, 1634), 66–8.
203 Ibid. 169.

deception. If for that reason the need arose to discipline the elders, Robinson taught that private members should 'solemnly . . . examine, admonish, silence, and suppress their teachers'.[204] The minister was like the pilot of a ship, who, 'if he either ignorantly or desperately will run upon the sands, may be displaced by his passengers'.[205] While Robinson always affirmed this congregational liberty, he also added a most significant clause that would come into play should the elders believe they were 'wrongfully accused' by the congregation. In that event, the elders could perform what Robinson called 'a special work of their government, not only in preserving order, but in directing, instructing, and guiding the church by the Word of God in her whole proceedings'.[206] Tied with his conviction that, as ministers of the Word, the elders were 'absolutely and simply to be obeyed', it is perhaps more faithful to the evidence to conclude that, far from subordinating the ministry to the people, the structure of his polity ensured that the executive role of the eldership would not be seriously disturbed.

Yet, true to the form of most radical churchmen, Robinson was ultimately unable to leave the issue as ill-balanced as this, and so he added that while the elders could carry out their 'special work' of government, they could never rule against the will of the people;[207] as in civil court cases, the people played the role of the jury by possessing the power of veto which the judge could not overrule. Just who would win in this struggle between the ministers of the Word, who were to be obeyed absolutely, and the people, who possessed the 'negative voice', Robinson never finally determined—though he did try when he reasoned 'that the judging of sin and power to suppress it is one thing, and government for the right use and ordering of the same another thing. The officers which are judged do govern, and the body of the church which judges them is governed by them.'[208] Tenable as this may have been within the subtle dialectics of seventeenth-century scholastic debate, it is not very conclusive in terms of resolving the tension between executive and popular rule, but serves rather

[204] Ibid. 201, 418.

[205] Ibid. 213–14.

[206] From his letter to Francis Johnson, in Ainsworth, *Animadversion*, 112.

[207] Ibid. 113.

[208] Ibid.

as further evidence that the congregational separatism espoused by Robinson did not appreciably upset the sensitive balance of power that characterized reformed protestant views in the government of the gathered church. However extreme in his activities as a renegade, separatist churchman—denouncing the established ecclesiastical order, erecting a separate church outside the law, and fleeing the country as a fugitive—the congregational model he proposed for this bold experiment was ecclesiologically no more radical than the polity outlined by other contemporary left-wing puritans and separatists. Far from subordinating the eldership to the rule of ordinary saints, Robinson aspired, like other English radicals of the time, to grant the people ownership of ecclesial government while firmly upholding the governing function of the faithful shepherds of the flock of Christ.

6

AUTONOMY AND UNIFORMITY BETWEEN THE GATHERED CONGREGATIONS

Elizabethan Radical Puritans

LEFT-WING puritan ecclesiology, in contrast with the more centralized, hierarchical structure of the established church order, emphasized congregational participation in the affairs of the gathered church. Several convictions encouraged this trend toward decentralization, such as the notion many radical puritan churchmen held concerning the size of a local church community. As William Fulke said with grave simplicity in his Hampton Court sermon of 1570, 'the church of Christ, as he himself said, is a small flock'.[1] Ideally, Elizabethan puritans like Fulke desired that each church should assemble in one place and remain small enough to ensure the full participation of every member. From the example of the primitive church in the New Testament, Chaderton drew attention to the significant fact that 'the apostles, disciples and all continued together in one place'.[2] While he apparently felt that church affairs could be lawfully settled when some members were physically absent, Dudley Fenner also affirmed the concept of the church as a gathered community in which all members exercised their right of participation. If a member was 'absent, sick, or employed', but had something 'of weight to signify to the church, the church was to harken unto them by whomsoever they send their advice'. And if private members wilfully neglected their

[1] William Fulke, *A sermon preached at Hampton Court on Sunday being the 12. day of November, in the year of Our Lord, 1570* (London, 1570), Sig. Hiv.

[2] Laurence Chaderton, *A fruitfull sermon, vpon the 3. 4. 5. 6. 7. & 8. verses of the 12 chapters of . . . Romans* (London, 1584), 43.

'liberty' of co-operation in the ongoing life of the congregation, Fenner advised that, after a warning, 'the whole church is not to depend upon them'.[3] It was Travers who perhaps expressed the most pronounced concern that the local manifestation of the visible church need be limited in the size of membership, small enough, at least, so that the gathered congregation could 'hear the voice of one man speaking'.[4]

While emphasizing in this and other ways the significance of understanding the church to be a small, gathered community, there was at the same time another inclination among many radical puritans that acted in some measure as a counterforce to this congregational impulse. They wished to establish a national synodical superstructure which would provide a source of unity for the otherwise disparate cells of the committed that together would comprise the visible church in England. Their general idea was to alter the existing diocesan structure of the church of England into local, provincial, and national assemblies of ministers and lay assistants drawn from the parish churches.

In 1572, the plan was clearly set out by Throkmorton in *A Second Admonition*. There he sought to establish conferences of 'some certain ministers, and other brethren' from the parishes, comprising a local deanery for the purpose of disciplining wayward ministers and creating the opportunity for ordination candidates to prophesy and interpret scripture. Throkmorton intended that these conferences should meet regularly at set times, though he added that they could also be called whenever the need arose.[5] While the participating divines were entitled to share equal authority among themselves, it was suggested that one ordained member of the conference could be appointed to moderate the proceedings. This appointment, however, was not perpetual; neither was the moderator allowed authority to exercise pre-eminence over even the simplest member, but 'to propose things to be deliberated upon, gathering other men's voices, bidding silence and such like that nothing be done disorderly, which

[3] Dudley Fenner, *A counter-poyson* (London, 1584), 34.

[4] Albert Peel (ed.), *The Seconde Parte of a Register* (Cambridge, 1915), i, 168.

[5] W. H. Frere and C. E. Douglas (eds.) *Puritan Manifestoes* (reprint. edn., London, 1954), 107–8.

synods and councils being once ended, he to remain as before his choosing to that office'.[6]

According to the model proposed in *A Second Admonition*, matters of serious concern to the church which could not be determined either by the local church or by the local conference were to be decided at a provincial synod and, if necessary, at a national assembly.[7] Unlike the local conferences which primarily served the purpose of examining and training candidates for the ordained ministry, the provincial synods, according to one anonymous puritan source, were to be called primarily for the purpose of maintaining uniformity among the churches by offering advice and deciding controversies.[8] Throkmorton argued that the provincial synods possessed more authority than local conferences because the provincial and national synods represented a larger cross-section of the thinking of the church. Unresolved controversies were to be decided on the basis not only of an appeal to the greater number involved in provincial and national bodies, but also to the greater learning of their participants: the 'ready' and 'right way . . . to pacify all controversies of the church' was 'to pass from one or few to more, and from more to more godly and learned'.[9]

As to the extent of power wielded by conferences and synods over the local church, Throkmorton insisted that they had the power to decide and determine matters of controversy according to the dictates of the Word.[10] But just how far this power could be exercised to overturn the will of individual gathered churches was not always so clear. Thomas Cartwright's views were decidedly ambiguous when he explained that 'no particular church has power over another, yet every particular church of the same resort, meeting and counsel ought to obey the opinion of more churches with whom they communicate'.[11] Dudley Fenner, however, was less uncertain about his intention of preserving the primacy and autonomy of

[6] *A parte of a register countayning sundrie memorable matters, for the reformation of our church* (n.p., 1593), 541; Cartwright, *The second replie of Thomas Cartwright* (n.p., 1575), 492.

[7] Frere and Douglas (eds.), *Puritan Manifestoes*, 108.

[8] Peel (ed.), *Seconde Parte*, i. 166–7.

[9] Frere and Douglas (eds.), *Puritan Manifestoes*, 111.

[10] Ibid. 108–9.

[11] Thomas Cartwright, *A directory of church government* (London, 1644), as reprinted in C. A. Briggs, *American Presbyterianism* (New York, 1885), app. 6.

the local congregation in cases of church discipline. As he explained, 'it belongs to the pastor and the eldership to excommunicate by the consent of the people. If our Saviour Christ [in] Matthew 18, when he says tell the church means not one bishop . . . neither can it be meant of many churches . . . but do mean upon these reasons a particular congregation.'[12] William Fulke apparently would have agreed. While he believed that a national synod had the authority to make decrees, its authority stopped short of enforcing uniformity: 'The wisdom of the synod therefore ought to have such regard of all churches, that they have special respect to everyone. Wherein we of long time in England have been carried away with an untrue principle, that uniformity must be in all places.'[13]

While the concern for a national synodical structure received closer attention in the 1580s from some puritans after presbyterianism had been successfully established in Scotland and the puritan classical movement consolidated in England,[14] it is surprisingly not a pronounced feature in the published manifestos of most extremists during the Elizabethan era. Among many radicals there is indeed very little surviving evidence that they had much, if any, interest in the role that presbyterian synods would occupy in a reformed national church. In the extant writings of Laurence Chaderton and John Udall, for example, the subject was ignored altogether. Walter Travers, typed by his modern biographer as a paragon of puritan presbyterianism, made only a passing reference to 'conferences and synods' in *Ecclesiastical discipline*, as did Dudley Fenner in *A counter-poyson.*[15] Indeed, Travers's *A full and plaine declaration of ecclesiastical discipline*, which has been identified by S. J. Knox as 'a full statement of the presbyterian system',[16] appears to favour a more decentralized 'congregational' model than is usually granted to classical presbyterianism. While Travers conceded conferences and synods a

[12] Fenner, *Counter-poyson*, 116–17.

[13] Leonard J. Trinterud, *Elizabethan Puritanism* (New York, 1971), 290.

[14] A. F. Scott Pearson, *Church and State: Political Aspects of Sixteenth Century Puritanism* (Cambridge, 1925), 102.

[15] Walter Travers, *A full and plaine declaration of ecclesiastical discipline* (n.p., 1574), 178; Fenner, *Counter-poyson*, 182.

[16] S. J. Knox, *Walter Travers: Paragon of Elizabethan Puritanism* (London, 1962), 46.

right to decree 'that which is for the wealth and commodity of the church', he added the significant proviso that implementation of synodical decisions depended upon the 'good will' and 'allowing' of the people, to whom Travers also offered the high privilege of making the decisions of synods 'void and of no effect if they be not such as in the last state wherein the people have to rule and govern'.[17]

In spite of the continued association between Scottish presbyterians and radical protestants in England, illustrated by the invitations extended to Cartwright and Travers to take up chairs at the University of St Andrews in 1580, the principles of Travers expressed here are striking by virtue of their congregational complexion. They stand in marked contrast to the rule of a synodical oligarchy of clerics which, as Gordon Donaldson claims, increasingly characterized presbyterianism to the north.[18] Indeed, the lack of any clear evidence of a uniform synodical instinct among the radicals, combined with the often pronounced attention they paid to congregational participation and authority, indicates that many were less inclined to promote a full-blooded presbyterian system than is implied by the 'Presbyterian' label that historians almost universally and uncritically apply to radical puritans of the Elizabethan period.[19] As Patrick Collinson has observed:

> some of the theoretical literature of the period was reticent on the delicate question of how these structures were to be related to local churches, and it may be that whenever their own interests were involved, most Elizabethan puritans would have been reluctant to concede to synods anything beyond the power to 'counsel' and 'advise' allowed in later years by the independents.[20]

[17] Travers, *Ecclesiastical discipline*, 178.

[18] Gordon Donaldson, *The Scottish Reformation* (London, 1960), 187; 190–1.

[19] Knox, *Walter Travers*, 37. G. Bolam, however, recognized that while Cartwright and Travers advocated a graduated scale of classes, they nevertheless preserved the autonomy of the gathered church. C. Gordon Bolam *et al.* (eds.), *The English Presbyterians* (Boston, Mass., 1968), 32.

[20] Patrick Collinson, 'Towards a Broader Understanding of the Early Dissenting Tradition', in C. Robert Cole and Michael E. Moody (eds.), *The Dissenting Tradition: Essays for Leland H. Carlton* (Athens, Ohio, 1975), 16; see also George Yule, 'Some Problems in the History of the English Presbyterians in the Seventeenth Century', *Journal of the Presbyterian Historical Society of England*, 13 (1965), 4.

While there were undoubtedly presbyterian tendencies at work within Elizabethan puritan circles, the evidence of a drift toward congregationalism is a marked feature among many left-wing puritans. It is this evidence which makes the development of 'congregationalism' among the Elizabethan separatists and the non-separating congregationalists of the early Stuart period less innovative than many ecclesiastical historians have supposed and which also serves as a caveat that the identification of Elizabethan left-wing puritanism with presbyterianism should be made, if at all, with considerable caution.

Jacobean Radical Puritans

In his seminal study of new England orthodoxy, Perry Miller argued that the roots of New England Congregationalism were to be discovered not in the ideology of separatism, but in the small group of early seventeenth-century English radical puritans he identified as 'non-separating congregationalists'. According to Miller, the five radical puritans who comprised this avant-garde of the puritan left (Jacob, Parker, Ames, Bradshaw, and Baynes) made a significant shift from the presbyterianism of Elizabethan puritans to congregationalism by advocating the two essential features of a congregational polity: 'restriction of church membership to the proved elect and the autonomy of particular congregations'.[21] Exactly how they came to espouse congregationalism remained a complete mystery to Miller, but in order to underscore the radical nature of their departure from the previous generation of presbyterians, Miller quoted the notorious testimony of William Ames in the preface to Bradshaw's *English puritanisme*: 'Thou may herein observe what a terrible popedom and primacy these rigid presbyterians desire.'[22] Accordingly,

[21] Perry Miller, *Orthodoxy in Massachusetts 1630–1650* (New York, 1970), 78. Essentially, Miller was following a distinction between Elizabethan presbyterians and Jacobean congregationalists first made by Champlin Burrage, *The Early English Dissenters* (Cambridge, 1912), i, 187–9.

[22] As quoted in *Orthodoxy in Massachusetts*, 78. Miller actually attributed the words to Bradshaw, but the preface was written by Ames. See Keith Sprunger, *The Learned Doctor William Ames* (Urbana, Ill., 1972), 36.

Miller concluded that Bradshaw and the other 'non-separating congregationalists' were as much opposed to the polity of Elizabethan puritanism as to episcopacy.

Miller's use of the statement by Ames is a good example of the way in which the anachronistic denominational categories under which he worked often controlled and, at times, distorted his reading of the sources. Apparently under the influence of this denominationally predisposed thesis, Miller missed the irony in Ames's remark: the 'rigid presbyterians' mentioned by Ames were, indeed, not the Elizabethan puritans but early Stuart radical puritans like himself, who advocated the polity described in Bradshaw's *English puritanisme*; and his retort was directed not against his fellow puritans but against those bishops who had recently complained that the polity of left-wing puritanism was leading to a 'terrible popedom and primacy' of the elders. The point Ames wished to make was that the bishop's complaint was an unfounded caricature of the puritan position and that he, at least, was completely convinced Bradshaw's treatise provided a convincing rebuttal which would lay to rest not only that particular criticism, but the many other misleading portraits of English puritanism which had been created over the years by the opposition. In fact, it is doubtful that the major gulf that Miller posited between his Elizabethan 'presbyterians' and Jacobean 'non-separating congregationalists' ever existed at all.

As we have seen in the previous section of this chapter, the concept of gathered, autonomous churches struck a resonant chord in the writings of many Elizabethan radicals. With that in mind, the 'congregational' inclination among Jacobean left-wing puritans was neither so novel nor so mysterious a development as Miller claimed, for the ecclesiological principles of their Elizabethan forerunners in radical protestant religion very likely provided the seed-bed of their convictions. That, at least, appears to be the explanation if one takes seriously their own self-understanding and considers the number of references to Cartwright, Travers, Fenner, Fulke, Whitaker, and others employed by radical puritans in the two decades following the Hampton Court Conference. Indeed, in the same preface quoted by Miller, Ames himself claimed that 'Cartwright,

Fenner, Fulke, Whitaker, Reynolds [and] Perkins' walked in 'the same way and steps' as Bradshaw. He then proceeded to admit that 'most of those, and those most celebrious, were not so rigid in all things' as Bradshaw. While this last statement has been taken by some historians to support Miller's thesis, it is much too vague to be conclusive and is open to other interpretations. Very likely he was not referring here to Cartwright and other Elizabethan radicals after about 1570, but to earlier English protestants cited in the same list, such as Wyclif, Tyndale, Rogers, Bradford, Goodman, Gilby, Foxe, and others. They were the ones Ames probably intended when he referred to 'those most celebrious'. The reason he said they 'were not so rigid in all things' is that Ames recognized, as Elizabethan radicals themselves had, that the earlier generations of English protestants were not as ecclesiologically advanced because they viewed matters of church government as an *adiaphora* issue. At the same time, Ames shared with the Elizabethan radicals a deep reverence for these earlier reformers despite this failing, and defended the more 'rigid' ecclesiology of later radicals like himself on the basis of the puritan 'further light' argument.[23] As for many of the Elizabethan left-wing puritans who stood in the more radical tradition of Cartwright and Fulke, Ames apparently saw no significant difference between their ecclesial convictions and Bradshaw's. Given the 'congregational' disposition of many Elizabethan radicals discussed above, it appears that Ames was not overclaiming the degree of compatibility that actually existed between Bradshaw and his predecessors.

The writings of the early Stuart left-wing puritans reveal substantial agreement over the important issues of congregational autonomy and the authority of synodical government. William Ames talked about the visible church as neither a national, provincial, nor diocesan body but only as several distinct companies, 'the members whereof are combined among themselves, and do ordinarily meet into one place to the public exercise of religion'. While particular churches were not dependent upon a large ecclesiastical superstructure,

[23] See Ames's preface to William Bradshaw's *English puritanisme, containing the main opinions of the rigidest sort of those that are called puritans* (n.p., 1604), not paginated. For the *adiaphora* and 'further light' themes, see above, ch. 1, 2.

Ames nevertheless advised churches to enter into a synodical relationship one with another for mutual help in matters 'of great moment'. This did not constitute a new church and, like Travers, Ames argued that 'neither ought it to take away or diminish any way that liberty and power which Christ has left to his churches'.[24]

Paul Baynes agreed with William Bradshaw that all ecclesiastical power was bound 'within the limits only of one particular congregation'.[25] Concerning the extent of synodical power, Bradshaw explained that even when particular churches went astray doctrinally, synods had no coercive or judicial power but could offer only advice and counsel.[26]

Of all the Jacobean radicals, with the possible exception of Henry Jacob,[27] Robert Parker produced the most extensive examination of synodical theory in Chapters 13–22 of book iii in *De politeia*. While Parker was willing to call synods a kind of 'church' (unlike Ames, Bradshaw, and Baynes), he nevertheless subordinated synodical authority to the gathered church. A synod, Parker said, was a 'consociation' of two or more particular churches which joined together through a mutual exchange of either letters or delegates to consider problems that could not be solved at the local level.[28] Synods derived whatever authority they did possess directly from the participating churches which, according to Parker's reading of Whitaker's *De conciliis*, implied that 'this authority must rest more principally and essentially in those churches'. A synod could neither deprive individual churches of their liberties in elections and discipline nor 'obtrude anything upon churches unwilling'.[29]

But the five 'non-separating congregationalists' studied by

[24] William Ames, *The marrow of sacred divinity*, 177–9, in *The workes of the reverend and faithful minister of Christ William Ames* (London, 1643), 177–9.

[25] William Bradshaw, *Several treatises of worship and ceremonies by the reverend Mr. William Bradshaw* (London, 1660), 85; Paul Baynes, *The diocesans tryall* (London, 1621), 8.

[26] Bradshaw, *Several treatises*, 37.

[27] See below, nn. 60–83.

[28] Parker MS, iii, 14. Cf. Ames, *Marrow*, 179, in *Workes*; Baynes, *Diocesans tryall*, 8; Bradshaw, *Several treatises*, 37.

[29] Parker MS, iii, 13, 14, 23; Frank Benjamin Carr, 'The Thought of Robert Parker (1564?–1614) and His Influence on Puritanism Before 1650', (London University Ph.D. thesis, 1964), 184.

[30] Stuart Barton Babbage, *Puritanism and Richard Bancroft* (London, 1962), 139.

Miller were not the only Jacobean radicals advocating congregational autonomy. Although the evidence is not as conspicuous, even William Stoughton, whose 'presbyterianism' has been contrasted with the 'congregationalism' of Bradshaw and Jacob,[30] provides little indication of any fundamental deviation from his more extreme contemporaries. Stoughton, whose advocacy of congregational participation in the government of the gathered church we have already noted,[31] also acknowledged that councils, canons, and princes could 'reform', 'bridle', and 'direct' unruly individuals and churches,[32] but that they could never take the right of 'free election' into their own hands.[33] In sympathy with Elizabethan radicals like Cartwright, Fenner, and Udall,[34] Stoughton also advocated a form of congregational discipline by individual parishes in which the ministers and the 'faithful inhabitants of the same parish', rather than a consistory or presbytery, would 'exercise all manner of spiritual justice within their own parish'.[35]

While Jacobean advanced puritans in this way affirmed the autonomy of the gathered church, it is of interest ecclesiologically to observe that, paradoxically, some passages in their writings tended to modify, however marginally, their commitment to the principles of congregationalism. For example, although William Ames said the administration of censures 'ordinarily' pertained to the governors of the church, he also added that 'it belongs to assemblies and synods, when any difficulty does arise, by common consent to declare and discern who are to be excommunicated'. If this appeared to give synods the authority to excommunicate, Ames explained that 'properly' they could not: 'Yet they may for manifest heresies or crimes be condemned, forsaken, rejected, which

[31] See above, ch. 5, n. 76.

[32] This was perhaps not much more than the 'congregational classis' in Holland allowed when, in their petition to James I of 1621, they claimed that the purpose of the classis was the 'redresse of all enormities . . . in deporting or putting away some scandalous persons and putting in their places persons more fit'. R. P. Stearns, *Congregationalism in the Dutch Netherlands* (Chicago, 1940), 80.

[33] William Stoughton, *An assertion for true and christian church-policie* (Middelburg, 1604), 214.

[34] Ibid. 331–2.

[35] Ibid. 385.

has an analogy with excommunication.'[36] In another curious passage, Ames remarked that a minister could be removed from one church to another 'upon the judgement of other churches and by the consent of that church to which he is bound for *further* fruit of edification'.[37] Surprisingly, given the emphasis we have seen in the views of radical puritans on the inseparable link between ordination and the congregation to which the ordained person administered, Ames said nothing about the necessity of consent from the church in which the candidate was already an officer. Paul Baynes appears to have left the door slightly more ajar for synodical control in special cases. At least, he said that particular churches, like the synagogues of the Jews, held the power of government in 'ordinary matters' while admitting that the temple at Jerusalem (and so by parallel, a synodical body) possessed the power in 'some reserved causes'.[38]

If, indeed, these remarks tended to dilute the congregationalism of Miller's non-separating congregationalists, the next generation of Jacobean radicals, who formed the 'congregational classis' between 1621 and 1633 in the Netherlands, found themselves in a better position to conduct what R. P. Stearns has called 'one of the earliest experiments in congregational polity'.[39] As the apparent ecclesiological debtors of their Elizabethan and Jacobean radical puritan predecessors, the ministers of this new classis movement were equally adamant in rejecting the ruling power of all classes of synods. In perhaps the clearest statement of their intentions, Thomas Hooker explained to John Paget that a congregation possessed its own authority to choose a minister 'without or against the approbation of the classis if they saw good reason'.[40] Carried into practice in Holland, the theoretical literature of Elizabethan and Jacobean radicals thus spawned a small but vigorous experiment in congregational autonomy during the 1620s and 1630s. It was comprised of several independent congregations

[36] William Ames, *Conscience with the power and cases thereof*, iv, 89, in *Workes*.

[37] Ibid. 70–1.

[38] Baynes, *Diocesans tryall*, 8; and 13 where, while hesitant to grant real power to a diocesan government, he does not reject the synagogue/temple model. See also Carr, 'The Thought of Robert Parker', 192, who claims that Parker believed a 'synod was superior to the prime churches under certain circumstances'.

[39] Stearns, *Congregationalism*, 17.

[40] Ibid. 109.

bound together in fellowship through the advice and counsel of the classis structure, and it provided yet another avenue of practical experience for the emergence of Independency and the Congregational Way in Old and New England of the 1640s.

Elizabethan and Jacobean Separatists

Much like the Jacobean non-separating congregationalists, one of the hallmarks of separatist churchmanship was a concern for the primacy of the individual church. Rejecting what they understood to be the comprehensive, national structure of the church in the Old Testament, separatists argued that each congregation should stand independent and free of the controlling influence and power of any other ecclesiastical body. Nevertheless, the concept of a synodical forum within which autonomous churches could associate for reasons of mutual encouragement, exhortation, and guidance also comprised a prominent feature of their ecclesiological designs. Although driven by circumstances into the isolation of exiled and beleaguered underground religious enclaves, their separatism did not thereby foster a policy of unrestrained congregational autonomy; they only rejected, in varying degrees, the absolute subordination of local congregations to the authority of larger synodical bodies, while at the same time they intended to safeguard and preserve, albeit in their own highly restricted way, the ancient ideals of catholicity and uniformity between true churches of Christ.

Among those who made up the separatist mainstream during the Elizabethan and early Stuart period, Robert Browne appears to have conceded to synods more authority over particular churches than other spokesmen within the tradition. In what seems to have been an extension of a principle by which he justified the involvement of lay members in the affairs of the local church, Browne disclosed what he believed was a need for some kind of synodical assembly that would carry greater weight in the determination of controversial issues than individual congregations. Just as the authority of the whole church was superior to that of the elders because their numbers were greater, so, in words reminiscent of *A Second Admonition*, Browne reasoned that the 'joining and partaking of many churches together and of the authority which many have must needs be greater and more weighty than the authority of any single person'.[41] Earlier, he had defined a 'synod' as 'a joining or partaking of the authority of many churches met together in peace for redress and deciding of matters which cannot well be otherwise taken up'.[42]

As B. R. White has observed, Henry Barrow seems to have seen the need more acutely than Browne for limiting synodical power.[43] Like Browne before him, he believed that churches should join together when the need arose into 'a synod or council of sundry churches for the deciding of controversies and doubts' so that 'all churches in all places might walk by one rule in the unity of the spirit'. The scriptural precedent for this was to be sought in the example of the Jerusalem council recorded in Acts 15, where it was clear to Barrow that synods were to comprise 'certain chosen elders of the churches . . . thereunto assembled, together with such faithful of any church as will be present without shutting out any of them' and where each one 'has free liberty and place to relate or debate his own cause without interruption or prejudice'.[44] He did, however, include one limitation upon the liberty of lay participants that corresponded with the more conservative side of separatist notions concerning ministerial authority. In his reply to Gifford's *Treatise against the Donatists*, Barrow attenuated to a degree the liberty of 'popular' participation with the qualification that private members should:

use this power and liberty aright, not disturbing the holy order of the church, presuming to speak before their ancients or against anything by them said, without showing just cause, etc., always keeping

[41] Robert Browne, *The Writings of Robert Harrison and Robert Browne*, ed. Albert Peel and Leland H. Carlson (London, 1953), 41, 399; see also Frere and Douglas (eds.), *Puritan Manifestoes*, 111, and Cartwright, *Directory of church government*, 14.

[42] *Browne*, 271.

[43] B. R. White, *The English Separatist Tradition* (Oxford, 1971), 75.

[44] Henry Barrow, *The Writings of Henry Barrow, 1587–1590* ed. Leland H. Carlson (London, 1962), 665–6.

themselves within the compass of faith and sobriety. Who so does otherwise is reproved of all and judged of all as a disturber.[45]

He went on to say that while uniformity of practice between churches was the expected end-product of synodical associations, the essential autonomy of each church was not to be infringed upon: 'so has not this council any power or authority over any church or any member of the church to censure, excommunicate, erect or depose any'.[46]

Barrow had harsh words for those Elizabethan puritans who, he believed, were espousing a presbyterian structure, a concept he thought 'as new, strange, and antichristian' as episcopacy itself. He indicted them on seven counts for: (1) restricting participation to ministers only; (2) privately judging all church affairs, not just doubts and questions; (3) meeting at predetermined places and times instead of when the need arose; (4) electing a single moderator or 'judge' to govern the sessions; (5) making decrees that were by majority vote absolutely binding for all churches; (6) executing censures which by right all belonged to local churches; and (7) planning to establish a hierarchy of ruling bodies from a national council down to district classes.[47] If Barrow had in mind radical puritans like Field, Travers, and others, his criticisms were a serious distortion of their declared intentions. They did not restrict participation only to ordained men, nor grant to synods imperious powers to determine all matters of discipline, nor expect that larger assemblies would meet only at predetermined times, nor intend that the election of a moderator would impugn the ideal of ministerial equality.[48]

Like many other radical puritans and separatists, Francis Johnson drew the boundaries of a true church rather tightly round the concept of the gathered church, which he defined as 'a distinct and entire body' with its own church officers and government, being small enough for the whole church to gather ordinarily in one place. If a church became too large to maintain a disciplined fellowship, it should then divide into

[45] Henry Barrow, *The Writings of Henry Barrow, 1590–1591* ed. Leland H. Carlson (London, 1966), 151.

[46] *Barrow, 1587–1590*, 665–6.

[47] Ibid. 669–70; 696.

[48] See above.

two smaller independent bodies.[49] Nevertheless, he determined that even though churches were 'distinct and several bodies every one as a compact city in itself, yet are they all to walk by one and the same rule and by all means convenient to have the counsel and help one of another in all needful affairs of the church'.[50] While Johnson came to reject the conventional separatist interpretation of Matthew 18: 17,[51] he did not change his mind about the power of church synods. In his last publication, Johnson maintained that churches should join together in 'synods, classes, assemblies, or councils for mutual help and advice in cases of question, controversy and difficulties about religion'. Yet he, too, remained adamant that synods must 'not challenge or usurp any unlawful jurisdiction or power over the particular churches or their pastors and governors'.[52]

Early in his career, at a time when the Ancient Church in Amsterdam stood alone and marred by internal dissension, Henry Ainsworth expressed a deep desire for Christian communion and spiritual unity between sister churches in his masterful little treatise of separatist ecclesiology, *The Communion of Saints*, 1607. Although true churches were to be 'disjoined in place', he believed they should be 'united in heart and spirit, so as they generally are but one body or church under one head Christ, called in one hope of their vocation by one God and Father of all, and must endeavour to keep the unity of the spirit in the bond of peace'.[53] This communion included participation in the Lord's Supper for all members of other recognized congregations of believers and the privilege of transferring membership from one true church to another by letter of recommendation.[54] Unlike most separatists, however, Ainsworth did not believe that elders from outside a church should administer ordination when a church was without its

[49] Henry Ainsworth and Francis Johnson, *An apologie or defence of svch trve Christians as are commonly (but vniustly) called Brownists* (Amsterdam, 1604), 60; Francis Johnson, *A treatise of the Ministery of the Church of England* (Amsterdam, 1595), 250–1.

[50] Francis Johnson, *A Trve confession of the faith* (Amsterdam, 1596), art. 38.

[51] White, *English Separatist Tradition*, 141–9.

[52] Johnson, *Ministery*, 251.

[53] Henry Ainsworth, *The communion of saincts* (Amsterdam, 1607), 290.

[54] Ibid. 213–4.

own elders.[55] Smyth, who it appears would have agreed with Ainsworth on this latter point, nevertheless thought it might be possible for officers to be transferred from one church to another, while Johnson saw the fraternal relationship between churches extending even to financial help in situations where churches were unable to support their own ministers.[56]

Like Barrow, Ainsworth believed that the unity of the faith among dispersed congregations should be preserved primarily through observing 'the duties between churches' established in Acts 15, where, he said,

> when there grew a dissension by means of false doctrine sown among them, [the church at Antioch] sent the said Paul and Barnabas for advice and help unto Jerusalem;. which church after great disputation even by the apostles themselves, sent back chosen and chief men of their own company to Antioch with Paul and Barnabas and wrote letters also of the same matter.[57]

As it turned out, Ainsworth soon found himself in just such a situation when the Ancient Church, of which he was teacher, became embroiled in the dispute over John Smyth's se-baptism, and further dissension broke out between Ainsworth and Johnson over the latter's reinterpretation of Matthew 18: 17. The resulting controversy is a good illustration of an inherent tension in separatist polity between the competing demands for congregational autonomy on the one hand, and uniformity of doctrinal practice among gathered churches on the other.

The controversy began when Ainsworth insisted on retaining the traditional separatist rendering of Matthew 18: 17, after it became apparent that he and Johnson were at loggerheads over the issue. Ainsworth invoked article 38 of the 1596 *Confession*, suggesting that they seek the counsel and help of another true church 'as members of one body in the common faith'. But much to his dismay, Ainsworth recorded that 'here when differences had arisen about our common faith . . . [Johnson and his followers] would not desire nor consent to have desired the help of our sister church at Leiden'.

[55] Henry Ainsworth, *An animadversion to Mr. Richard Clyftons Advertisement* (Amsterdam, 1613), 58; cf. *Barrow, 1590–1591*, 233.

[56] John Smyth, *The Works of John Smyth* (ed. W. T. Whitley (Cambridge, 1915), 258; Francis Johnson, *A Christian plea conteyning three treatises* (Leiden, 1617), 317.

[57] Ainsworth, *Communion*, 290–2.

Apparently Johnson assumed that Leiden would side with Ainsworth; for this reason, while admitting that seeking advice was permissible, Johnson evidently decided to insist more firmly on the separatist principle of congregational autonomy, making the claim that article 38 was an indifferent matter and therefore not always binding. Ainsworth shot back with the example of the Jerusalem assembly in Acts 15, which he believed proved that seeking advice from other churches was prescribed.[58]

Eventually, the Leiden separatist congregation did become involved at the request of 'some 30' members of the Ancient Church who sided with Ainsworth. Although Johnson continued to drag his feet on the matter, the Leiden church at length sent a delegation 'not to oppose any person or to maintain any charge of error', as Robinson and elder William Brewster explained to the church at Amsterdam, 'but by all other brotherly means to help forward your holy peace'. The dispute limped on for almost a year. Several plans were proposed, including a compromise whereby matters of discipline would be brought 'first to the elders' and then, if not settled, to the church. In the end, nothing was resolved. Ainsworth concluded the matter with the melancholy realization that 'the practice of their [Johnson's] errors was established . . . the Lord's Supper of a long time not administered among us . . . [and] open war proclaimed against us'.[59]

Thus, the first serious attempt by a separatist church to resolve a dispute by a representative, interchurch council ended in failure, the weakness being that the polarity of the two ideals of congregational independence and interdependence that marked separatist views about associations between churches was open to manipulation—like so many aspects of their ecclesiology—according to the exigencies of particular situations. There was, however, one other avenue that they believed would be lawful for maintaining unity in the church: this was the authority of the civil magistrate, a subject to which we shall turn in Chapter 7.

58 Ainsworth, *Animadversion*, 107–8.

59 Ibid. 133–7.

Henry Jacob

As discussed in Chapter 1, Jacob repeatedly portrayed Christ throughout his writings as the supreme lawgiver who, in that respect, performed much the same role for the people of Israel under the law as he did for Christians under the gospel: 'as Christ was in general unto the Jews the institutor and framer of the form of their visible and ministerial church and government and worship absolutely and only, so he is also the same unto us'.[60] Yet with the establishment of the new covenant, there also followed a radical disjunction between the church of the Old and the New Testaments through the new form of ecclesial government instituted by Christ in the New Testament. Under the old covenant, Jacob explained that the form of the church had been a 'national, or rather . . . a universal church and government', whereas under the 'spiritual body politic' of the new covenant inaugurated by Christ the catholic church was now divided into particular congregations, 'which in number are many and distinct; howsoever in nature they are all one and the same'.[61]

Ideally, Jacob held, particular churches should be small enough for members to gather in one place. If not, 'they ought to distinguish and distribute themselves into diverse competent set congregations which should be so many proper and entire churches'. This particular aspect of church polity was transgressed, he said, by 'some reformed churches beyond [the] seas'.[62] It was perhaps this principle, in part, that motivated the division of the Southwark church on 12 September 1633, when 'the church being now become so large yet it might be prejudicial' dismissed ten members who in turn became 'an entire church' of their own.[63] Jacob did not, however, make the restriction on size mandatory: 'my

[60] Henry Jacob, *The divine beginning and institution of Christs true or visible Ministeriall church* (Leiden, 1610), Sig. C7.

[61] Ibid.; Henry Jacob, *A plaine and cleere exposition of the 2d. commandement* (Leiden, 1610), Sig. D7.

[62] Henry Jacob, *Reasons taken out of Gods Word* (Middelburg, 1604), 65–6.

[63] Stinton MSS, 6. There were probably other reasons for the division, not least of which was the real danger of persecution under Laud. A smaller company would be all the less noticeable to the authorities.

meaning is not that all Christ's true visible churches evermore contain (each of them) no more people than do make only one congregation. But I mean that none consists of many ordinary and constantly set congregations.'[64]

Discarding what he understood to be the national church structure of the Old Testament, Jacob also disapproved of the national, provincial, and diocesan structure of the established church in England; each parish congregation, he believed, should be independent of outside ecclesiastical authority.[65] At the same time, he did not entirely condemn the concept of a larger synodical superstructure within which autonomous churches could associate, but, like other radical puritans and separatists, only rejected the subordination of local congregations to either episcopal or presbyterian tribunals.

Jacob advocated what he and Robert Parker called the occasional 'consociation' of congregations 'by way of synods'.[66] These were 'meetings of choice men out of many churches' that could be convened (or dissolved) at the request of the magistrate. They were to be accorded special respect in the churches, he argued, because the 'counsel, advice, and determinations' emanating from them 'are most expedient and wholesome always'.[67] Nevertheless, Jacob insisted that their decisions possess no binding authority over the gathered church: 'We hold likewise that ruling synods and united presbyteries exercising government and imposing laws and decrees upon several churches and the pastors of them are . . . human institutions' not to be found 'either expressly or by necessary consequence in any part of Christ's Testament'.[68] Agreeing with William Whitaker, Jacob remarked, 'If councils were simply necessary, Christ somewhere would have commanded to keep them, or at least his apostles, which yet we read that they do nowhere.'[69]

[64] Henry Jacob, *A declaration & plainer opening of certaine points in the divine beginning* (Middelburg, 1611), 10.

[65] Jacob, *Reasons*, 5; *Declaration & plainer opening*, 13.

[66] Henry Jacob, *A confession and protestation of the faith of certaine Christians in England* (Amsterdam, 1616), Sig. B2. The word 'consociation' seems to be unique to Henry Jacob and Robert Parker among the Elizabethan and Jacobean radicals. For Parker, see above, n. 28.

[67] Jacob, *Reasons*, 31; Henry Jacob, *A humble supplication for toleration, and libertie* (Middelburg, 1609), 13.

[68] Jacob, *Humble supplication*, 13; *Reasons*, 31.

[69] Jacob, *Reasons*, 31.

In fact, there was one passage which apparently proved problematic for Jacob: Acts 15, where 'we find . . . a kind of likeness to such synods' that have the 'power to prescribe and rule ecclesiastically . . . even sundry whole churches though they severally consent not'.[70] In 1604, Jacob took a position, adopted by Paul Baynes and also Francis Johnson in his controversy with Ainsworth, explaining that the council of Jerusalem as discussed in Acts 15 did not qualify as a model for seventeenth-century polity because it was 'a very extraordinary office and power'.[71] In 1613, however, Jacob gave the passage a more traditional reading: he now concluded, as had other radical puritans and separatists, that 'the apostles' practice in Acts 15 [was] . . . both a synod and an authentic rule and pattern for synods'. This interpretative adjustment apparently occurred through his discovery that, while the apostles made decrees and 'delivered the same to diverse churches to be kept', they did not impose those decrees on the churches without their consent. He based this new interpretation on an argument from silence:

> To the church of Antioch, whom it most concerned, only this they [the apostles] say: if you observe these things, you shall do well. They say not, the minister that embraces not these ordinances is deprived of his ministry; the person receiving them not is excommunicated *ipso facto*; or, he is *anathema* accursed.[72]

As von Rohr has noted about Jacob's re-evaluation of Acts 15, there was a modification of his exegesis, but not of his understanding of the authority of church synods.[73] While there ought to be a consociation of congregations, Jacob consistently asserted that there should not be a 'subordination, or surely not a subjection of the congregations under any higher spiritual authority, save only Christ's and the holy scriptures'.[74] Synods could deliberate on important matters and even apply what Jacob vaguely called 'persuasive'

[70] Jacob, *Reasons*, 31.

[71] Ibid. 32. Baynes, *Diocesans tryall*, 18–19; for Johnson, see above, n. 58.

[72] Henry Jacob, *An attestation of many learned, godly and famous divines* (Middelburg, 1611), 116–17.

[73] John von Rohr, 'The Congregationalism of Henry Jacob', *Transactions of the Congregational Historical Society* (1962), 112–13.

[74] Jacob, *Confession*, Sig. B2.

pressure on the churches to accept their decisions, but they could not demand obedience.[75]

Jacob envisaged the relationship between individual churches and their pastors to be one based on equality:

One visible church cannot be more a church than any other, though some may be greater, some smaller, some richer, some poorer. Yet as churches, they are all equally churches, and one has as much ecclesiastical or spiritual right, power, and authority as any other. Even so it is with their pastors being compared (I say) together as pastors among themselves.[76]

It was this very idea of equality, of course, that proved so troublesome to many seventeenth-century readers. Equality and autonomy, the argument ran, would inevitably destroy the unity of church and society and bring about discord, anarchy, and eventually total chaos. The unifying effect of the centralized hierarchy of authority in the old order, Jacob acknowledged, was a feature that commended episcopacy to many order-loving people. They were persuaded that 'making peace and unity and consent among Christian people' was considered 'proper to diocesan and provincial bishops', while they also believed that a parity of churches and pastors was 'the cause of strife and discord in the churches'.[77] Over this one issue of congregational autonomy, Jacob conceded that differences sometimes existed between his own polity and that of 'sundry' other less doctrinaire puritans in the land.[78]

In an attempt to provide a satisfactory solution to the conflict between, on the one hand, a fear of anarchy and, on the other, the desire for congregational liberty, a relatively conservative streak appeared in Jacob's views on the social structure of synods. He was confident his position on synods would maintain a reasonable level of unity between particular churches because first, he did not wholly reject a hierarchical structure for the organization of ecclesiastical synods and, second, he thought a godly magistrate could, if necessary, be relied upon to suppress those churches that continued to act in a disorderly fashion. Thus, while he consented to the reformed

[75] Jacob, *Humble supplication*, 14.

[76] Jacob, *Reasons*, 38–9.

[77] Jacob, *Attestation*, 15; *Reasons*, 39.

[78] Jacob, *Reasons*, 31, though he does not identify them.

concern for parity between 'pastors among themselves in their common office', there should nevertheless be, he said, a kind of hierarchy within each synod: 'where many pastors meet, we do not only allow but require a disparity and priority also, namely in the president or moderator'.[79] This 'divine disparity' (as opposed to the 'human disparity' of episcopacy) Jacob believed was

> the true cause of peace and unity. For where, in what place can discord be: in every church we acknowledge a superior, and in every meeting out of many churches a superior likewise. Now no other place can be imagined where discord and strife ecclesiastical can arise. If therefore superiority and disparity will cause peace, we through God's goodness and blessing shall both have and keep peace everywhere.[80]

It was, it seems, in this effort to deflect attacks by conservative officials within the established church and, at the same time, to find favour for the ideals of radical protestantism among those in civil authority in a class-conscious society, that the more democratic and emancipatory sentiments of his congregationalism quickly receded behind these elements of disparity and submission. Jacob intended to ensure that a measure of traditional social control remained which would forestall the many-headed 'monster' of unchecked popularity that could easily arise, he believed, through an ecclesiology that advocated an absolute parity; unbridled autonomy held a frightening and objectionable potential for social anarchy, even for one as radically committed to the overthrow of the existing regime at Canterbury as Henry Jacob.

Finally, even though Jacob repudiated 'any higher spiritual authority, save only Christ and the holy scriptures',[81] the civil magistrate possessed the authority not only 'to enact and ordain laws ecclesiastical', but also to superintend the management of maverick congregations. 'We acknowledge . . . no other power and authority for the overseeing, ruling and censuring of particular churches . . . in the case of their

[79] Jacob, *Reasons*, 37–8.

[80] Ibid. 40. This, of course, was not unique among the radicals or separatists, most of whom also insisted upon the presence of an elected moderator for synodical sessions.

[81] Jacob, *Confession*, Sig. B2.

misgovernment', Jacob wrote in his supplication addressed to James I, 'than that which is originally invested in your royal person, and from it derived to such of your laity as you shall judge worthy to be deputed to the same under you.'[82] As he answered the question raised in his catechism of 1605 about how unity might be preserved when each congregation remained fundamentally independent of the spiritual authority of others:

> Unity in conscience stands not upon one church or pastor over the rest, but upon the one Word and Testament of Christ taught ordinarily by that church unto us whereof we are, as God's ordinance is. Also thus most easily may the meanest next dwelling magistrate rule any church in outward peace; yea in peace and concord of religion far more easily and more readily than otherwise.[83]

If the Bible was the heart of ecclesiastical unity, the magistrate, as will be discussed below in Chapter 7, would be expected to provide the coercive rod to maintain conformity between the gathered churches.

John Robinson

In one of his earliest controversies as an advocate of separatist ecclesiology, Robinson was confronted by his anonymous puritan opponent with the question of whether a diocesan or national synod could act as the governing body for particular churches. Much of the debate arising from this issue hung on the use of the word 'church' in scripture. His puritan adversary in this small skirmish maintained that an assembly of elders drawn from many churches could properly be construed a 'representative church, as Solomon's assembly, 1 Kings 8, is called the congregation of all Israel'.[84] Robinson agreed that the word *ecclesia* in the scriptures was sometimes used indefinitely for all particular churches, but whenever this occurred, he argued, the church should be taken to indicate only that all particular churches were 'one in nature, form,

[82] Jacob, *Humble supplication*, 13–14.

[83] Champlin Burrage, 'Lost Prison Papers of Henry Jacob', *Review and Expositor*, 5 (1908), 506.

[84] Champlin Burrage, *An Answer to John Robinson of Leyden* (London, 1920), 7.

definition, essential parts and properties, though not in existence'.[85] While admitting that the Old Testament church was organized on the basis of a national structure 'having one high priest, one temple, one altar, one sacrifice', Robinson averred that the visible church under the New Testament was understood to be made up of 'many distinct and entire churches'.[86] Each congregation was a complete spiritual corporation within itself having the right to administer all the ecclesiastical ordinances of preaching, prayers, the sacraments, and censures, because 'Christ speaks immediately without diocesan or provincial churches' to each particular congregation.[87]

For Robinson, the only true visible church was, therefore, a particular congregation. Sharing a point of agreement with views expressed earlier by Thomas Cartwright, Robinson declared that the notion of a universal church was a mere abstraction with no concrete point of reference in the real world.[88] Visible churches were 'particular assemblies of faithful people, separated from all other assemblies which, like so many distinct flocks, do ordinarily herd together and so communicate in Word, prayer, sacraments and censures'.[89] Because he believed it was a 'necessity' that the whole membership 'be present at and in all the public administrations and actions of communion in the church's holy things', the size of a gathered congregation also proved to be an important consideration. He thus shared the concern voiced earlier in the writings of Travers and Johnson that a church should be small enough to allow everyone 'ordinarily' to meet in one place.[90] If a church outgrew these numerical boundaries, Robinson—like Johnson—called for 'a dispersion' and 'a multiplication of more particular assemblies'. Perhaps the most valuable benefit of gathering in one place was, he explained, that the church became more visible in society:

[85] Burrage, *Answer to John Robinson*, 4; cf. John Robinson, *A just and necessarie apologie* (Amsterdam, 1625), 13.

[86] Burrage, *Answer to John Robinson*, 8; John Robinson, *A justification of separation from the Church of England* (Amsterdam, 1610), 174.

[87] Burrage, *Answer to John Robinson*, 14.

[88] Robinson, *Apologie*, 12, 14.

[89] Robinson, *Justification*, 196.

[90] Ibid. Robinson also agreed with Jacob and other radicals and separatists, that the large congregations of many Continental reformed churches were a serious defect in their polity: *Justification*, 196.

'Now that the church . . . is then most truly visible indeed, when it is assembled in one place . . . no man admitting a due thought of things, can make doubt of.'[91]

Robinson wrote very little on the issue of interchurch relationships. While he initially appeared to reject the concept of a provincial or national representative church in his first apology as a separatist, he nevertheless seems quickly to have moderated these convictions to the extent that, by 1610, he was willing to agree with Paul Baynes that a synodical meeting could indeed be called a church, though he denied that such a body possessed any judicial power over particular churches:

> But it will be said, may not the officers of one or many churches meet together to discuss and consider of matters for the good of the church or churches and so be called a church, synod, or the like? I deny it not, so they infringe no order of Christ, or liberty of the brethren, they may so do and so be called in a sense.[92]

Like most radical puritans and separatists, Robinson refused to grant any binding authority to the proclamations and decisions of such interchurch assemblies. As he explained it to Bernard, 'neither has any one church in the world that power over another, nor all the churches in the world over any one, which the meanest church has over any her member or members whomsoever. One church may forsake another, but judicially to censure or excommunicate it may it not.'[93]

The brevity with which Robinson, and, indeed, radical puritans and separatists generally, treated the subject of interchurch structures is not surprising, since neither tradition had much occasion to put theory into practice, nor had they an extended history of intercongregational experience in which their views could have been matured and sharpened. Rather than using well-developed, institutionalized channels of interchange characterized by a formal, graduated system of authority, relations between various separatist congregations —as well as those that occurred between puritan parishes—

[91] Robinson, *Apologie*, 10. The Leiden separatist church was reported to have had over 300 members at one point. See F. J. Powicke, *John Robinson (1575?–1625)* (London, 1920), 50. For Johnson, see above, n. 49.

[92] Robinson, *Justification*, 199–200.

[93] Ibid. 196.

tended toward the informal. The bond between them was more often formed through a web of mutual friendships and shared religious experiences of godly life in the midst of an unregenerate and unreceptive world. In this situation, the need for a developed policy of interchurch relations was not an urgent one. Reacting vehemently to what they perceived to be the tyrannical rule of a worldly episcopal hierarchy, the separatists, like other radicals, knew one thing for certain: they would no longer condone the 'monstrous interposition and intrusion betwixt the head and the body' created by the existence of diocesan bishops. But beyond a few rudimentary discussions about procedures regarding intercommunion, transfer of membership, and ordination (in which there was not total agreement),[94] and a conviction that synods should offer only advice and not binding pronouncements, separatist thinking on the subject remained relatively unexplored.

While it is evident that the synodical theory proposed by Robinson helped to ensure the autonomy of particular churches, it did so, of course, at the expense of any ecclesiastical disciplinary apparatus for the enforcement of uniformity between congregations. This was the weak link in Robinson's polity, according to one contemporary critic who reasoned that by not granting judicial power to provincial or national ecclesiastical councils, 'the particular churches shall be without bond or order. So unwisely do you provide for each particular congregation a liberty which must needs prejudice the universal.'[95] Robinson, as he himself later explained in 1625, remained unconvinced by the arguments of those who claimed that a catholic unity between churches could be preserved only through the constraints of ecclesiastical councils which possessed compulsory powers.[96] But the fact remains that, considering Robinson's failure to settle the internal congregational dispute between Ainsworth and Johnson on the basis of interchurch advice that we noted earlier in this chapter, the objection raised by Robinson's critic would have possibly appeared very much more persuasive an argument to

[94] Stephen Brachlow, 'Puritan Theology and Radical Churchmen in Pre-Revolutionary England' (Oxford University D.Phil. thesis, 1979), 337, n. 2.

[95] Burrage, *Answer to John Robinson*, 45.

[96] Robinson, *Apologie*, 13.

those radicals inclined toward a more rigid and authoritative structure of synods.

Not only did Robinson's attempt to settle the dispute between Ainsworth and Johnson through the advice and counsel of a sister church end in failure, but so did similar attempts on his part in the mid-1620s to resolve the controversy over Sabine Staresmore's application for membership in the Ancient Church of separatists at Amsterdam. Apprently Staresmore had moved from London to Leiden where he was accepted for membership in Robinson's congregation on the basis of the covenent he had made with Henry Jacob's church in Southwark. Staresmore then attempted to transfer his membership to Amsterdam on the same basis, only to find himself rebuffed by a rigorist faction within that congregation.[97] To judge from the correspondence by Robinson and the church at Leiden dealing with the subject, the exchange of letters between London, Amsterdam, and Leiden over the issue was fruitless. In the end, Robinson wrote a warning to the Amsterdam church about their unscriptural proceedings in handling the Staresmore case and concluded by saying that since he knew they were unwilling to listen to outside advice, he would no longer trouble them about the matter.[98] Thus, the autonomy of the particular churches remained intact, but not without seriously weakening the possibility of maintaining a uniformity of practice and communion. There was, however, one other means of safeguarding uniformity, according to Robinson and other separatists and radical puritans: that was through the instrument of a godly civil magistrate.

[97] See John Robinson, *An appeale on truths behalf* (Leiden, 1624), *passim*; and 'Letter to the church at London', in *The lawfulnesse of the hearing of the ministers of the Church of England* (Leiden, 1634), 74.

[98] Robinson, *An appeale on truths behalf*, Sig. C3.

7

CHURCH AND MAGISTRATE

Elizabethan Radical Puritans

THE preceding two chapters have explored the structures envisaged by left-wing puritans and separatists for governing the visible church with respect to the distribution of power within the gathered congregation and the limits of synodical authority. While we have considered these two issues in isolation from other potentially competing forces, there was a third dimension in the overall configuration of their polity that stood outside the ecclesial sphere, but which, nevertheless, could exert a considerable influence in ecclesiastical matters: this was the place and function occupied by the civil magistate in a reformed church.

If the structures puritan radicals developed for governing the church were, as we have seen, laden with the ambiguities inherent in the Calvinist penchant for mixed forms of polity, then the relationship they described between church and magistrate was equally subject to what David Little has described as the 'dilemma of earthly power' that haunted puritan ideals. It was a dilemma they faced on two fronts. First, there was the clash between viewing the civil and ecclesiastical orders as two distinct spheres of divinely ordained power while, at the same time, subjugating magistracy to the ministry by granting ministers the final responsibility for interpreting the meaning of scripture in matters of church reform. In the second place, there was the apparent anomaly of pressing the coercive powers of the civil arm into the service of an institution that insisted upon the preservation of voluntarism in religion.[1] While recognizing, like Calvin, that true faith could never be established in the hearts of people by

[1] David Little, *Religion, Order, and Law* (Oxford, 1970), 129.

force,[2] the coercive role attributed to the magistrate for maintaining ecclesiastical uniformity and suppressing demonstrable idolatry meant that, in the final analysis, neither the separatists nor the radical puritans could be said to have embraced a theory of religious liberty in any modern sense.[3]

Throughout the pages of the *Institutes*, Calvin often defined the role and place of civil magistracy in the exalted terms that he believed their divinely instituted functions in church and society earned for them. Magistrates were 'invested with divine authority'; they acted as 'God's representatives' (or 'vice-regents') and, therefore, they deserved to be called 'gods'.[4] Calvin required that every citizen conform to the government of the higher authorities as a form of pious duty even when subjected to the rule of ruthless tyrants.[5] Civil disobedience to an ungodly prince, he warned, was tantamount to a wilful resistance of the king of kings: 'Let no man deceive himself here, the magistrate cannot be resisted without God being resisted at the same time.'[6]

While insisting that church and state must be considered as 'things completely distinct', Calvin nevertheless appreciated the part that civil governments held in maintaining doctrinal and ecclesiastical orthodoxy: 'the civil government has as its appointed end . . . to cherish and protect the outward worship of God, to defend sound doctrine of piety and the position of the church'.[7]

The radical puritans of Elizabeth's reign were no less conservative with respect to their veneration for social order and the reverence they believed was due to God's earthly representatives in the political sphere. As Chaderton explained, the disciplinarians were soundly persuaded by scripture that 'God is not the author of confusion, but of good order, and necessary distinction'.[8] Ideologically, it seems it was never the

[2] W. K. Jordan, *The Development of Religious Toleration in England* (London, 1932), i, 251–9. For Calvin, see Harro Hopfl, *The Christian Polity of John Clavin* (Cambridge, 1982), 191.

[3] J. W. Allen, *A History of Political Thought in the Sixteenth Century* (London, 1928), 229–30.

[4] John Calvin, *Institutes of the Christian Religion*, ed. J. T. McNeill, trans. F. L. Battles (London, 1960), bk. 4, ch. 20, s. 4.

[5] Ibid., ss. 8, 25–6. [6] Ibid., s. 24. [7] Ibid., s. 1.

[8] Chaderton, *A fruitfull sermon*, as quoted in Patrick Collinson, *The Religion of Protestants: The Church in English Society 1559–1625* (Oxford, 1982), 162.

intention of the Elizabethan puritans, as Patrick Collinson has forcefully argued, 'to demolish the world to which they so securely belonged, nor is there much evidence that their religion implied dissatisfaction with the positions of social dominance which they had inherited or acquired'.[9] Like Calvin, they maintained traditional values and views about the exalted nature of magistracy and its role in preserving true Christian religion. Cartwright, for example, said that the queen possessed 'chief authority' in the land to 'set up and defend not only the civil government, but also the true reformation of the church'.[10]

As we shall see, there were dynamics within radical puritan views of magistracy that subordinated civil rulers to ecclesiastical authority. Yet it does not do full justice to the rich texture of their views simply to assert that in left-wing puritan polity the sovereign of the state would be considered, in Gordon Donaldson's words, '*only* a member of the church . . . over which he was not permitted to exercise any authority'.[11] Travers made clear his own perception that the duty of magistrates to 'set in order and establish the state of the church by their authority and to preserve and maintain it' conferred an honour that elevated them well 'above the rest of the faithful'.[12] In the event of ecclesiastical disorder, idolatry, schism, or heresy, the magistrate possessed the right to punish transgressors, be they fellow magistrates or members of the clergy. As Edward Dering explained: 'Princes have full authority over all ecclesiastical and civil persons, and equally over both to punish the offenders.'[13] While the church was in charge of religious discipline, the extent of its own punitive powers was strictly limited to the administration of spiritual punishment. The civil magistrate, however, possessed the right to punish corporally or by confiscation of material goods

[9] Chaderton, *Fruitfull sermon*, 181.

[10] W. H. Frere and C. E. Douglas, *Puritan Manifestoes* (reprint. ed., London, 1954), 85–6.

[11] Gordon Donaldson, *The Scottish Reformation* (London, 1960), 186 (my italics).

[12] Walter Travers, *A full and plaine declaration of ecclesiastical discipline* (n.p., 1574), 187.

[13] *A parte of a register countayning sundrie memorable matters, for the reformation of our church* (n.p., 1593), 79.

any who rejected the discipline of the church or failed to respond positively to the preaching of the gospel.[14]

At the same time, there were ideas within radical puritan ecclesiology that, as David Little has said, would have attenuated all forms of 'involuntary domination' and 'political–legal coercion' over the church.[15] In what was surely Cartwright's most significant gesture toward the preservation of religious voluntarism and freedom, pregnant with momentous possibilities for the development of the ideal of religious toleration in the seventeenth century, he maintained that it was not lawful for the prince to force subjects to participate in the sacraments of the church. The sacraments were, of course, a central rite of ecclesial life. By removing the coercive hand of the political powers from this fundamental institution, Cartwright provided—albeit in a highly limited way—room for the free exercise of individual conscience in the life of faith. Nevertheless, it is characteristic of the ambiguities in the radical puritan vision that the restraining power of the state was encouraged by Cartwright with respect to the other central feature of reformed ecclesiology, the preaching of the Word. Cartwright believed that while coercion was not appropriate for the sacraments, the magistrate could compel subjects to hear the Word preached and punish those who did not outwardly reform accordingly; indeed, Cartwright insisted that flagrant idolaters should suffer capital punishment like murderers and traitors.[16]

Possessing executive powers in ecclesial as well as civil matters, the magistrate was also expected to summon, as the need arose, national assemblies of ministers. The 1586 'Acts for the reformation of the ministerie in the churche of England', for example, explicitly discouraged the assembling of general synods except by appointment of the queen, her Privy Council or Parliament.[17] Fenner indicated that by virtue of his office, the magistrate was 'a principal member of the congregation where he is', so that if there was an unlawful

[14] Frere and Douglas (eds.), *Puritan Manifestoes*, 122, 129–30; see also Albert Peel (ed.) *The Seconde Parte of a Register* (Cambridge, 1915), i, 169.

[15] Little, *Religion, Order, and Law*, 130.

[16] A. F. Scott Pearson, *Church and State: Political Aspects of Sixteenth Century Puritanism* (Cambridge, 1928), 105–6; 109–10.

[17] Peel (ed.), *Seconde Parte*, i, 308.

election in his church, the magistrate 'lawfully may and by duty ought not only to disannul whatsoever election the elders and people have unlawfully made, but also by his civil pre-eminence to compel them to make a new election according to the Word of God'.[18]

The puritan convinction about the role of the magistrate in arbitrating cases of ecclesiastical error and disorder thus reflected in some measure the dominant political views of church and state in sixteenth-century England where the two powers, political and ecclesiastical, were conceived as two sides of one and the same order. Consequently, the attempt by radical puritans to remould the established church could easily be regarded as an assault not simply on the ecclesial order, but on the entire political-social edifice, as well.[19] For traditionalists within the established church, this apparent conflict in the puritan campaign between their conservative political ideals and their radical religious activities, proved to be their most frequent line of attack against left-wing puritans. So, while paying tribute to royal supremacy, radical puritans had to answer the perpetual accusations of sedition raised by the civil and ecclesiastical hierarchy. As Udall paraphrased the argument of the conformists, 'you cannot be the queen's friend that thus look for innovations in the state'.[20] Alterations in the religious sphere implied alterations in the civil.

In light of their high view of magisterial authority as an institution of God, it is not surprising to find that Elizabethan radical churchmen always disavowed the charges of sedition and did so with a conviction that they were being entirely consistent within the framework of their ideals. In response to the allegation by the bishops that the *First Admonition* degraded the authority and sovereignty of the queen, Cartwright protested: 'Her Majesty shall not find better subjects in her land than those that desire a right reformation.'[21] The extremists saw themselves as lawful and utterly loyal subjects of Elizabeth I. In his sermon of 1584, for example, Chaderton fervently swore 'before God, his angels and you all, that to save Her Majesty's life, I would give my right hand . . . Nay . . .

[18] Dudley Fenner, *A counter-poyson* (London, 1584), 28–9.

[19] Pearson, *Church and State*, 6–8, 42.

[20] *Parte of a register*, 352.

[21] Frere and Douglas (eds.), *Puritan Manifestoes*, 85–6.

pour out all the blood in my heart, though it should run a thousand years.'[22] A party of zealous puritan magnates in Suffolk expressed a similar sentiment in their letter of protest over the humiliation of leading puritan ministers and gentlemen of the county by the justices of assize. The letter, addressed to the Privy Council in 1583, indicates their common conviction that 'we serve Her Majesty and the country not according to our fancies . . . but according to the law and statutes of the realm of England: we reverence both the law and the lawmakers. When law speaks, we keep silence. Law commands, and we obey.'[23]

But while radical puritans appeared in this way to make generous concessions to conventionally accepted theories of state sovereignty, they did in fact adopt a political posture quite different from many of their religiously more conservative contemporaries. Whitgift, for example, propounded a theory of the monarch's role in church and state which gave Elizabeth 'absolute authority to make ecclesiastical laws as well as to apply them'. By contrast, Cartwright limited the queen's jurisdiction in ecclesiastical matters by the dictates of scripture.[24] So while advocating royal supremacy, puritan extremists did so in a restricted sense by insisting upon the crucial proviso that the monarch must rule according to the dictates of scripture: the Word alone was supreme.[25] As the ejected preacher from Norwich, Richard Gawton, explained under intense interrogation by church officials, 'though the queen have ecclesiastical jurisdiction, yet it is not absolute to do what she list: but with all humble submission I acknowledge all such jurisdiction as she claims, for her own words declare she claims no further jurisdiction that the Word of God does allow'.[26] Gawton's response precisely mirrored puritan expectations for a godly magistracy as expressed earlier by, for example, Walter Travers, who had explained that magistrates should 'rule not as they themselves list according to their own will, but only according to this Word and commandment'.[27]

[22] Chaderton, *Fruitfull sermon*, 45.

[23] *Parte of a register*, 129. See also Diarmaid MacCulloch, *Suffolk and the Tudors: Politics and Religion in an English County 1500–1600* (Oxford, 1986), 207–9; 343.

[24] Pearson, *Church and State*, 30.

[25] Allen, *History of Political Thought*, 220.

[26] *Parte of a register*, 395–6.

[27] Travers, *Ecclesiastical discipline*, 185.

A. F. Scott Pearson concluded many years ago in his classic work on puritan political doctrines that the qualification of royal jurisdiction in ecclesiastical matters by the less tolerant disciplinarians so narrowed their recognition of traditional concepts of royal supremacy as to have rendered their views thoroughly suspect.[28] Certainly, the distinction that puritan dissidents drew between church and state and the priority they granted to biblical (as opposed to merely human) authorities provided their radical activism with ideological sanctions that effectively freed them from the necessity of conforming to even royal mandates if those laws stood contrary to a puritan interpretation of scripture. Throkmorton made it plain that while he acknowledged Elizabeth as the 'supreme governor in all causes', he was, nevertheless, ready to obey the Bible before the sovereign in word and deed. 'We are forced to speak for [reformation] and to use it,' Cartwright said, even though in so doing they clearly contravened the law of the land.[29] Even among the earliest agitators in the vestiarian controversy of the 1560s, reform-minded protestants were summoned passively to resist the higher authorities whenever their laws contravened biblical injunctions: 'The minister of the Word must rather obey God than man. But when he does obey the prince in ceremonies and in fashion of apparel, he does not obey God more than man. Therefore he must not obey in these things.'[30]

These sanctions in the political theories of puritan propaganda that justified puritan radical activities had roots extending back at least as far as Calvin's *Institutes*. While defending the right of secular governments to repress the instabilities and errors of a fallen society and demanding filial obedience to the magistrate from every subject, Calvin nevertheless opened the way for godly disobedience when civil law stood in opposition to the law of God. At the end of the *Institutes*, after what could easily, though erroneously, be read as 'twelve hundred pages culminating in a defense of absolutism',[31] Calvin inserted the potentially subversive re-

[28] Pearson, *Church and State*, 37.
[29] Frere and Douglas (eds.), *Puritan Manifestoes*, 130.
[30] *Parte of a register*, 48.
[31] Perry Miller, *Orthodoxy in Massachusetts 1630–1650* (New York, 1970), 31.

mark based on Acts 5: 29: 'If they [the magistrates] command anything against him [God], let it go unesteemed. And here let us not be concerned about all that dignity which the magistrates possess; for no harm is done to it when it is humbled before that singular and truly supreme power of God.'[32]

Despite what has recently been called Calvin's 'almost inflexible opposition to political resistance',[33] Calvin thus became, as Michael Walzer has argued, an 'inexhaustible source of sedition and rebellion' for succeeding generations of Calvinists.[34] While radical puritans shared much of the Genevan reformer's conservative bias and the intensity of his passion for order at any price, it is likely that his acknowledgement of the validity of resistance in certain circumstances also provided a kind of ideological grammar for the political rhetoric of the more rigorous disciplinarians in Elizabethan England, as it did throughout the wider international Calvinist community.[35]

If left-wing puritans were willing to acknowledge royal supremacy, provided the prince submitted to the supremacy of the Word, the really crucial question, then, was not whether the final authority lay with the magistrate or the Bible, but who was to provide the final court of appeal in relevant matters of biblical interpretation. The Elizabethan radical puritans believed that the responsibility for this belonged entirely with the elders so that, in theory at least, the ruling

[32] Calvin, *Institutes*, bk. 4, ch. 20, s. 31–2.

[33] Hopfl, *Christian Polity of John Calvin*, 171–2.

[34] Michael Walzer, *The Revolution of the Saints: A Study in The Origins of Radical Politics* (New York, 1976), 23. This is not to suggest that Calvin provides the only source for the radical dimensions in puritan political thought. The revolutionary aspects of Calvinism were even more fully revealed by other Calvinists, such as Beza, Knox, Pierre Viret, and the English radical protestant, Christopher Goodman. See Robert M. Kingdon, 'The First Expression of Theodore Beza's Political Ideas', *Archiv für Reformationsgeschicte*, 46 (1955), 88–100; Robert D. Linder, 'Pierre Viret and the Sixteenth-Century English protestants', *Archiv für Reformationsgeschicte*, 58 (1967), 149–71; Dan G. Danner, 'Christopher Goodman and the English Protestant Tradition of Civil Disobedience', *Sixteenth Century Journal*, 8 (1966), 62–73; David H. Wollman, 'The Biblical Justification for Resistance to Authority in Ponet's and Goodman's Polemics', *Sixteenth Century Journal*, 13 (1982), 29–41; and Richard L. Greaves, *Theory and Revolution in the Scottish Reformation: Studies in the Thought of John Knox* (Grand Rapids, Mich., 1980), 126–56.

[35] Little, *Religion, Order, and Law*, 33.

structures of the state in ecclesial matters should be firmly subordinated to the overriding claims of a puritan ministerial élite. Fenner has already been cited as saying that the magistrate was considered a 'principal member' of his congregation, possessing a special authority to command new elections of ministers if the first were judged unlawful. But this would be valid only so long as the elders believed the civil ruler had determined the matter according to the Word. As Fenner explained elsewhere, the magistrate must not require ministers to act contrary to consciences which had been tutored by the Word. Moreover, as a member of the church and, therefore, subject to spiritual discipline, the magistrate, 'be he never so mighty', was in this sense considered 'inferior' to the elders.[36] Thus, one of the first puritans to be suspended from his living in the vestiarian controversy of 1565, a Mr Broklesby, had claimed that 'in the time of ministration, he [the minister] was above the queen'.[37]

It was Cartwright and Travers who addressed themselves most directly to the problem, and they unquestionably granted priority to the ministers.[38] Travers explained that the magistrate, like any other church member, must be subject to the spiritual government of the elders because 'the . . . Apostle . . . charges everyone to be subject to those who in the Lord are set over them, for seeing they ought to be careful as well of the salvation of the magistrate as of others'.[39] Cartwright did not deny that the Christian magistrate may 'be assistant, and have his voice' in the decision-making process of the congregation, but only as one 'of the people admitted unto these consultations', *any* of whom were to be allowed to give their consent and 'sometime also their speech'. Finally, Cartwright ascribed 'unto the ministry the decision of matters in controversy and the making of church ceremonies'. The elders were 'the fittest judge of the church matters'.[40]

Theoretically, then, Cartwright and the Elizabethan radicals

[36] Fenner, *Counter-poyson*, 149–50, 175.

[37] Peel (ed.), *Second Parte*, i, 52. The entry lists Broklesby as 'the first put out of his living for the surplice'. See, however, M. M. Knappen, *Tudor Puritanism: A Chapter in the History of Idealism* (Chicago, 1939), 193, n. 13.

[38] Travers, *Ecclesiastical discipline*, 185.

[39] Jordan, *The Development of Religious Toleration*, 244.

[40] Thomas Cartwright, *The rest of the second replie* (n.p. 1577), 167, 170.

turned sixteenth-century theories of royal absolutism upside down. While the prince was encouraged to 'make laws of matters ecclesiastical', it was not lawful, according to William Fulke, 'for him to make laws in ecclesiastical causes contrary to the knowledge of his learned pastors'.[41] Thus, as Pearson summarized the position of the disciplinarians, 'the final arbitrament of the magistrate is thus accepted if he enforces the principles of Puritanism and so the Puritan is the final judge after all.'[42] In the end, the Crown was left, as Cartwright put it with perhaps less political tact than religious zeal, 'to lick the dust of the feet of the church'.[43]

Jacobean Radical Puritans

In his recent study of moderate puritans, Peter Lake made the remarkably novel claim that Jacobean non-separating congregationalists like William Bradshaw developed their polity in order 'to avoid the clash with Royal Supremacy' which, Lake believed, had proved to be such a liability to the presbyterians of the Elizabethan era. Bradshaw's experiment in congregationalism was, therefore, 'a device', according to Lake, designed 'to circumvent the stock charges of subversion that had so been levelled against the puritan position'. The assumption behind this hypothesis is that Bradshaw had consciously conceived a new polity—congregationalism, as distinct from presbyterianism—in order to alleviate the contradiction in the ecclesiology of Elizabethan puritans between the governing authority they granted presbyterian synods and their avowals of royal supremacy. Dr Lake argued that by his modified polity, Bradshaw 'infinitely strengthened the power of the king' since he eliminated the competing power of a 'comprehensive hierarchy of presbyterian synods' and passed the jurisdictional powers of synods into the hands of the monarch. Lake further argued:

> Since, for Bradshaw it was only individual churches or congregations that existed as jurisdictional bodies, and not the national church, he

41 Leonard J. Trinterud, *Elizabethan Puritanism* (New York, 1971), 298.

42 Pearson, *Church and State*, 75.

43 *The Works of John Whitgift*, ed. John Ayre (Cambridge, 1851), iii, 189.

could not be accused of submitting the power of the prince to the authority of the church. Under Bradshaw's scheme the king could only be subject to the purely spiritual powers of that particular congregation which he honoured with his presence.[44]

While this is a remarkably novel reconstruction of Bradshaw's views, the writings of Bradshaw do not in fact lend themselves very well to the interpretation offered by Dr Lake, for at least two reasons. First, there is simply no evidence to support the claim that Bradshaw had 'devised' a congregational form of church government for the particular purpose of avoiding a conflict with royal supremacy. Second, Lake's entire premiss appears to rest on something very much like the assumptions of Perry Miller, who portrayed the congregationalism of Bradshaw and other Jacobean radicals as a momentously new polity within the puritan movement that differed markedly from the presbyterianism espoused by the Elizabethan disciplinarians. But, as discussed in the previous chapter, Miller's non-separating congregationalists did not promulgate anything qualitatively different from views on reform than had already been expressed in the literature of the Elizabethan extremists. Many of the Elizabethan radicals demonstrated similar inclinations toward upholding the primacy of the gathered congregation, and they were as often just as reluctant as Bradshaw to grant any determinative power to synods. Indeed, the political concepts of Bradshaw seem not to have differed at all appreciably from those rendered by Cartwright and other radical ideologues during the puritan campaigns of the 1570s and 1580s.

Sharing with the Elizabethan radical puritans many of the same ideals about church government, the Jacobean non-separating congregationalists, as a whole, also shared a common conviction about the relationship between church and magistrate. While it is true that in Bradshaw's view the king would be subject only to a *spiritual* censure from the particular church to which he belonged, this also stood in fundamental agreement with the intentions of Elizabethan radical puritans. They consistently maintained that the primacy of ecclesiastical governors over the prince must be

[44] Peter Lake, *Moderate puritans and the Elizabethan church* (Cambridge, 1982), 269–71.

taken as a primacy of the Word (and not, strictly speaking, the elders) over all the other authorities. With respect to magisterial authority, the judgement of the elders extended only to purely spiritual matters so that clerical jurisdiction could not infringe upon the supremacy of the sovereign in civil affairs.[45] Furthermore, it is difficult to see how the polity of Bradshaw and other non-separating congregationalists avoided, as Dr Lake suggests, the accusation of 'submitting the power of the prince to the authority of the church'. While Bradshaw quite naturally stressed the more conservative aspects of puritan political ideology in his many affirmations of the king's supremacy, there is no doubt, as we shall see, that he and his co-religionists accepted the limitations to that supremacy in ecclesiastical matters imposed by the radical Calvinist tradition.

For this reason, Jacobean left-wing puritans like Bradshaw often found themselves liable to the very same accusations of disloyalty and derogating from the royal prerogative encountered by the puritan campaigners of the 1570s and 1580s. In response to those renewed accusations, the Jacobeans reiterated much of the same conventional rhetoric about their absolute loyalty to the Crown and their generous advocacy of magisterial supremacy. Although Bradshaw believed that James I's understanding of English puritanism had been 'exceedingly abused with fogs and mists . . . breathed out of the mouths of the prelates', he nevertheless optimistically assured the king in his *Protestation of the kings supremacy*, 1605, that James could discover 'no Christians in the world' willing to grant as much authority in the church to their monarch as the more militant protestant ministers.[46] He insisted that Jacobean noncomformists supported 'the same authority and supremacy in all causes . . . without limitation or qualification', an honour which, like Calvin, they were committed to pay to even a ruthless tyrant who persecuted the truth.[47] According to William Ames, the office of the magistrate, as instituted by God, owned 'the greatest of human powers'. Contempt of that

[45] Jordan, *Development of Religious Toleration*, 243–8.

[46] William Bradshaw, *Several treatises of worship and ceremonies by the reverend Mr. William Bradshaw* (London, 1660), 83.

[47] Ibid. 82–3 (second time).

authority could be, therefore, nothing less than 'a sin against the law of God'.[48]

While thus functioning as the supreme earthly authority in all affairs of the church and state, the monarch's 'chief care' ought to be, said Ames, the promotion of true religion and the suppression of every impiety.[49] The extent of magisterial authority over churches was so broad, Bradshaw explained, that magistrates possessed the power to redress erroneous ecclesiastical practices even 'without the consent and against the will of the ecclesiastical governors', a right that Bradshaw extended to 'the meanest civil officer in a kingdom, city, or town'. Moreover, the monarch alone possessed the right to convene ecclesiastical synods and ratify synodical decrees without which 'no man can force any subject to yield any obedience unto the same'.[50]

In effect, the king would assume something of the role held by the archbishop; or, as Bradshaw said, the monarch 'ought himself to be as it were, archbishop and general overseer of all the churches within his dominions'.[51] In the event that a synod could not resolve a particularly knotty issue, the magistate was to act as the final court of appeal,[52] and if a congregation stumbled, the magistrate alone possessed the power to coerce that church into correcting its error.[53]

While militant early Stuart puritans believed that it was unlawful for the civil authorities to compel unbelievers to make a profession of faith or join the church,.[54] they nevertheless allowed public officials a considerable degree of coercive power over the spiritual affairs of their subjects.[55] For example, although magistrates could not force citizens into church membership, which was possible only by a voluntary profession of faith, they nevertheless could (and indeed *should*)

[48] William Ames, *Conscience with the power and cases thereof*, v, 164–7, in *The workes of the reverend and faithfull minister of Christ William Ames* (London, 1643). While seeking toleration to practice their own polity (e.g., Bradshaw, *Several treatises*, 87), the Jacobean radicals did not therefore advocate a blanket religious toleration. That, they believed, was a scandalous policy, even as it was practiced in the Dutch provinces. Parker MS, iii, 17.

[49] Ames, *Conscience*, v, 165.

[50] Bradshaw, *Several treatises*, 47, 83.

[51] Ibid. 86.

[52] Ibid. 37; Parker MS, iii, 25.

[53] Bradshaw, *Several treatises*, 86.

[54] Ames, *Conscience*, iv, 9; Bradshaw, *Several treatises*, 67–8; Parker MS, iii, 17.

[55] William Ames, *The marrow of sacred divinity*, 313, in *Workes*.

compel the whole populous into the churches to hear the Word preached; citizens who failed to respond in repentance and profession of faith were 'to be allured with favours and if that will not do to be moved by loss of favour'.[56] Finally, like Cartwright, Ames even affirmed that the Deuteronomic law requiring the death penalty for religious disobedience was to be maintained under the new covenent, though he hoped it would not be too rigorously enforced![57]

Considering the powers for ecclesiastical jurisdiction that Bradshaw so willingly appears to lavish on the monarchy, it is understandable how he could be thought to have 'infinitely strengthened the power of the king'.[58] And in one sense (and by his own admission), Bradshaw did—not relative to the Elizabethan puritan platform, however, but, as he saw it, in relation to the English prelacy. It was the power and influence wielded by the episcopal hierarchy and courts, Bradshaw insisted, that severely diminished royal prerogatives, not the humble and obedient godly pastors of the reformist party. Indeed, Bradshaw was convinced (perhaps naïvely so, it would seem) that the puritan mandate favouring ministerial parity 'was no more derogatory and repugnant to the state and glory of a monarch than the parity or equality of schoolmasters of several schools, captains of several camps, shepherds of sheep or masters of several families'.[59]

In addition, Bradshaw's willingness to grant to magistracy the authority to frame and execute laws pertaining to the well-being of the church, to call and preside over synods, and to redress ecclesiastical abuses was, far from a device to strengthen the power of the king, substantially no more generous a provision than Throkmorton had offered in *A Second Admonition*.[60] At the same time, all of these rather conservative sentiments about royal supremacy as expressed

[56] Ames, *Conscience*, iv, 9.

[57] Ibid. v, 172 (printed in error as 142).

[58] See above, n. 44.

[59] Bradshaw, *Several treatises*, 39. Bradshaw's accusation that the bishop's use of power undermined the royal supremacy was not original to him. This was an old claim, popular among Elizabethan disciplinarians. It also formed the heart of Sir Francis Knolly's campaign against the *jure divino* claims of episcopacy in 1588. See W. D. J. Cargill Thompson, *Studies in the Reformation: Luther to Hooker* (London, 1980), 98.

[60] Frere and Douglas (eds.), *Puritan Manifestoes*, 130.

by Bradshaw most certainly may not be taken to imply that he, or any other Jacobean puritan radical, would thereby have been willing to concede unlimited sovereignty to any earthly monarch over ecclesial affairs. Throughout Bradshaw's *Protestation of the kings supremacy*, he unapologetically drew the very same lines of limitation around royal prerogatives that had been laid down originally in the manifestos of Elizabethan radical puritans. 'We deny no authority to the king in matters ecclesiastical,' wrote Bradshaw,

> but only that which Christ Jesus, the only head of the church, has directly and precisely appropriated unto himself . . . For we hold that Christ alone is the doctor of the church in matters of religion and that the Word of Christ, which he has given unto his church, is . . . a perfect direction in all ecclesiastical matters whatsoever.[61]

Behind Bradshaw's extravagant assertions of what he called a royal 'supremacy . . . without limitation or qualification'[62] lay the massive and impregnable puritan assumption that this was operative only so long as the king presided over the church in harmony with scripture i.e., as interpreted in a reformed fashion.[63] This, however, was not the only restriction on traditional views of royal supremacy which could have fuelled the well-known fears of James I that a puritan polity would undo the monarchy and lead to democratic forms of civil government. Ames said that monarchical power was 'not absolute, but carried a double limitation, one from the will of God . . . another from that will of man which is included in those conditions and laws in which the power of rule is founded'.[64] According to puritan radicals, 'the power of rule' was founded originally not in the monarchy itself, but in the people. As Baynes explained: 'In a politic body, power is *first* in the community, in the king *from them*.'[65] Presumably on the basis of these two limitations, Ames was in a position to say that even private citizens were qualified to question whether

[61] Bradshaw, *Several treatises*, 91.

[62] Ibid. 82–3 (second time).

[63] Bradshaw, *Several treatises*, 90.

[64] Ames, *Conscience*, v, 164.

[65] Paul Baynes, *The diocesans tryall* (London, 1621), 83 (my italics). The theory of popular sovereignty expressed here by Ames and Baynes was a common feature of Calvinist political theory, with roots in scholastic thought, and proved to be a potent source for protestant resistance theories in the 1560s and 1570s. See Quentin Skinner, *The Foundations of Modern Political Thought*, (Cambridge, 1978), ii, 332–45.

public laws or edicts were 'lawfùl, convenient and binding'.[66] If those edicts proved unlawful, dissident puritans declared that 'then we may disobey it and not sin'.[67]

All the same, it would be a serious distortion of their own self-understanding to suggest that the Jacobean radicals therefore held populist political views. Congregational in church polity, they made it clear that they believed a monarchical state, as Bradshaw said, was the most appropriate civil polity for English society.[68] Although James I took the puritan theory of royal limitations as a serious threat to his prerogatives,[69] the radicals were convinced that neither their political theories nor their nonconformist practices disparaged royal supremacy in the least.[70] In fact, through a particularly deft, but entirely commonplace, piece of puritan casuistry, militants like Bradshaw reasoned that passive resistance to unbiblical civil laws was a way of performing 'more true and loyal obedience unto his [the magistrate's] authority therein, than any of those that shall yield obedience to any laws of that kind enacted by never so good a magistrate'.[71] Ames added the further insight—which lays bare the potential for social disorder implicit in their ideals—that 'if in some case the law cannot possibly be observed, but some great damage, scandal or inconvenience must needs follow, it is to be presumed that the lawgiver never intended that the law in such a case should be observed'.[72]

Ultimately, then, as with Cartwright and other Elizabethan left-wing puritans, the Jacobean radicals made the magistrate liable to the rule of the elders in spiritual matters. They assumed that James I, as a Christian monarch, would have subjected himself to the spiritual regimen of a particular church, even 'as the meanest subject in the kingdom'.[73] If a

66 William Ames, Preface, to *English puritanisme, containing the main opinions of the rigidest sort of those that are called puritans* (n.p., 1604), not paginated; *Marrow*, 314, in *Workes*.

67 Baynes, *Diocesans tryall*, 24.

68 Ibid. 39.

69 Kenneth Shipps, 'The "Political Puritan"', *Church History*, 45 (1976), 197.

70 Parker, MS, iii, 41.

71 Bradshaw, *Several treatises*, 15.

72 Ames, *Conscience*, v, 168.

73 Bradshaw, *Several treatises*, 47. Though in his petition to James I Bradshaw softened the radicalism of this statement by saying the censure of a sovereign should be administered by the elders with all due reverence to the monarchical office by kneeling before him 'and in the humblest manner to censure his faults': ibid., 44–5.

conflict ever arose between the clergy and the Crown over an interpretation of a particular biblical passage, the clergy possessed conclusive authority to adjudicate the matter. Thus, while assuring the conformist, Thomas Chester, that Ames believed all citizens were 'bound in conscience to observe the just laws of magistrates', Ames added that if in the judgement of the ministers the magistrate should err, 'obedience is to be yielded unto lawful ecclesiastical governors'.[74] It was Thomas Hooker, in writing the preface to one of Ames's posthumous publications during the repressive anti-puritan period of the 1630s, who exposed more clearly the theocratic dimensions of Ames's political theory when he stipulated that the duties of the magistrate were to be judged, determined, and delivered by the elders.[75]

Elizabethan and Jacobean Separatists

Within the broad framework of left-wing puritan thought concerning the relationship between church and magistrate, there existed a diversity of possibilities and contrasting impulses which, as David Little observed, involved the proponents of radical protestantism 'in some wondrous ambiguities'. At the centre of these ideological cross-currents lay the puritan dilemma of preserving the coercive function of the state in ecclesiastical affairs while simultaneously insisting on the voluntary character of faith and the essentially consensual nature of church polity.[76] In the historiography of English dissent, the separatists have often been cast as political innovators who exposed and rejected this puritan dilemma by advocating a complete separation of the religious and secular spheres and promoting the notion of religious toleration.[77] Upon further examination, however, it appears that—despite the radical nature of their act of separation—the

[74] William Ames, *A reply to Dr. Mortons general defence of three nocent ceremonies* (n.p., 1622), 95–6.

[75] Preface to William Ames, *A fresh suit against human ceremonies* (Rotterdam, 1633), not paginated.

[76] See the discerning analysis of this dilemma in Little, *Religion, Order, and Law*, 81–131.

[77] See below, nn. 87–93.

separatists actually embraced within their own understanding of magistracy the very same contending ideological forces that characterized left-wing puritan thought; rather than describing them as politically innovative, it is perhaps more accurate to say that the separatists tended to exploit to their own purposes convictions that were already present within radical puritanism. While they certainly did not simply reiterate verbatim the formulas of left-wing puritan propagandists, neither did they reshape in any appreciable measure the fundamental posture of English radical Calvinism.

If the intractable nonconformity of radical puritans raised serious questions about their allegiance to the Crown, the outright separatism of those 'hasty puritans' who severed their ties with the English parish system served only to validate the suspicions of conformists that puritanism was fundamentally anti-monarchical and anarchic.[78] By way of reply, the separatists, like the radical puritans, insisted that they did not, either in theory or by their practice, intend to debase royal supremacy. On the contrary, they too believed a prince possessed the divine right to preserve and enforce religious uniformity. As for themselves, they claimed their loyalty to the English Crown was unassailable. Browne insisted that, as civil magistate, the queen's power was

> highest under God within her dominions, and that over all persons and causes. By that she may put to death all that deserve it by law, either of the church or commonwealth, and none may resist her or the magistrates under her by force or wicked speeches, when they execute the laws.[79]

Having repeatedly affirmed his loyalty to the queen and traditional maxims about the monarch's position as 'supreme governor of the whole land and over the church also',[80] Henry Barrow protested in a letter shortly before his death: 'I have everywhere in my writings acknowledged all duty and obedience to her Majesty's government, as to the sacred ordinance of God the supreme power he has set over all causes

[78] Robert Browne, *The Writings of Robert Harrison and Robert Browne*, ed. Albert Peel and Leland H. Carlson (London, 1953), 152.

[79] Ibid.

[80] Henry Barrow, *The Writings of Henry Barrow, 1587–1590*, ed. Leland H. Carlson (London, 1962), 198.

and persons, whether ecclesiastical or civil, within her dominions.'[81] His plea, however, fell on deaf ears; Barrow, who had spent almost three years in prison, was hanged shortly thereafter, along with John Greenwood, for political insubordination, having, as the sentence read, 'most maliciously written and published against her Majesty's government'.[82]

Nevertheless, the godly advocates of separatism continued to defend both their own innocence and the ecclesiastical prerogatives of the throne. 'Neither I myself, nor any other (to my knowledge) that professes the same course of true religion with me,' explained the separatist leader of Great Yarmouth, William Euring in 1617, 'did ever intend or once conceive so much as in thought any one point or part of sedition or evil conspiracy against . . . the king's majesty, his royal state and government.'[83] Some years earlier, before his conversion to baptist convictions, John Smyth had called the puritan Richard Bernard a 'malicious or an ignorant slanderer' for having accused the separatists of traducing the honour and authority of the Crown. Smyth replied with the commonplace that all separatists believed in the divinely ordained concept of monarchy, in which 'the princes and civil estates are the Lord's blessed ordinance'.[84] Not only did the separatists teach absolute submission to their sovereign, but also that 'a prince has power in a particular visible church to punish any wickedness anyone commits and to cause that visible church to assume and practice any truth God's Word teaches'. In saying this, Smyth echoed the highly 'Erastian' sounding words of article 39 in the 1596 *Confession*, which claimed that magistrates should 'enforce all their subjects, whether ecclesiastical or civil, to do their duties to God and men . . . punishing and restraining the evil according as God has commanded, whose lieutenants they are here on earth'.[85]

[81] As printed in Henry Ainsworth and Francis Johnson, *An apologie or defence of svch trve Christians as are commonly (but vniustly) called Brownists* (Amsterdam, 1604), 92.

[82] F. J. Powicke, *Henry Barrow, Separatist (1550?–1593) and the Exiled Church of Amsterdam 1593–1622* (London, 1900), 76.

[83] William Euring, *Ten Covnter Demands* (London, 1617), 8. For Euring's life, see Champlin Burrage, *The Early English Dissenters* (Cambridge, 1912), i, 191–2.

[84] John Smyth, *The Works of John Smyth*, ed. W. T. Whitley (Cambridge, 1915), ii, 519.

[85] Ibid., Francis Johnson, *A trve confession of the faith* (Amsterdam, 1596), art. 39.

However, if in this respect the separatist's perception of the coercive role of the magistrate in ecclesiastical matters resonates with contemporary radical puritan views, there were other dimensions within their understanding of magistracy that historians have suggested distinguish them from left-wing puritans. It has been argued that the separatists stood apart from the puritans by their rejection of the compulsory power of the state over the church. This conclusion is very often based upon the celebrated passage in Robert Browne's *Treatise of reformation without tarying for anie*, 1582, a passage that has routinely been cited as evidence that the separatist commended a policy of religious toleration and radical separation of the civil and religious spheres. As the passage reads, Browne explained that magistrates

> may do nothing concerning the church, but only civilly and as civil magistrates; that is, they have not that authority over the church as to be prophets or priests or spiritual kings, as they are magistrates over the same: but only to rule the commonwealth in all outward justice, to maintain the right, welfare and honour thereof with outward power, bodily punishment and civil forcing of men. And therefore also because the church is in a commonwealth, it is of their charge: that is concerning the outward order provision and outward justice, they are to look to it, but to compel religion, to plant churches by power and to force a submission to ecclesiastical government by laws and penalties belongs not to them.[86]

According to these and other comparable statements, separatist views have often been set over against the views of radical puritans. A. F. Scott Pearson, for example, argued that while Cartwright and other Elizabethan disciplinarians would have enlisted the sword of the magistrate to enforce uniformity, the separatists would have refused it.[87] In like manner, W. K. Jordan contended that, in contrast to the Elizabethan puritans, Robert Browne 'completely dissociated the Church and State', recognizing 'that it was no part of the duty of the ruler to maintain the true religion'.[88]

Similar assessments of Browne have been made more recently by B. R. White and Timothy George. Dr White claimed that Browne limited the queen's coercive authority

[86] *Browne*, 184. [87] Pearson, *Church and State*, 105–6.

[88] Jordan, *Development of Religious Toleration*, i, 263–75.

only to civil, earthly, and secular matters and 'did not shrink from the possible consequences of his position that the magistrate must not be allowed to exercise any power in spiritual matters'.[89] Although Dr George admitted that Browne 'had only an inchoate theory of toleration', he was nevertheless convinced that Browne's 'emphasis on the voluntary church and the unforced conscience went beyond the thinking of any other English leader of his time'.[90]

In two other recent studies, Richard Reinitz and George Selement have observed that Browne and his colleague Robert Harrison justified their rejection of state interference in religious matters by interpreting typologically the role that the kings of Israel had assumed over the church in the Old Testament.[91] Accordingly, the separatists denied that English magistrates could function like the theocratic kings of Israel in establishing true religion because Christ had inaugurated a new order that displaced any parallel with Old Testament models of monarchy. Consequently, the separatists believed that the kings of Israel should now be understood to have commenced a reformation of the church as 'figures of Christ'. The monarchs of Israel reformed the church 'by the civil sword', Harrison explained, 'for they had authority in both cases that our kings and princes want, for the figurative manner was ended in Christ'.[92] According to George Selement's analysis, 'the crux of the matter involved the radical division that Separatists made between the Abrahamic covenant, which they asserted no longer applied to Christians, and the covenent of the New Testament. Christ, in short, made the Jewish system of theocracy obsolete.' In this new order, Christ alone was the head of the church, while the Old Testament monarchs no longer provided an appropriate paradigm for the English Crown.[93]

[89] B. R. White, *The English Separatist Tradition* (Oxford, 1971), 58–60.

[90] Timothy George, *John Robinson and the Separatist Tradition* (Macon, GA, 1982), 43–4.

[91] Richard Reinitz, 'The Separatist Background of Roger Williams' Argument for Religious Toleration' in Sacuan Bercovitch (ed.), *Typology and Early American Literature* (Amherst, Mass., 1972), 107–37; George Selement, 'The Covenant Theology of English Separatism and the Separation of Church and State', *Journal of the American Academy of Religion*, 41 (1973), 66–74.

[92] *Browne*, 41; see also 163, for similar views by Browne.

[93] Selement, 'Covenant Theology of English Separation', 68.

Each of these recent authorities have proposed, then, that Browne and Harrison had in some measure significantly transformed the puritan view of godly magistracy by rejecting Old Testament parallels, positing a complete separation of church and state, and repudiating the use of force in religious matters. However, neither Browne and Harrison, nor any other figures within the later history of separatism, rejected so unambiguously as these accounts suggest the police value of the civil sword in ecclesial affairs[94] and the Old Testament models of monarchical sovereignty in church affairs. Furthermore, none of the studies cited above has taken into account expressions within left-wing puritan thought which, as we shall see, also denied forms of involuntary domination over the spiritual affairs of individuals, as well as similar interpretations by radical puritans of monarchy in the Old Testament.

In the first place, Browne's conviction that magistrates ought not to interfere in determining ecclesial matters has parallels in left-wing puritan literature as, for example, when Cartwright explained to Whitgift that the 'making of the orders and ceremonies of the church' pertains 'unto the ministers of the church and unto the ecclesiastical governors; and that as they meddle not with the making of civil laws and laws for the commonwealth, so the civil magistate has not to ordain ceremonies pertaining to the church'.[95] In addition, Cartwright was quite clear that, whereas the state carried out its divinely ordained function as servant of the church by coercive means, the church itself functioned in an entirely different mode as a consensual or voluntary society. As Cartwright informed Whitgift: 'We do not use any compulsion or violence over any.'[96]

Secondly, and more significantly, the context of Robert Browne's assertion that magistrates should not 'compel in matters of religion' is far more ambiguous than the statement appears if quoted (as it usually is) in isolation. A few pages

[94] e.g., ibid. 70–6. To which I take exception, as the following discussion bears out.

[95] As quoted in Donald J. McGinn, *The Admonition Controversy* (New Brunswick, 1949), 415.

[96] Ibid. ii, 208. Note the discussion of Cartwright's views in Little, *Religion, Order, and Law*, 81–104; also Collinson, *Religion of Protestants*, 242–83, esp. 247, where he comments that 'voluntary religion . . . was the significance and the near uniqness of English puritanism'.

earlier Browne had said, 'indeed the magistrate may *force*' a minister in matters of reform.[97]

Thirdly, Browne did not, by his typological interpretation of the kings of Israel, thereby, discard entirely the parallels between monarchy in the Old Testament and the nursing role of magistrates in the contemporary church. Within the immediate context of his famous assertion against civil coercion, Browne acknowledged that, just like the theocratic kings of Israel, modern monarchs possessed the power to 'rule the commonwealth in all outward justice . . . with outward power, bodily punishment, and civil forcing of men'. Moreover, this authority was not limited to civil matters alone, as White suggests,[98] but applied to the maintenance of the ecclesiastical affairs as well, for Browne goes on to say that 'therefore also because the church is in a commonwealth, it is of their charge; that is, concerning the outward provision and outward justice, they are to look to it'.[99] Thus, civil magistrates, to repeat Browne's words, 'have not that authority over the church as to be prophets, or priests, or spiritual kings, as they are magistrates over the same'.[100] In other words, the secular rulers do not act in church affairs as spiritual authorities but only as civil authorities with custodial functions. This conviction, like so many of Browne's, had been fully anticipated by Cartwright several years earlier when the puritan explained to Whitgift that, according to Old Testament precedents, the magistrate did not have authority in the church as a priest or Levite but only as a civil magistrate, with the task of ensuring, by his power, that true religion would be maintained in the land.[101]

In much the same manner as Browne, Harrison also equated the duties of modern magistracy with Old Testament examples, specifically saying that 'as the kings of Judah did

97 *Browne*, 161 (my italics).

98 White, *English Separatist Tradition*, 58.

99 *Browne*, 164.

100 Ibid. 164.

101 A deduction from Cartwright, *The rest of a second replie*, 153, where Cartwright responds to Whitgift's claim that the example of Jehoshaphat, King of Judah allows Elizabeth to assume all power in ecclesiastical and civil causes: 'Whereunto I reply that he (Jehoshaphat) committed not those ecclesiastical matters unto priests and Levites as those which he might have retained with himself or as a thing in his own discretion but used only his princely authority to put in execution that which the Lord commanded.'

reform by their civil power . . . so also it appertains to the magistrates now to break down the idolatrous altars . . . and to slay those which have revolted'.[102] More to the point, Henry Barrow, in a statement paralleling the convinctions of Cartwright and Browne, argued that although the prince could not '*make* any a member of the church', he could nevertheless '*compel* all his subjects to the hearing of God's Word, *punishing* the deriders and contemners of the same'.[103]

The paradoxical claims of the separatists, in which the magistrate was summoned to protect the voluntary nature of church membership with coercive power, could appear 'obviously contradictory', as George Selement has concluded.[104] However, they were not if they are understood from within the radical puritan and separatist frame of reference. From their perspective, compelling the citizenry to hear biblical sermons and punishing the recalcitrant did not violate the voluntary quality of their congregational polity; rather, it created opportunities in which the Spirit could work persuasively and savingly in individual lives through the hearing of the Word which, in turn would hopefully issue in a free, willing profession of faith. The separatists, like the radical puritans, thus intended that the compulsive powers of the magistrate be brought to bear unrelentingly upon the lives of all men and women, driving them, as David Little has said about Cartwright's concept of civil compulsion, 'toward that community whose mark of membership is the consent of the free conscience'.[105]

By modern standards, the use of bodily coercion for the purpose of extracting a voluntary decision appears, of course, morally perverse; but the separatists did not think so, and evidently believed they were being entirely consistent in their proposals. Indeed, through their willingness thus to preserve the punitive powers of the state for the maintenance of an outward, biblical ecclesiastical order, the separatists believed they possessed a solution to the dilemma raised by their

[102] *Browne*, 119.

[103] *Barrow, 1587–1590*, 158 (my italics). For Cartwright, see above, n. 16.

[104] Selement, 'Covenant Theology of English Separatism', 71. See also Michael R. Watts, *The Dissenters* (Oxford, 1978), 31, for a similar assessment.

[105] Little, *Religion, Order, and Law*, 103–4.

synodical theory.[106] If unity between churches could not be enforced by synods, it could be, ideally, by the magistrate. After conceding that synods should not 'challenge or usurp any unlawful jurisdiction or power over the particular churches', Francis Johnson proceeded to address himself to the problem this raised for preserving religious uniformity:

If any ask to whom then the churches shall be subject, if there be no diocesan or other like prelates set over them, I answer, that the churches and all the officers and members thereof, are to be subject to the princes, states, and magistrates under whom they live; according as the apostles do teach us, saying, Let every soul be subject to the higher powers, etc., Romans 13 . . . The magistrates are under the Lord to be keepers of both the tables of the law of God: to whom all persons ought to be subject, even for conscience sake, and to yield obedience unto them.[107]

Within the separatist tradition, the magistrate's coercive function as safeguard of religious uniformity was considerably weakened and finally rejected altogether, only within the ranks of those who had jettisoned their radical Calvinist ecclesiology for believers' baptism.[108] In Smyth's first avowedly anabaptist tract, *The character of the beast*, 1609, he still expressed a high view of monarchical authority, but, significantly, he bypassed in silence the crucial issue of the king's duty to order or preserve true religion.[109] It was not until he published *Propositions and conclusions* three years later that he unequivocally denied a custodial role for the magistrate in church affairs with the simple assertion: 'the magistrate is not by virtue of his office to meddle with religion or matters of conscience, to force and compel men to this or that form of religion or doctrine, but to handle only civil transgressions, injuries, and wrongs of men against men'.[110]

For those who remained true to central separatist political ideals, however, the grand assumption underlying all their

[106] See above, ch. 6.

[107] Francis Johnson, *A Christian plea conteyning three treatises* (Leiden, 1617), 252.

[108] Timothy George, 'Between Pacifism and Coercion: The English Baptist Doctrine of Religious Toleration', *Mennonite Quarterly Review*, 58 (1984), 30–49.

[109] *Smyth*, ii, 572.

[110] Ibid., 748; see also Thomas Helwys, *A short declaration of the mystery of iniquity* (London, 1612), 44; John Murton, *Objections answered by way of dialogue* (n.p., 1615), 27

affirmations about state prerogatives in ecclesiastical causes was, of course, that obedience would be due only so long as the magistrate ruled 'according as God has commanded'.[111] In the event that a prince or magistrate ruled contrary to the law of God, that felicitous partnership between church and state collapsed: 'if the magisrates set up false relgion or neglect their duty, the faithful must avoid false worship and practice the truth, patiently undergoing what may be laid upon them for the same'.[112] The separatists all agreed that under ideal conditions church and state should work harmoniously as 'distinct yet cooperating departments'.[113] To the extent that this happened, the magistrate was to be obeyed 'as God himself', but always only so long as 'it be lawful and warrantable by the Word'.[114]

This last qualification, the 'one utterly crucial reservation' that dominated puritan political thought,[115] ensured that, ideologically at least, the separatists were never in a dilemma over whether to offer their loyalty to the monarch or to Christ;[116] there may have been conflicting claims imposed upon their conscience by those two authorities, but the separatists knew exactly with whom their first allegiance lay. Obedience to the magistrate, said Barrow, 'must always be in the Lord'.[117] This was the principle followed by the earliest Christians, explained the separatist John Canne, for the 'primitive Christians had not the magistrates' leave to serve God, yet they did whatsoever [God] commanded them; their practice is an example for us'.[118]

As with so much of their ecclesiology, the overriding concern in this question of obedience to state authorities centred on the compelling puritan issue of eternal salvation. The Word always took precedence over human statutes simply because more was at stake should they transgress the

[111] Johnson, *True confession*, art. 39.

[112] *Barrow, 1587–1590*, 158–9.

[113] Miller, *Orthodoxy in Massachusetts*, 240.

[114] *Barrow, 1587–1590*, 406.

[115] J. Sears McGee, *The Godly Man in Stuart England* (New Haven and London, 1976), 124. The concept of a qualified obedience was not peculiar to puritans and separatists alone, as McGee notes, ibid., 117.

[116] *Contra* Perry Miller, *Orthodoxy in Massachusetts, passim*. Note David Hall's critical appraisal of Miller's thesis in his introduction to the Harper Torchbook edn., 19–22.

[117] *Barrow, 1587–1590*, 406–7.

[118] John Canne, *A necessitie of separation* (Amsterdam, 1630), 155.

laws of God. As Johnson argued near the end of his last work, if the magistrate would not give his support to the building of true churches, 'yet ought we notwithstanding so to do, obeying God rather than man, and patiently to suffer what they shall lay upon us . . . knowing that [God] does regard and will require it at their hands; and will give a crown of life to such as are faithful to death'.[119]

Henry Jacob

The political views of Henry Jacob illustrate how intimately his ecclesiology was tied to the prevailing left-wing puritan and separatist conception of magisterial function, though in repeated efforts to exhibit an acceptable face of the puritan proposals for James I he was often less outspoken about subordinating civil law to the authority of scripture. From the beginning of his public campaign for radical reform in 1604, Jacob was sensitive to the imputation of treachery and treason that puritan propaganda and dissent had elicited from conservative prelates. As he concluded at that time: 'Finally our adversaries will object that by these assertions and defences we detract from the king's authority and power: namely thus misliking that which he allows and specially holding an authority ecclesiastical not derived from him.'[120] It was an accusation he confronted at various points throughout his career, and by way of an answer he expended much of his energy attempting to prove his fealty to the Crown rights.[121]

From Jacob's perspective, the charge of political insubordination levelled against strict disciplinarians by the bishops was nothing less than 'a malicious surmise of that whereof there is no ground'.[122] He flatly denied that nonconformists were in any way 'schismatics, seditious persons, enemies to

[119] Johnson, *Christian plea*, 323.

[120] Henry Jacob, *Reasons taken out of Gods Word* (Middelburg, 1604), 57.

[121] e.g. Champlin Burrage, 'Lost Prison Papers of Henry Jacob', *Review and Expositor*, 5 (1908), 493, 512–13; Henry Jacob, *A Christian and modest offer of a most indifferent conference* (Middelburg, 1606), 35; *The Divine beginning and institution of Christs true or visible Ministeriall church* (Leiden, 1610), Sig. A3; *An attestation of many learned, godly and famous divines* (Middelburg, 1613), 115.

[122] Jacob, *Modest offer*, 3, 35.

the king's supremacy, nor any way undutiful to king or state'.[123] On the contrary, Jacob claimed in a preface addressed to James I that 'we come nothing short' of the prelates 'touching any duty to Your Highness' Crown and dignity'.[124] In fact, the primary line of defence that Jacob erected throughout his publications was to say, as William Bradshaw had said before him, that the reformist version of magistracy actually enhanced royal supremacy far more than did episcopacy. The thirteenth proposition of Jacob's *A Christian and modest offer*, published a year after Bradshaw's *Protestation of the king's supremacy*, echoed the latter's views in every respect when Jacob claimed: 'The church government desired is more agreeable to the state of monarchy and to the king's supremacy in all causes ecclesiastical and more easy and safe both for church and commonwealth than is the present government by prelates.' Later in the same work, he averred that royal sovereignty was not only dangerously impeded by episcopacy, but that in time the bishops would prove to be the ones 'who (we doubt not) will appear to be enemies (though in a mystery) to God, to the king and to his people'.[125]

It was not until 1609, in his *Humble supplication* for toleration addressed to James I, that Jacob outlined in considerable detail eight reasons in support of this claim. Most of them were largely made up of the subtle and sometimes superficial charges and countercharges of puritan propaganda rather than assertions of high principle. He argued, for example, that while the civil government in England was politically independent of all foreign powers, 'the prelates . . . hold their office and ministry to be essentially derived and conferred upon them not by any authority domestic and proper to the state but by virtue of such ordination as was conveyed to their predecessors from the church of Rome'. In this way, Jacob believed the bishops 'disclaim the sovereign absoluteness and independence of the state wherein they live and make both your majesty and themselves tied, in regard of their said ministry so received, to acknowledge some obligation and

[123] Ibid.

[124] Jacob, 'To the high and mightie Prince Iames', in *Reasons*, Sig. A3.

[125] Jacob, *Modest offer*, 3, 37. For Bradshaw, see above, n. 59.

homage to the see of Rome'. The reformists, on the other hand, advanced the nationalistic interests of the English political system by deriving their 'whole spiritual office and power of administration' not from foreign sources, but from among themselves.[126]

But among the eight reasons, the sixth was very likely the one he hoped would be the most persuasive to the Scottish monarch. There Jacob presented the very same policy that had been expressed in Bradshaw's *Protestation* some four years earlier. Jacob thus argued that the king's prerogatives would be greatly strengthened by the reformist platform because of the wide-ranging powers it granted the magistrate in ecclesiastical affairs: 'We hold that all officers and ministers of the Gospel ought to be subject to your Highness and to all and every your subordinate civil magistrates. And that the civil magistrates only ought to be the overseers of provinces and dioceses, and of the several churches therein.'[127] Just as Bradshaw had defined the role of the civil authorities, Jacob explained that the magistrate would assume the functions formerly exercised by the episcopate. While always careful to distinguish the magistrates' power in religious affairs as something civil rather than spiritual, the power granted to the civil arm in the ecclesial arena would be, Jacob believed, quite generous. In *A Modest offer*, the proposed reforms included making civil magistrates 'overseers' of diocesan structures and of each particular congregation[128] for the purpose of maintaining order when the rule of the eldership was either ineffective or misguided.

If anywhere it should fall out that this people thus guided and being so few, will yet presume to be . . . unruly and violent, then the prince's next dwelling officers of justice may and ought to make them keep peace and quietness . . . all which verily being well considered . . . it is childish and without all wit to cry out against us (as our adversaries do) *popularity, anarchy, and enmity to princes*.[129]

The same consequence, Jacob later added, awaited all 'misgoverning or ill teaching of any . . . church officer'.[130]

[126] Henry Jacob, *A humble supplication for toleration, and libertie* (Middelburg, 1609), 9–10.

[127] Ibid. 12.

[128] Jacob, *Modest offer*, 2.

[129] Jacob, *Reasons*, 28.

[130] Jacob, *Modest offer*, 2–3.

Throughout his writings Jacob often sought from James I legal tolerance for the policies of the reformists that would have enabled them to practice without molestation—at least in private—the form of church government they desired;[131] but like other radicals, Jacob did not by so requesting intend a blanket toleration for all religious dissent. Furthermore, *A Christian and modest offer* made it abundantly clear that Jacob believed militant puritans, once in power, would be sure the tables were turned on the nefarious prelates: the king would be expected to coerce the bishops into conformity with the new reformed order 'under such penalties as the ministers are [now] urged to subscribe unto the articles devised by the prelates'.[132] While such belligerent treatment of former ecclesiastical dignitaries would seem to contradict a standard puritan conviction that individuals should not be compelled—as Jacob put it—'against their will',[133] Jacob evidently believed that it did not. In part this was because what might be called Jacob's 'anti-compulsion' clause applied only to the elders, not magistrates who, by their civil office, possessed constraining powers inappropriate to spiritual guides.

> Though nothing may be imposed on the Christian people of a congregation against their wills by any spiritual authority (for so we intend) yet we affirm withal that the civil magistrate may impose on them spiritual matters by civil power (yes, whether they like or dislike) if he sees it good. This we all gladly acknowledge.[134]

If necessary, the royal prerogative could also entail the use of government-sanctioned violence against schismatics, heretics, and idolators. For this reason, Jacob felt perfectly justified in saying that the church polity he and other precisionists advocated 'neither is, nor ever has been, nor can be in the least sort dangerous to any civil state whatsoever, but may easily, yes, with violence be resisted and punished by any the meanest next dwelling officer of justice' if it could be proved incompatible with the Word of God.[135]

In this way, Jacob's political views consistently reflected the ideological tactics marshalled by radical puritans after the

131 Ibid. 61 (*sic* 16).
132 Ibid. 16.
133 Jacob, *Attestation*, 24.
134 Ibid. 115–16.
135 Jacob, *Divine beginning*, Sig. A3.

Hampton Court conference in their campaign to win the approval of James I, and to indict Bancroft's episcopal regime as offering the real threat to royal supremacy. So Jacob reminded the king that, as matters stood, the tyrannical arm of the usurping bishops reached like tentacles 'from Dover in Kent to the Mount in Cornwall, and . . . they proceed to the extremest censures'. They 'imprison, they deprive, they degrade, they excommunicate, they anathematize'.[136] But as for the reformist party, Jacob assured the disbelieving king that 'we acknowledge . . . no other power and authority for the overseeing, ruling and censure of particular churches . . . in the case of their misgovernment, than that which is originally invested in your royal person'.[137]

As it turned out, the king was patently unimpressed by Jacob's assessment of the current religio-political situation. Jacob's *An humble supplication* was one of the few puritan petitions ever to receive the direct attention of an English monarch. From the king's own heavily annotated copy of the petition, preserved in the Lambeth Palace Library, it is evident how ridiculous Jacob's whole scheme appeared from the royal chambers. At times contemptuous, but mostly amused, James cast off as 'a notorious and shameless lie' Jacob's assertion that because English episcopacy had historic links with Rome, the English Crown was, *ipso facto*, subservient to a foreign power.[138] As to Jacob's claim that puritans like himself acknowledged no other 'overseers' of particular churches 'than that which is originally invested in your royal person', James queried with what must have been genuine exasperation: 'Why then do you not obey the king's laws that are already made, by whom you grant to be your supreme magistrate?'[139]

The answer was, of course, to be found in the reformed proviso that obedience to civil authorities in divine things was lawful only so long as the magistrate ruled according to the Word. While the thrust of Jacob's theory of magistracy was, as we have noted, directed almost entirely to a vain attempt at persuading James of the reformist's fidelity to royal prerogatives, Jacob never relinquished his fundamental commitment

[136] Jacob, *Humble supplication*, 15.
[137] Ibid. 13.
[138] Ibid., Lambeth Palace copy, 9.
[139] Ibid. 12.

to the potentially subversive puritan principle of the Word's priority. From 1604 on, this commitment was always assumed, though rarely explicitly stated until his very last publication. It was even present, though obliquely, at the heart of his assertion of royal supremacy in *An humble supplication*. There he said that the more forward puritans would willingly submit to the king's jurisdiction 'in the case of their [the puritan's] misgovernment',[140] the implication being that they would submit to James' supremacy in ecclesial concerns only if it could be proved that the puritan cause violated the plain meaning of scripture. The answer, then, to the question that the annoyed king scribbled in the margins of Jacob's *Supplication* was that Jacob believed the ecclesiastical laws already endorsed by royal mandate could not be obeyed because they were unbiblical. In this typically puritan fashion, Jacob limited royal supremacy by the supremacy of Christ. 'The king is *custos* and *vindex*, the keeper and maintainer (by compulsive power) of the whole state of religion,' Jacob explained in 1604. 'But', he hastened to add, 'he is not *author* or *minister* of any ecclesiastical thing or constitution whatsoever';[141] that right and title belonged to and was derived from 'Christ only'.[142]

Although Jacob's very genuine affirmations of royal supremacy very likely proved to be a source of personal conflict for him when they collided with his loyalty to Christ, as a puritan propagandist he was, theoretically, never confronted with the dilemma of whom to obey first. If the ecclesiastical laws endorsed by the English king clashed with laws of the heavenly king, the choice between the two was clear; one must obey God before human authorities.

While this formed the foundation for understanding magisterial functions in ecclesiastical matters, it did not become a prominent theme in Jacob's writings until his last publication. In *Sundry matters*, ten reasons were offered why it was necessary visibly to obey God before the magistrate in matters of church government. The first was for soteriological assurance: 'the only sure way for the comfort of our souls is the practice of God's ordinances for his visible church under the gospel.

140 Ibid. 13.

141 Jacob, *Reasons*, 58.

142 Jacob, *Attestation*, 314.

Therefore we are bound to practice the said ordinances, notwithstanding the magistrate do forbid the said practice.'[143] Neither was it acceptable to show outward obedience to civil laws while reserving inward obedience for the laws of God. Thus, as Jacob put it, 'the magistrate forbidding the practice of this [the reformist's] way is not *actually* to be obeyed'.[144]

Finally, a radical political stand was considered unavoidable on the basis of Jacob's perception of Christ as the Mosaic lawgiver for the church under the gospel, a motif which, as we observed above in Chapter 4, weighed heavily in Jacob's ecclesiology. He explained in the tenth and final reason that Christ required the same absolute obedience from Christians to the ecclesiastical laws of the New Testament as he had from the Jews under the law: 'Christ is our prophet, king and priest', he concluded, 'whence also it necessarily follows (and it is to be concluded) that our obedience and practice in these points must now, as well as under the law, agree to Christ and his Word, and depend on it and not on the magistrate if he differ from it.'[145]

John Robinson

If Robinson's synodical theory proved ineffective in practice as a means of maintaining uniformity between the squabbling exiled separatist congregations in Holland,[146] his conviction about the role of the magistrate as civil governor of the church would have provided the restraining instrument, at least in theory, for securing visible religious conformity in society. He concurred with the principle embraced by other separatists and puritan radicals that 'religious actions [may] be punished civilly by the magistrate which is the preserver of both the tables and so to punish all breaches of both'.

Formally, Robinson's Christian magistrate would have lived a double life. As an active member of a congregation he would have been considered no higher than any other member and, like everyone, would have been subject to the spiritual

[143] Henry Jacob, *A collection of sundry matters* (Middelburg, 1616), Sig. B4.
[144] Ibid., Sig. B5 (my italics).
[145] Ibid., Sig. B8.
[146] See above, ch. 6.

censures of the church; but as a civil officer, his duties would have entailed the solemn responsibility of imposing a biblical polity on all the churches of his realm. In the rare event that a magistrate should be excommunicated from the fellowship of the church for some gross and unrepented sin on his part, Robinson accepted the Calvinist verdict that, while thus stripped of his spiritual credentials, the magistrate would yet possess a legitimate civil authority to 'censure and punish civilly the whole church and every member of it if there be cause, whether in matters of church or commonwealth'.[147]

Like Calvin, Robinson saw the magistrate primarily as an impersonal functionary whose own personage, private creed, and moral character was irrelevant to the execution of his civil duties.[148] Thus, he warned that it would be a grave transgression of a divine institution for the saints to differentiate between the obedience due to a godly prince and to a pagan tyrant; that would leave society vulnerable to anarchic forces, justifying 'seditious subjects under the pretext (specially catholic) [of] religion, to raise tumults in kingdom'.[149]

This concern of Robinson's to honour the authority of magistracy regardless of the magistrate's personal estate surfaced as a prominent feature in his advice to the departing *Mayflower* Pilgrims at Delftshaven in 1620. Robinson counselled them to take care to elect civil governors who would love them and promote the common good. He then admonished them to prove their own 'godliness' by 'yielding unto' the newly elected magistrates 'all due honour and obedience in their lawful administrating, not beholding in them the ordinariness of their persons'.[150] In the young and isolated Pilgrim settlement, where the social structure would be relatively unstratified and homogeneous, magistrates would have to depend more than ever upon the Calvinist principle of the objective and impartial authority of magisterial office, rather

[147] John Robinson, *A justification of separation from the Church of England* (Amsterdam, 1610), 265, 184, 224–5; *A just and necessarie apologie* (Amsterdam, 1625), 57.

[148] On Calvin, see Walzer, *Revolution of the Saints*, 45.

[149] Robinson, *Apologie*, 57–8.

[150] 'Certaine useful advertisements', xlvi. Note J. T. McNeill's observation about the striking similarities between Robinson's advice and Calvin's pre-election sermons in *History and Character of Calvinism* (Oxford, 1954), 335–6.

than religious, economic, or social rank.[151] For this same reason, Robinson's view of magistracy, as he explained in 1625, followed the *Belgic Confession* in allowing the authority of the civil arm to extend 'indefinitely, and absolutely to the magistrate whether Christian or heathen'.[152]

Thus, Robinson identified substantially with the judgement of Calvinist radical churchmen on both sides of the puritan–separatist divide. This was, for the most part, also true of his verdict concerning the extent to which the civil sword could be lawfully wielded in ecclesiastical matters. While Barrow and Cartwright, as we have seen, agreed that it was lawful for the magistrate to compel subjects to listen to godly sermons, neither would have allowed the state compulsory power at the centre of the church's life, be that the church covenant or the Lord's Supper. Robinson also disapproved the use of coercive force for church membership, since he believed that membership in Christ's church was a matter of 'faith and devotion in the heart of the doers'.[153]

For this reason, Robinson (like other separatists) has often been hailed by historians for what his most recent biographer has called his 'well-known advocacy of religious toleration'.[154] But this is surely an anachronistic rendering of his concept of magisterial function, and seriously fails to reflect other more traditional values that are to be found within the wider scope of his views on the subject. When, for example, John Smyth parted company with the separatists over believer's baptism, Robinson not only condemned Smyth's novel ecclesiology, he also renounced his remodelled 'anabaptist' views of magistracy. It was Smyth who first unambiguously refused the state any coercive nursing role in ecclesial affairs. On the contrary, Robinson said the magistrate could lawfully 'further' Christ's kingdom and repress the malevolent forces of Antichrist not

[151] T. H. Breen, *The Character of the Good Ruler* (New York, 1974), 65–6.

[152] Robinson, *Apologie*, 56.

[153] John Robinson, *Observations divine and morall* (Amsterdam, 1625), 51.

[154] Timothy George, 'Predestination in a Separatist Context: The Case of John Robinson', *Sixteenth Century Journal*, 15 (1884), 73–85. See also Jordan, *Development of Religious Toleration*, ii, 242–7; and George, *John Robinson*, 131, n. 158, where he briefly discusses Robinson's understanding of the coercive powers of the magistrate in religious affairs but fails to integrate this with his portrait of Robinson as advocate of religious toleration

simply with 'spiritual weapons', as Smyth now argued, but also by their 'civil power'.[155] Robinson was confident that the magistrate could, by his coercive civil powers, repress idolatry and require the Word to be preached in rightly ordered churches, adding that it would also be lawful for civil authorities to force their citizens to hear the Word and penalize those who, after sufficient teaching, failed to respond:

> That godly magistrates are by compulsion to repress public, notable idolatry as also to provide that the truth of God in his ordinance be taught and published in their dominions, I make no doubt; but it may be also, it is not unlawful for them by some penalty or other, to provoke their subjects universally unto hearing for their instruction, and conversion, yes, to grant they may inflict the same upon them if after due teaching they offer not themselves unto the church.[156]

Just how Robinson reconciled punishing those who failed to join the church with his commendation of a voluntary profession of faith and covenant as the basis for church membership is an issue he never directly addressed, but from the above statement it is clear that his own position concurred in essentials with views expressed much earlier by Cartwright and, of course, other separatists. While rejecting the use of 'any compulsion or violence over any', Cartwright had nevertheless affirmed that every citizen should be compelled to hear the Word preached, adding, 'if they profit not, nor with sufficient teaching correct not themselves, that then they should be punished'.[157]

For radical puritans and separatists like Cartwright and Robinson, embracing both voluntarism and magisterial coercion in religious causes did not, as we have discussed above, constitute a contradiction of terms: rather, these two seemingly incongruous modes of operation were understood to work in a harmonious sequence, the one preparing the indisposed outer man for the inner work of the Spirit. For this reason, Robinson acknowledged that although the civil sword should not (nor could) compel a human conscience in religious matters, it

[155] John Robinson, *Of religious communion private and publique* (Amsterdam, 1614), 128.

[156] Robinson, *Justification*, 298; see also *Observations*, 51.

[157] As quoted in Pearson, *Church and State*, 106.

could (and *should*!) root out idolatry and compel individuals to that place where their consciences could be freely persuaded by the sword of Christ's Spirit to *choose* the way of faith.

While Robinson in this way shared the fundamental tenets of left-wing puritan and separatist political ideology, his views on the severity of magisterial repressive powers represent a notable departure from both traditions. On the basis that the Mosaic judicial laws were still binding under the new covenent, Cartwright had defended the use of the death penalty for religious idolatry. In the separatist party, Browne and Harrison also appear to have favoured capital punishment of idolaters by drawing an analogy between the powers exercised among the kings of Old Testament Judah and those of the English monarchy in their own time. Barrow openly lamented the fact that 'so many capital mischiefs as God punished by death', such as 'blaspheming the name of God' and 'open idolatry', were 'not by law punished at all' in England.[158]

While Robinson justified the use of 'bodily vengeance' by the magistracy,[159] he accepted capital punishment only for serious moral transgressions such as murder, adultery, and sedition, but not religious offences of idolatry or heresy. He discarded, at this point, the analogy between the English monarchy and the kings of Judah, arguing that no 'king now upon earth is by the Word of God to . . . inflict death upon all that refuse [to join the church] or remain wicked and unrepentant, as the kings of Judah were to do'.[160] Religious transgressions, he believed, would not have as damaging an impact on civil harmony as social offences. So he cautioned:

> That as the greater sins of other kinds do not violate and dissolve the marriage-bond, as adultery does by reason of its direct opposition there against; so neither do idolatry or heresy (how great sins soever in themselves) so outlaw a subject civilly as do seditions, murders, adulteries, and the like directly violating and disturbing civil societies.[161]

158 For Browne and Harrison, see above nn. 85–100. For Barrow, note the discussion by P. D. L. Avis, 'Moses and the Magistrate: A Study in the Rise of Protestant Legalism', *Journal of Ecclesiastical History*, 26 (1975), 167–70.

159 Robinson, *Justification*, 136; *Of Religious communion*, 83.

160 Robinson, *Justification*, 298.

161 Robinson, *Observations*, 52.

Considering Robinson's emphasis on visible churchmanship,[162] it is interesting to note further that he rejected the penalty of banishment for idolatry on the basis of inward, not visible, faith.[163] He offered no indication that his views on magisterial authority were in this way a departure from the puritan, as well as separatist norm, much less why he chose to adopt a more moderate position, except in so far as such conclusions 'derived directly from his doctrine of election'.[164] Whatever the reasons, it is evident that in Robinson's writings, separatist political ideology appears, at least in this respect, to be somewhat less menacing than Professor Woodhouse has suggested about the tradition as a whole.[165]

Otherwise, Robinson remained generally faithful to the prevailing view of magistracy promulgated by English radical puritan and separatist dissenters. While advocating filial loyalty to the Crown, he resolutely affirmed that the authority of the prince in ecclesiastical affairs was always subordinate to scriptural precedents. With reference to the biblical texts of Daniel 3: 18 and Acts 5: 29, he explained why separatists like himself had been persuaded to follow Christ without the approval of the king: 'knowing that as his approbation in such points of God's worship, as [God's] Word warrants not, cannot make them lawful; so neither can his disallowance make unlawful such duties of religion as the Word of God approves, nor can he give dispensation to any person to forbear the same'. Succinctly put, in words that sum up the one truly radical feature of godly religion in puritan and separatist England, Robinson said he acted and lived by the simple claim: 'There is no king of the church but Christ.'[166]

[162] See above, ch. 3.

[163] Robinson, *Observations*, 52. Because 'there is hardly any sect so antichristian or evil otherwise in church profession, in which there are not divers truly, though weakly led with the Spirit of Christ in their persons and so true members of his mystical body'. This, of course, put him at odds with the practice of Geneva, though he was unwilling to admit it. While he did not specifically support the Genevan practice of banishing the irreligious, he certainly did not criticize it either: John Robinson, *The manvmission to a manvdvction* (Amsterdam, 1615), 21.

[164] George, 'Predestination in a Separatist Context', 85.

[165] A. S. P. Woodhouse, *Puritanism and Liberty* (London, 1966), 44.

[166] Robinson, *Justification*, 14.

CONCLUSION

'ONE quality that tends to be shared by historians of pre-revolutionary Puritanism', Michael G. Finlayson has observed, 'is the dependence of their analysis upon a logical model that may be described as essentially dualistic.'[1] This has certainly been true of the assessment made by historians of the ecclesiological proclivities of separatists and left-wing puritans. The two parties have often been sharply differentiated by historians as representatives of distinct and, in several respects, clearly opposed ecclesiological currents within the broad stream of protestant dissent. It has been the concern of this study, however, to underscore the continuity of ideas between advanced puritan and separatist perceptions about the nature and structure of the church. Instead of revealing a distinct ideological demarcation between the two, the theoretical literature of puritan radicals and separatists during the Elizabethan and Jacobean eras exhibits an often fluid, but none the less shared, doctrinal vision of a truly reformed church of Christ. Throughout the period it is apparent that, while often locked in bitter controversy over their respective views of the established church, left-wing puritans and separatists were essentially of one mind about what they believed constituted a biblical polity for the church.

Separatists and radicals, for example, each approached their ecclesiology from within a 'mutualist,' reciprocal view of the covenant, which in turn tended to cast their discussion about church polity into the sometimes legalistic, combative forms generated by the need to fulfill the exacting conditions of the convenant relationship. True churchmanship, they believed, was determined by observing the letter of the scriptures with respect to Christ's ecclesiastical ordinances;

[1] Michael G. Finlayson, 'Puritanism and Puritans: Labels or Libels?', *Canadian Journal of History*, 8 (1973), 201.

and according to their understanding of saving faith, the practice of biblical churchmanship formed an important basis upon which troubled souls could obtain assurance of their election. When confronted by those who stood ecclesiologically to the left of themselves, both separatists and advanced puritans tended to draw back from their usual insistence that a biblical polity was vital to salvation. Nevertheless, the puritan commonplace that a scriptural polity was 'necessary . . . to our salvation' provided the theological rationale for the militant posture of each party whenever they opposed those less radical than themselves.

A similar ideological congruity has been observed in the eschatological temperament of separatists and radicals. While we have noted some evidence of a millenarian inclination in the non-separatist, Robert Parker, and possibly in a few Jacobean separatists, the two parties generally appear to have shared very similar views about history and the future. Some variations in detail are, of course, apparent and to be expected, but on the whole the radicals and separatists seem, however subtly, to have been moving by the turn of the century toward the modified Augustinian eschatology espoused by Thomas Brightman. At least, there was a tendency to depart from Foxe's glorified view of the Constantinian era, and there are occasional suggestions, tantalizing in their obscurity, of the expectation of a coming, imminent 'latter day glory', a motif so fundamental to seventeenth-century millenarianism.

Although there is no evidence that any of the Elizabethan and Jacobean radicals or separatists would have required the saints to provide a personal relation of experiential faith, they all agreed that the membership of gathered churches should be confined to the visibly elect and faithful. The two criteria required for membership—sound doctrine and good conduct—were, in the context of puritan soteriology, considered the 'infallible marks' of election.[2] For separatists and radical puritans alike, entrance into church fellowship through a profession of faith, therefore, offered a public affirmation that would have been reinforced in the continuing, weekly life of

[2] William Perkins, *The works of that famous and worthie minister of Christ . . . M. W. Perkins* (London, 1605), 374.

the congregation by the tightly disciplined Christian communities that were the ideal of left-wing puritan and separatist congregational polity.

Among the two groups, the issue of ministerial authority for the government of the gathered church also received parallel treatments: while wanting to grant genuine power to the people, by which they intended only adult male members of the congregation, they nevertheless fully intended to preserve the special status and authority of the reformed ministry. The result was a complex, sometimes equivocal paradigm of the power structure for individual churches that left the issue of authority in the gathered congregation poised between the two organizational models of aristocracy and democracy. In this regard, it appears that separatists were hardly more democratically inclined than their left-wing puritan counterparts. This is also true of their respective synodical theories; among the Elizabethan and Jacobean advanced puritans there seems to have often been little interest in giving much more to church synods than the power of advice and counsel allowed by the separatists.

Finally, radical puritans and separatists shared considerable common ground regarding views about the relationship between the magistrate and the church. While they both affirmed royal supremacy and granted considerable coercive power to the civil arm by encouraging magistrates to compel their citizens to hear the Word preached, both radical puritans as well as separatists were equally concerned to protect the voluntary nature of true church membership. While in this way they paid tribute to the sovereignty of the State in church affairs, radical puritans and separatists both accepted the priority of the reformed proviso that obedience was due only so far as the Word of God allowed. Thus, while separatists openly advocated a reformation 'without tarrying' for the magistrate outside the institutional church, radical puritans commenced their own reformation 'without tarrying' from within the parish structures, claiming that they felt compelled to 'use' as well as 'speak for' the polity prescribed by Christ.[3] In light of the evidence of *de facto* separatism in

[3] W. H. Frere and C. E. Douglas (eds.), *Puritan Manifestoes* (reprint. edn., London, 1954), 130.

many puritan parishes, the practical difference between separatists who would not 'tarry', and radical puritans who would 'use' Christ's ordinances, although ideologically significant enough to distinguish the two at this one crucial point, was, nevertheless, not a very great one.

In short, the ecclesiological ideals of left-wing puritans and separatists were very close indeed, a fact which many radical puritans were unwilling to admit but most separatists and conformists readily recognized. As Richard Bancroft observed in the late 1580s, while Cartwright and Browne were clearly at odds over the issue of separation, 'the same order and government for a perfect reformation is of both parts equally urged'.[4] One should not, of course, be naïvely deceived by Bancroft's assertion into believing that the congregational polity of separatism was the only direction that the puritanism of the Elizabethan disciplinarians could go. There was, within its many-sided organizational formulas, the potential for the later development of English Presbyterianism as well.

While this study has examined almost exclusively radical puritan and separatist printed literature, it also points up an important facet of godly life in England that local studies of grass-roots puritanism have uncovered: if the manuscript evidence reveals something of the broad diversity of puritan practice on the local level,[5] a close reading of the formal treatises written by puritan and separatist divines reveals that their programmes for reform were not always so fully developed as to provide easy classification. Indeed, they were subtly textured enough to suggest several organizational possibilities. Even among the more purposeful and militant members of the Elizabethan puritan movement there was, thus, a nagging 'unsettledness', as Richard Rogers of Wethersfield complained in his diary, concerning the 'variety of opinions' that puritans shared regarding questions of church government.[6] It was an opinion also shared by Francis Johnson in 1617, when he remarked about the fluidity of the

[4] Quoted in Stuart Barton Babbage, *Puritanism and Richard Bancroft* (London, 1962), 22.

[5] W. J. Sheils, *The Puritans in the Diocese of Petterborough, 1558–1610* (Northampton, 1979), 1–2.

[6] M. M. Knappen (ed.), *Two Elizabethan Diaries*, (Chicago, 1933), 98–9.

ecclesial ideals that he observed among radical puritans: 'some say one thing, some another; some speaking of one church, some of another; some to one purpose, some to another; sometimes more plainly and directly, sometimes with shifts and pretences, more deceiving the simple and betraying their own iniquity'.[7]

Thus, the outlines of radical protestant ecclesiology were not always clearly fixed nor fully developed. At the same time, they were subject to the often manipulative conventions of contentious debate. In the welter of charges and counter-charges, affirmations and qualifications of which so much of their theoretical writings consisted, any attempt by historians to posit distinct ecclesiological divisions between puritan presbyterians and congregational separatists will also be fraught with the pitfalls of scholastic subtleties that so encumbered the views of Elizabethan and Jacobean radical protestants.

While radical puritans and separatists saw themselves on opposing sides of the thin line that formally ran between those who did or did not acknowledge the English church as true, they nevertheless shared many of the same ecclesiological ideals about what constitutes the polity of a true church. Some puritans were, no doubt, inclined to favour policies of church organization that anticipated, in an inchoate way, mid-seventeenth-century Presbyterianism. Others, however, were feeling their way through the paradoxical features of a reformed ecclesiology towards a congregational structure which was clear enough for the Congregational Independents of the Interregnum to claim kinship with them,[8] and which, in their own time, formed the basis of an often unrecognized ideological consensus between radical puritans and separatists in Elizabethan and early Stuart England.

[7] Francis Johnson, *A Christian plea conteyning three treatises* (Leiden, 1617), 30.

[8] Philip J. Anderson, 'Presbyterianism and the Gathered Churches in Old and New England 1640–1662: the Struggle for Church Government in Theory and Practice' (Oxford University D. Phil. thesis, 1979), 7, 117, 127.

REFERENCES

PRIMARY SOURCES

Manuscripts

Angus Library, Regent's Park College, Oxford, Stinton MSS.
Bodleian Library, Oxford, MS Eng. Misc., th. e. 158 (cited as Parker MS).
Corpus Christi College Library, Oxford, CCC Admissions Register.

Printed Works

AINSWORTH, HENRY, *The communion of saincts* (Amsterdam, 1607).
—— *Counterpoyson* (Amsterdam, 1608).
—— *A defence of the holy scriptures and ministery* (Amsterdam, 1609).
—— *An animadversion to Mr. Richard Clyftons advertisement* (Amsterdam, 1613).
—— *A reply to a pretended christian plea* (Amsterdam, 1620).
—— *An arrow against idolatry* (n.p., 1640).
—— and JOHNSON, FRANCIS, *An apologie or defence of svch trve Christians as are commonly (but vniustly) called Brownists* (Amsterdam, 1604).
AMES, WILLIAM, 'Preface' to William Bradshaw, *English puritanisme, containing the main opinions of the rigidest sort of those that are called puritans* (n.p., 1640).
—— *A maniduction to Mr. Robinson* (Dort, 1614).
—— *A second manvdvction* (n.p., 1615).
—— *A reply to Dr. Mortons generall defence of three nocent ceremonies* (n.p., 1622).
—— *Reply to Dr. Mortons particular defence* (n.p., 1623).
—— *A fresh suit against human ceremonies* (Rotterdam, 1633).
—— *The workes of the reverend and faithfull minister of Christ William Ames* (London, 1643).
—— *The svbstance of Christian religion* (London, 1659).
BAILLIE, ROBERT, *A dissuasive from the errours of the time* (London, 1645).
BANCROFT, RICHARD, *A survay of the pretended holy discipline* (London, 1593).
BARROW, HENRY, *The Writings of Henry Barrow, 1587–1590*, ed. Leland H. Carlson (London, 1962).

BARROW, HENRY, *The Writings of Henry Barrow, 1590–1591*, ed. Leland H. Carlson (London, 1966).

BARTON, T. F. (ed.), *The Registrum Vagum of Anthony Harrison*, vol. i (Norfolk Record Society, 1963).

BASTWICK, JOHN, *The utter routing of the whole army of all the independents and sectaries* (London, 1646).

BAYNES, PAUL, *Brief directions vnto a godly life* (London, 1618).

—— *The helpe to trve happiness* (London, 1618).

—— *A commentarie upon the first chapter of the epistle of Saint Paul, written to the Ephesians* (London, 1618).

—— *The diocesans tryall* (London, 1621).

BERNARD, RICHARD, *Christian advertisements and counsels of peace* (London, 1608).

BEZA, THEODORE, *The judgement of a most reverend and learned man from beyond the seas, concerning the threefold order of bishops* (London, 1580).

—— *A discourse, of the true and visible markes of the catholique churche* (London, 1593).

BRADFORD, WILLIAM, 'Governor Bradford's First Dialogue' (1648), *Old South Leaflet*, (Boston, n.d.).

—— *History of Plymouth Plantation, 1606–1646 (2 vols.; Boston, 1912).*

BRADSHAW, WILLIAM, *English puritanisme, containing the main opinions of the rigidest sort of those that are called puritans* (n.p., 1604).

—— *A treatise of justification* (London, 1615).

—— *Several treatises of worship and ceremonies by the reverend Mr. William Bradshaw* (London, 1660).

BROWNE, ROBERT, *The Writings of Robert Harrison and Robert Browne*, ed. Albert Peel and Leland H. Carlson (London, 1953).

CALVIN, JOHN, *Institutes of the Christian Religion*, ed. J. T. McNeill, trans. F. L. Battles (London, 1960).

CANNE, JOHN, *The necessitie of separation* (Amsterdam, 1630).

—— *A Stay against straying* (Amsterdam, 1639).

CARTWRIGHT, THOMAS, *A reply to an answere made of M. Doctor Whitgifte* (n.p., 1574).

—— *The second replie of Thomas Cartwright* (n.p., 1575).

—— *The rest of a second replie* (n.p., 1577).

—— *A directory of church government* (London, 1644), reprinted in C. A. Briggs, *American Presbyterianism* (New York, 1885) app. 1–17.

—— *Cartwrightiana*, ed. Albert Peel and Leland H. Carlson (London, 1951).

CHADERTON, LAURENCE, *A fruitfull sermon, vpon the 3. 4. 5. 6. 7. & 8. verses of the 12 chapters of . . . Romans* (London, 1584).

CLAPHAM, HENOCH, *Error on the left hand* (London, 1608).

CLARKE, SAMUEL, *Lives of two and twenty* (London, 1660).

COTTON, JOHN, *The way of the congregational churches clear'd* (London, 1648).

EURING, WILLIAM, *Ten covnter demands* (London, 1617).

FENNER, DUDLEY, *A counter-poyson, modestly written for the time* (London, 1584).

—— *A defence of the reasons of the counter-poyson* (n.p., 1586).

—— *A briefe treatise upon the first table of the lawe* (Middelburg 1587).

FIELD, JOHN, *The judgement of a most reverend and learned man from beyond the seas, concerning a threefold order of bishops* (London, 1580).

FRERE, W. H. and DOUGLAS, C. E. (eds.), *Puritan Manifestoes*, (reprint edn., London, 1954).

FULKE, WILLIAM, *A sermon preached at Hampton Court on Sunday being the 12. day of November, in the year of our Lord. 1570* (London, 1570).

Genevan Bible (Frankfurt, 1599).

HALL, JOSEPH, *A common apologie of the church of England* (London, 1610).

Harmony of confessions (London, 1634).

HELWYS, THOMAS, *A short declaration of the mystery of iniquity* (London, 1612).

JACOB, HENRY, *A treatise of the suffering and victory of Christ* (Middelburg, 1598).

—— *A defence of the chvrches and ministery of Englande* (Middelburg, 1599).

—— *Reasons taken out of Gods Word* (Middelburg, 1604).

—— *A Christian and modest offer of a most indifferent conference* (Middelburg, 1606).

—— *A humble supplication for toleration, and libertie* (Middelburg, 1609).

—— *The divine beginning and institution of Christs true or visible ministeriall church* (Leiden, 1610).

—— *A plaine and cleere exposition of the 2d. commandement* (Leiden, 1610).

—— *A declaration & plainer opening of certaine points in the divine beginning* (Middelburg, 1611).

—— *An attestation of many learned, godly and famous divines* (Middelburg, 1613).

—— *A collection of sundry matters* (Middelburg, 1616).

—— *A confession and protestation of the faith of certaine Christians in England* (Amsterdam, 1616).

JESSOP, EDMOND, *A discovery of the errors of the English anabaptists* (London, 1623).

JOHNSON, FRANCIS, *A treatise of the ministery of the Church of England* (Amsterdam, 1595).

Johnson, Francis, *A trve confession of the faith* (Amsterdam, 1596).
—— *An inquirie and answer of T. White* (n.p., 1606).
—— *Certayne reasons and arguments proving that it is not lawfull to heare the present ministerie of the Church of England* (Amsterdam, 1608).
—— *A brief treatise . . . against two errours of the Anabaptists* (Amsterdam, 1609).
—— *A short treatise concerning the words of Christ. tell the church* (Amsterdam, 1611).
—— *A Christian plea conteyning three treatises* (Leiden, 1617).
Lawne, Christopher, *The prophane schisme of the Brownists discovered* (London, 1612).
Murton, John, *A description of what God hath predestinated concerning man* (London, 1620).
—— *Objections answered by way of dialogue* (n.p., 1615).
Paget, John, *An arrow against the separation of Brownists* (Amsterdam, 1618).
Pagitt, Ephraim, *Heresiography: or a description of the hereticks and sectaries of these latter times* (London, 1645).
A parte of a register countayning sundrie memorable matters, for the reformation of our church (n.p., 1593).
Peel, Albert, (ed.), *The Second Parte of a Register* (2 vols.; Cambridge, 1915).
—— (ed.), *Tracts Ascribed to Richard Bandcroft* (Cambridge, 1953).
Perkins, William, *The works of that famous and worthie minister of Christ . . . M. W. Perkins* (London, 1605).
Robinson, John, *A justification of separation from the church of England* (Amsterdam, 1610).
—— 'An answer to a censouous epistle', printed in Joseph Hall, *A common apologie of the Church of England* (London, 1610).
—— *Of religious communion private and publique* (Amsterdam, 1614).
—— *The manvmission to a manvdvction* (Amsterdam, 1615).
—— *An appeale on truths behalf* (Leiden, 1624).
—— *A defence of the doctrine propounded by the synode at Dort* (Amsterdam, 1624).
—— *A just and necessarie apologie* (Amsterdam, 1625).
—— *Observations divine and morall* (Amsterdam, 1625).
—— *The lawfulnesse of the hearing of the ministers of the church of England* (Leiden, 1634).
—— *The peoples plea* (n.p., 1641).
—— 'An appendix to M. Perkins his six principles of Christian religion' in *A just and necessary apologie* (London, 1644).
—— 'Certain useful advertisements' in H. M. Dexter (ed.), *Mourts Relation* (Boston, 1865)

SMYTH, JOHN, *The Works of John Smyth*, ed. W. T. Whitley (2 vols; Cambridge, 1915).

STARESMORE, SABINE, *The unlawfulness of reading in prayer* (n.p., 1619).

—— *Certain notes of Henry Ainsworth His Last Sermon* (n.p., 1630).

STOUGHTON, WILLIAM, *An assertion for true and christian church-policie* (Middelburg, 1604).

TRAVERS, WALTER, *A full and plaine declaration of ecclesiastical discipline* (n.p., 1574).

—— *An harmony of confessions of the faith of the christian and reformed chvrches* (London, 1643).

UDALL, JOHN, *A demonstration of the trueth of that discipline which Christe hath prescribed in his worde for the gouernement of his Church* (n.p., 1588).

WILCOX, THOMAS, *A discourse, of the true and Visible Markes of the Catholique Church* (London, 1582).

WILKINSON, JOHN, *An exposition of the 13 chapter of the revelation of Iesus Christ* (Amsterdam, 1619).

WINSLOW, EDWARD, *Hypocrisie vnmasked* (London, 1646).

SECONDARY SOURCES

ALLEN, J. W., *A History of Political Thought in the Sixteenth Century* (London, 1928).

ANDERSON, PHILIP J., 'Presbyterianism and the Gathered Churches in Old and New England 1640–1662: the Struggle for Church Government in Theory and Practice' (Oxford University D.Phil. thesis, 1979).

ARBER, EDWARD, *The Story of the Pilgrim Fathers* (London, 1897).

ASHTON, ROBERT, *The Works of John Robinson* (3 vols.; London, 1851).

AVIS, P. D. L. 'Moses and the Magistrate: A Study in the Rise of Protestant Legalism', *Journal of Ecclesiastical History*, 26 (1975), 149–72.

—— '"The True Church" in Reformation Theology', *Scottish Journal of Theology*, 30 (1977), 319–45.

—— *The Church in the Theology of the Reformers* (London, 1981).

BABBAGE, STUART BARTON, *Puritanism and Richard Bancroft* (London, 1962).

BALL, BRYAN W., *A Great Expectation* (Leiden, 1975).

BALLARD, R. H., 'The Dynamic of Independency', *Baptist Quarterly*, 23 (1970), 241–50.

BALTZER, KLAUS, *The Covenant Formulary in Old Testament, Jewish, and Early Christian Writing* (Philadelphia, 1971).

BARTLETT, ROBERT, *The Pilgrim Way* (Philadelphia, 1971).
BAUCKHAM, RICHARD, 'Hooker, Travers and the Church of Rome in the 1580s', *Journal of Ecclesiastical History*, 29 (1978), 37–50.
—— *Tudor Apocalypse*, Courtenay Library of Reformation Classics, no. 8, ed. G. E. Duffield (Appleford, 1978).
BOLAM, C. GORDON, *et al.* (eds.), *The English Presbyterians* (Boston, Mass., 1968).
BRACHLOW, STEPHEN, 'Puritan Theology and Radical Churchman in Pre-Revolutionary England' (Oxford University D.Phil. thesis, 1979).
—— 'More Light on John Robinson and the Separatist Tradition', *Fides et Historia*, 2 (1980), 6–22.
—— 'John Robinson and the Lure of Separatism in Pre-Revolutionary England', *Church History*, 50 (1981), 288–301.
—— 'John Smyth and the Ghost of Anabaptism: A Rejoinder', *Baptist Quarterly*, 30 (1984), 296–300.
—— 'Puritan Theology and General Baptist Origins', *Baptist Quarterly*, 31 (1985), 179–94.
—— 'The Elizabethan Roots of Henry Jacob's Churchmanship: Refocusing the Historiographical Lens', *Journal of Ecclesiastical History*, 34 (1985), 228–54.
BREEN, T. H., *The Character of the Good Ruler*, Norton Library edn. (New York, 1974).
BRIDENBAUGH, CARL, *Vexed and Troubled Englishmen 1590–1642*, rev. edn. (Oxford, 1976).
BROOK, BENJAMIN, *The Lives of the Puritans*, 2 vols. (London, 1813).
BURGESS, WALTER H., *John Robinson, Pastor of the Pilgrim Fathers* (London, 1920).
BURRAGE, CHAMPLIN, *The Church Covenant Idea* (Philadelphia: 1904).
—— 'Lost Prison Papers of Henry Jacob', *Review and Expositor*, 5 (1908).
—— *New Facts Concerning John Robinson* (London, 1910).
—— *The Early English Dissenters*, 2 vols. (Cambridge, 1912).
—— (ed.), *An Answer to John Robinson of Leyden* (London, 1920).
CAPP, B. S., *The Fifth Monarchy Men* (London, 1972).
—— 'Godly Rule and English Millenarianism' in Charles Webster (ed.), *The Intellectual Revolution of the Seventeenth Century*, (London, 1974).
CARLSON, LELAND H., *Martin Maprelate, Gentleman: Master Job Throkmorton Laid Open in His Colors* (San Marino, Calif. 1981).
CARR, FRANK BENJAMIN, 'The Thought of Robert Parker (1564?–1614) and His Influence on Puritanism Before 1650' (London University Ph.D. thesis, 1964).

CARTER, ALICE CLARE, *The English Reformed Church in Amsterdam* (Amsterdam, 1964).
—— 'John Robinson and the Dutch Reformed Church', in G. J. Cuming (ed.), *Studies in Church History* (Leiden, 1966), 232–414.
CASWELL, R. N., 'Calvin's View of Ecclesiastical Discipline', in G. E. Duffield (ed.), *John Calvin* (Appleford, 1966), 212–221.
CHRISTIANSON, PAUL, *Reformers and Babylon: English apocalyptic visions from the reformation to the eve of the civil war* (Toronto, 1978).
—— 'Reformers and the Church of England under Elizabeth I and the early Stuarts', *Journal of Ecclesiastical History*, 31 (1980), 463–82.
CLANCY, THOMAS H., 'Papist–Protestant–Puritan: English Religious Taxonomy 1565–1665', *Recusant History*, 13 (1976), 227–53.
CLARK, ANDREW, (ed.), *Register of the University of Oxford* (London, 1887).
—— *Register of the University of Oxford* (London, 1888).
CLOUSE, ROBERT, 'The Apocalyptic Interpretation of Thomas Brightman and Joseph Mede', *Bulletin of the Evangelical Theological Society*, 11 (1968), 181–93.
—— 'Johann Heinrich Alsted and English Millenarianism', *Harvard Theological Review*, 62 (1969), 189–207.
—— 'John Napier and Apocalyptic Thought', *Sixteenth Century Journal*, 5 (1974), 101–14.
COGGINS, JAMES, 'Theological Positions of John Smyth', *Baptist Quarterly*, 30 (1984), 247–64.
COHEN, CHARLES LLOYD, *God's Caress: The Psychology of Puritan Religious Experience* (Oxford, 1986).
COHN, NORMAN, *The Pursuit of the Millennium* (London, 1962).
COLLINSON, PATRICK, *A Mirror of Elizabethan Puritanism: The Life and Letters of 'Godly Master Dering'* (London, 1964).
—— *The Elizabethan Puritan Movement* (London, 1967).
—— 'Toward a Broader understanding of the Early Dissenting Tradition', in C. Robert Cole and Michael E. Moody (eds.), *The Dissenting Tradition: Essays for Leland H. Carlson*, (Athens, OH, 1975).
—— 'A Comment Concerning the Name Puritan', *Journal of Ecclesiastical History*, 31 (1980), 483–8.
—— *The Religion of Protestants: The Church in English Society 1559–1625* (Oxford, 1982).
—— *Godly People: Essays on English Protestantism and Puritanism* (London, 1983).
—— 'England and International Calvinism, 1558–1640', in Menna

Prestwich (ed.), *International Calvinism 1541–1715*, (Oxford, 1985), 197–223.

Collinson, Patrick, 'The English Conventicle', in W. J. Sheils and Diana Wood (eds.), *Voluntary Religion* (Oxford, 1986).

Coolidge, John S., *The Pauline Renaissance in England* (Oxford, 1970).

Cross, Claire, *The Puritan Earl: The Life of Henry Hastings* (London, 1966).

—— *Church and People 1450–1660: The Triumph of the Laity in the English Church* (London, 1976).

Curtis, M. H., 'Alienated Intellectuals of Early Stuart England', *Past and Present*, 23 (1963), 25–43.

—— 'The Hampton Court Conference and its Aftermath', *History*, 46 (1961), 1–16.

Dale, R. W., *History of English Congregationalism* (London, 1908).

Danner, Dan G., 'Christopher Goodman and the English Protestant Tradition of Civil Disobedience', *Sixteenth century Journal*, 8 (1977), 62–73.

Davis, Horton, *The Worship of the English Puritans* (London, 1948).

Davis, Kenneth R., 'No Discipline, No Church: An Anabaptist Contribution to the Reformed Tradition', *Sixteenth Century Journal*, 12 (1982), 43–58.

Dent, C. M., *Protestant Reformers in Elizabethan Oxford* (Oxford, 1983).

Dexter, H. M., *The Congregationalism of the Last Three Hundred Years* (London, 1880).

—— and Dexter, M., *England and Holland of the Pilgrims* (London, 1905).

Donaldson, Gordon, *The Scottish Reformation* (London, 1960).

Donnelly, John Patrick, 'Italian Influences on the Development of Calvinist Scholasticism', *Sixteenth Century Journal*, 7 (1976), 81–101.

Emerson, Everett H., 'Calvin and Covenant Theology', *Church History*, 25 (1956), 136–44.

Finlayson, Michael G., 'Puritanism and Puritans: Labels or Libels?', *Canadian Journal of History*, 8 (1973), 227–53.

Firth, Katherine R., *The Apocalyptic Tradition in Reformation Britain 1530–1645* (Oxford, 1979).

Fowler, Thomas, *The History of Corpus Christi College* (London, 1893).

Geller, Lawrence D. and Gomes, Peter J., *The Books of the Pilgrims* (New York and London, 1975).

George, C. H., 'Puritanism as History and Historiography', *Past and Present*, 41 (1968), 77–104.

GEORGE, TIMOTHY, *John Robinson and the Separatist Tradition* (Macon, Ga., 1982).
—— 'Predestination in a Separatist Context: The Case of John Robinson', *Sixteenth Century Journal*, 15 (1984), 73–85.
—— 'Between Pacifism and Coercion: The English Baptist Doctrine of Religious Toleration', *Mennonite Quarterly Review*, 58 (1984), 30–49.
GOEHRING, WALTER R., 'Henry Jacob (1563–1624) and the Separatists' (New York University Ph.D. dissertation, 1975).
GREAVES, RICHARD L., 'The origins and Early Development of English Covenant Thought', *The Historian*, 31 (1968), 21–55.
—— 'The Nature of the Puritan Tradition', in R. Buick Knox (ed.), *Reformation Conformity and Dissent: Essays in Honour of Geoffrey Nuttall* (London, 1977), 255–73.
—— *Theology and Revolution in the Scottish Reformation: Studies in the Thought of John Knox* (Grand Rapids, Mich., 1980).
—— and ZALLER, ROBERT (eds.), *A Biographical Dictionary of British Radicals*, 2 vols. (London, 1982).
—— *Deliver Us From Evil: The Radical Underground in Britain, 1660–1663* (Oxford, 1986).
—— 'The Puritan–Noncomformist Tradition in England, 1560–1700: Historiographical Reflections', *Albion*, 17 (1987).
HAENDLER, GERT, *Luther on Ministerial Office and Congregational Function* (Philadelphia, 1982).
HALL, BASIL, 'Puritanism: The Problem of Definition' in G. J. Cuming (ed.), *Studies in Church History* (London, 1965).
—— 'Calvin Against the Calvinists', in G. E. Duffield (ed.), *John Calvin* (Appleford, 1966), 19–37.
HALL, DAVID, *The Faithful Shepherd: A History of the New England Ministry in the Seventeenth Century* (rev. edn., New York, 1974).
HALLER, WILLIAM, *Foxe's Book of Martyrs and the Elect Nation* (London, 1963).
—— *The Rise of Puritanism* (1st Penn. pbk. edn., Philadelphia, 1972).
HARRIS, RENDEL and JONES, STEPHEN K., *The Pilgrim Press* (Cambridge, 1922).
HEADLEY, JOHN M., *Luther's View of Church History* (New Haven, Conn., 1963).
HILL, CHRISTOPHER, 'History and Denominational History', *The Baptist Quarterly*, 21 (1968), 65–71.
—— *Economic Problems of the Church* (3rd edn. rev., Oxford, 1968).
—— *Society and Puritanism in Pre-Revolutionary England* (Panther edn., London, 1969).
—— *Antichrist in Seventeenth-Century England* (Oxford, 1971).

HILL, CHRISTOPHER, 'Occasional Conformity', in R. Buick Knox (ed.), *Reformation Conformity and Dissent* (London, 1977).

HOPFL, HARRO, *The Christian Polity of John Calvin* (Cambridge, 1982).

HORTON, DOUGLAS, *Congregationalism: A Study in Church Polity* (London, 1952).

HUNTER, JOSEPH, *Collections Concerning the Church or Congregation of Protestant Separatists Formed at Scrooby* (London, 1854).

JESSOPP, AUGUSTUS, ed., 'The Condition of the Archdeaconry of Norwich in 1603', *Original Papers of the Norfolk Archeological Society* (1888), vol. x.

JEWSON, C. B., *History of the Great Hospital Norwich* (Norwich, 1949).

—— *The Baptists in Norfolk* (London, 1951).

JOHNSON, STEPHEN M., 'The Soteriology of John Robinson, Pilgrim Pastor and Advocate of the Reformed Faith', *Westminster Theological Journal*, 44 (1982), 31–57.

JONES, R. TUDOR, *Congregationalism in England, 1662–1962* (London, 1962).

JORDAN, W. K., *The Development of Religious Toleration in England*, 2 vols. (London, 1932).

KEARNEY, HUGH, *Scholars and Gentlemen: Universities and Society in Pre-industrial Britain 1500–1700* (London, 1970).

KELLY, J. N. D., *Early Christian Doctrines* (New York, 1958).

KENDALL, R. T., *Calvin and English Calvinism to 1649* (Oxford, 1979).

KINGDON, ROBERT M., 'The First Expression of Theodore Beza's Political Ideas', *Archiv für Reformationsgeschicte*, 46 (1955), 88–100.

—— *Geneva and the Consolidation of the French Protestant Movement, 1564–1572 (Madison, Wis., 1967).*

—— *'Peter Martyr Vermigli and the Marks of the True Church'*, in F. Forrester Church and Timothy George (eds.), *Continuity and Discontinuity in Church History* (Leiden, 1979), 198–214.

KLIEVER, LONNIE, 'General Baptist Origins', *Mennonite Quarterly Review*, 36 (1962), 291–321.

KNAPPEN, M. M., *Tudor Puritanism: A Chapter in the History of Idealism* (Chicago, 1939).

KNOX, S. J., *Walter Travers: Paragon of Elizabethan Puritanism* (London, 1962).

LAKE, PETER, 'The Dilemma of the Establishment Puritan: The Cambridge Heads and the Case of Francis Johnson and Cuthbert Bainbrigg', *Journal of Ecclesiastical History*, 29 (1978), 23–35.

—— 'The Significance of the Elizabethan Identification of the Pope as Antichrist', *Journal of Ecclesiastical History*, 31 (1980), 161–78.

—— *Moderate puritans and the Elizabethan church* (Cambridge, 1982).

—— 'William Bradshaw, Antichrist and the Community of the Godly', *Journal of Ecclesiastical History*, 36 (1985), 570–89.

LAMONT, WILLIAM, *Godly Rule: Politics and Religion, 1603–1660* (London, 1969).

—— 'Puritanism as History and Historiography: Some Further Thoughts', *Past and Present*, 44 (1969), 133–46.

LANGDON, GEORGE, *Pilgrim Colony: a History of New Plymouth 1620–1691* (New Haven, 1966).

LINDER, ROBERT D., 'Pierre Viret and the Sixteenth-Century English Protestant', *Archiv für Reformationsgeschicte*, 58 (1967), 149–71.

LITTELL, FRANKLIN, 'The Periodization of History', in Timothy George and Francis Church (eds.), *Continuity and Discontinuity in Church History* (Leiden, 1979), 18–30.

LITTLE, DAVID, *Religion, Order, and Law* (Oxford, 1970).

LUOMA, JOHN K., 'Who Owns the Fathers? Hooker and Cartwright on the Authority of the Primitive Church', *Sixteenth Century Journal*, 8 (1977), 45–59.

MACCULLOCH, DIARMAID, *Suffolk and the Tudors: Politics and Religion in an English County 1500–1600* (Oxford, 1986).

MACLURE, MILLER, *The Paul's Cross Sermons 1534–1642* (Toronto, 1958).

MANNING, R. B., *Religion and Society in Elizabethan Sussex* (Leicester University Press, 1969).

MARCHANT, RONALD A., *Puritans and the Church Courts* (London, 1960).

MARSDEN, GEORGE M., 'Perry Miller's Rehabilitation of the Puritans: A Critique', *Church History*, 39 (1970), 91–105.

MARSHALL, JOHN S., *Hooker and the Anglican Tradition* (London, 1963).

MARTIN, J. W., 'English Protestant Separatism at its Beginnings: Henry Hart and the Free-Will Men', *Sixteenth Century Journal*, 7 (1976), 55–74.

MARUYAMA, TADATAKA, *The Ecclesiology of Theodore Beza* (Geneva, 1978).

MCGEE, J. SEARS, *The Godly Man in Stuart England* (New Haven and London, 1976).

MCGIFFERT, MICHAEL, 'Grace and Works: the Rise and Division of Covenant Divinity in Elizabethan Puritanism', *Harvard Theological Review* 75 (1982), 463–502.

MCGINN, DONALD J., *The Admonition Controversy* (New Brunswick, 1949).

McGrath, Patrick, *Papists and Puritans under Elizabeth I* (London, 1967).

McGregor, J. F. and Reay, B. (eds.), *Radical Religion in the English Revolution* (Oxford, 1984).

McNeill, John T., 'The Doctrine of the Ministry in Reformed Theology', *Church History*, 12 (1943), 77–97.

—— *History and Character of Calvinism* (Oxford, 1954).

Miller, Perry, *The New England Mind* (New York, 1939).

—— *Errand into the Wilderness*, Harper Torchbook edn. (New York, 1964).

—— *Orthodoxy in Massachusetts 1630–1650*, Harper Torchbook edn. (New York, 1970).

Milner, Benjamin, *Calvin's Doctrine of the Church* (Leiden, 1970).

Møller, Jens G., 'The Beginnings of Puritan Covenant Theology', *Journal of Ecclesiastical History*, 14 (1963), 46–67.

Morgan, Edmund S., *Visible Saints: The History of a Puritan Idea* (New York, 1963).

Morgan, Irvonwy, *The Godly Preachers of the Elizabethan Church* (London, 1965).

Muller, Richard A., 'Perkins' *A Golden Chaine*: Predestinarian System or Schematized Ordo Salutis?' *Sixteenth Century Journal*, 9 (1978), 69–81.

—— *Christ and the Decree: Christology and Predestination in Reformed Theology from Calvin to Perkins* (Durham, NC, 1986).

Neal, Daniel, *The History of the Puritans*, 2 vols., (London, 1794).

New, John F. H., *Anglican and Puritan: The Basis of Their Opposition, 1558–1640* (London, 1964).

Nuttall, G. F. *The Holy Spirit in Puritan Faith and Experience* (Oxford, 1946).

—— *The Puritan Spirit: Essays and Addresses* (London, 1967).

—— *Visible Saints 1640–1660* (Oxford, 1957).

O'Day, Rosemary, 'The Reformation of the Ministry 1558–1642', in Rosemary O'Day and F. M. Heal (eds.), *Continuity and Change* (Leicester, 1976), 55–75.

Olsen, V. Norskov, *John Foxe and the Elizabethan Church* (Berkeley and Los Angeles, 1973).

Paul, Robert S., 'Henry Jacob and Seventeenth-century Puritanism', *Hartford Quarterly*, 17 (1967), 92–113.

Payne, E. A., *Free Churchmen, Repentant and Unrepentant* (London, 1965).

Pearl, Valerie, *London and the Outbreak of Puritan Revolution* (London, 1961).

PEARSON, A. F. SCOTT, *Thomas Cartwright and Elizabethan Puritanism 1535–1603* (Cambridge, 1925).
—— *Church and State: Political Aspects of Sixteenth Century Puritanism* (Cambridge, 1928).
PORTER, H. C., *Reformation and Reaction in Tudor Cambridge* (Hamden, Conn., 1972).
POWICKE, F. J., *Henry Barrow, Separatist (1550?–1593) and the Exiled Church of Amsterdam 1593–1622* (London, 1900).
—— *John Robinson (1575?–1625)*, (London, 1920).
REINITZ, RICHARD, 'The Separatist Background of Roger Williams' Argument for Religious Toleration', in Sacvan Bercovitch (ed.), *Typology and Early American Literature*, (Amherst, Mass., 1972), 107–37.
SCHEFFER, J. DE HOOP, *History of the Free Churchmen called Brownists in the Dutch Republic* (New York, 1922).
SEAVER, PAUL S., *The Puritan Lectureships: The Politics of Religious Dissent 1560–1662* (Stanford, 1970).
SELEMENT, GEORGE, 'The Covenant Theology of English Separatism and the Separation of Church and State', *Journal of the American Academy of Religion*, 14 (1973), 66–74.
SELLERS, IAN, 'Edwardians, Anabaptists and the Problem of Baptist Origins', *Baptist Quarterly*, 27 (1981), 97–112.
SHANTZ, DOUGLAS, 'The Place of the Resurrected Christ in the Writings of John Smyth', *Baptist Quarterly*, 30 (1984), 199–203.
SHAW, MARK R., 'Drama in the Meeting House: The Concept of Conversion in the Theology of William Perkins', *Westminster Theological Journal*, 45 (1983), 41–72.
SHEILS, W. J., *The Puritans in the Diocese of Petterborough, 1558–1610* (Northampton, 1979).
SHIPPS, KENNETH, 'The "Political Puritan"', *Church History*, 45 (1976), 196–205.
SHRIVER, JAMES, 'Hampton Court Re-visited: James I and the Puritans', *Journal of Ecclesiastical History*, 33 (1982), 48–71.
SHUFFELTON, FRANK, *Thomas Hooker, 1586–1647* (Princeton, NJ, 1977).
SKINNER, QUENTIN, *The Foundations of Modern Political Thought*, 2 vols. (Cambridge, 1978).
SPRUNGER, KEITH, *The Learned Doctor William Ames* (Urbana, Ill., 1972).
—— 'Other Pilgrims in Leiden: Hugh Goodyear and the English Reformed Church', *Church History*, 41 (1972), 46–60.
—— 'English Puritans and Anabaptists', *Mennonite Quarterly Review*, 46 (1972), 113–28.

SPRUNGER, KEITH, *Dutch Puritanism: A History of English and Scottish Churches of the Netherlands in the Sixteenth and Seventeenth Centuries* (Leiden, 1982).
STARK, WERNER, *Sectarian Religion* (London, 1967).
STEARNS, R. P., *Congregationalism in the Dutch Netherlands* (Chicago, 1940).
STEARNS, RAYMOND and BRAWNER, DAVID, 'New England Church "Relations" and Continuity in Early Congregational History', *Proceedings of the American Antiquarian Society*, 75 (1965).
SYKES, N. F., *New Priest, Old Presbyter* (Cambridge, 1956).
THOMPSON, W. D. J. CARGILL, *Studies in the Reformation: Luther to Hooker* (London, 1980).
TIPSON, BAIRD, 'Invisible Saints: The "Judgement of Charity" in Early New England Churches', *Church History*, 44 (1975), 460–71.
TOLMIE, MURRAY, *The Triumph of the Saints: The Separate Churches of London 1616–1649* (Cambridge, 1977).
TOON, PETER, *Puritans, the Millenium and the Future of Israel* (London, 1970).
TRINTERUD, LEONARD J., 'The Origins of Puritanism', *Church History*, 20 (1951), 37–57.
—— *Elizabethan Puritanism* (New York, 1971).
TYACKE, N. R. N., 'Puritanism, Arminianism and Counter-Revolution' in C. Russell (ed.), *The Origins of the English Civil War* (New York, 1973), 119–43.
—— *Anti-Calvinists: The Rise of English Arminianism c. 1590–1640* (Oxford, 1987).
VAN BEEK, M., *An Enquiry Into Puritan Vocabulary* (Groningen, 1969).
VAUX, ROLAND DE, *Ancient Israel, its Life and Institutions* (London, 1961).
VON ROHR, JOHN, 'The Congregationalism of Henry Jacob', *Transactions of the Congregational Historical Society*, 19 (1962), 107–17.
—— 'Covenant and Assurance in Early English Puritanism', *Church History*, 34 (1965), 195–203.
—— '*Extra Ecclesiam Nulla Salus*: An Early Congregational Version', *Church History*, 36 (June 1967), 107–21.
WADDINGTON, JOHN, *Congregational History: 1567–1700* (London, 1874).
WALLACE, DEWEY W., *Puritans and Predestination: Grace in English Protestant Theology, 1525–1695* (Chapel Hill, NC, 1982).
WALZER, MICHAEL, *The Revolution of the Saints: A Study in the Origins of Radical Politics* (New York, 1976).
WATKINS, OWEN C., *The Puritan Experience* (London, 1972).
WATTS, MICHAEL R., *The Dissenters* (Oxford, 1978).

WENDEL, FRANÇOIS, *Calvin: The Origin and Development of his Thought* (London, 1976).

WHITE, B. R., 'Baptist Beginnings and the Kiffin Manuscript', *Baptist History and Heritage*, i, (1967).

—— 'The Doctrine of the Church in the Particular Baptist Confession of 1644', *Journal of Theological Studies*, 19, (1968), 570–90.

—— *The English Separatist Tradition* (Oxford, 1971).

—— 'The English Separatists and John Smyth Revisited', *Baptist Quarterly*, 30 (1984), 344–7.

WHITE, JOHN, *The Genesis of the New England Churches* (New York, 1874).

WHITLEY, W. T., 'Records of the Jacob–Lathrop–Jessey Church 1616–1641', *Transactions of the Baptist Historical Society*, i, (1908–9).

—— *The Works of John Smyth* (Cambridge, 1915).

WILLIAMS, G. H., 'Congregationalist Luther and the Free Churches', *Lutherian Quarterly*, 19 (1967), 283–95.

WILLIAMS, J. F. (ed.), *Bishop Redman's Visitation* (Norfolk Record Society, 1946).

WILLISON, GEORGE F., *Saints and Strangers* (London, 1946).

WILSON, JOHN F., 'Another Look at John Canne', *Church History*, 33 (1964), 34–48.

WOLLMAN, DAVID H., 'The Biblical Justification for Resistance to Authority in Ponet's and Goodman's Polemics', *Sixteenth Century Journal*, 13 (1982), 29–41.

WOOD, ANTHONY, *Athenae Oxonienses* (London, 1721).

WOODHOUSE, A. S. P., *Puritanism and Liberty* (London, 1966).

WOODHOUSE, H. F., *The Doctrine of the Church in Anglican Theology 1547–1603* (London, 1954).

YARBROUGH, SLAYDON, A., 'Henry Jacob, A Moderate Separatist, and His Influence on Early English Congregationalism' (Baylor University Ph.D. dissertation, 1972).

—— 'The Ecclesiastical Development in Theory and Practice of John Robinson and Henry Jacob', *Perspectives in Religious Studies*, 5 (1978), 183–97.

YULE, GEORGE, 'Continental Patterns and the Reformation in England and Scotland', *Scottish Journal of Theology*, 22 (1969), 305–23.

—— 'Some Problems in the History of English Presbyterians in the Seventeenth Century', *Journal of the Presbyterian Historical Society of England*, 13 (1965), 4–13.

ZARET, DAVID, *Heavenly Contract: Ideology and Organization in Pre-Revolutionary Puritanism* (Chicago, 1985).

ZIFF, LARZER, *The Career of John Cotton: Puritanism and the American Experience* (Princeton, 1962).

—— *Puritanism in America: New Culture in a New World* (Oxford, 1973).

—— 'The Social Bond of the Church Covenant', *American Quarterly*, 10 (1958), 454–62.

INDEX

Stephen Brachlow is Professor of Church History and Christian Spirituality at the North American Baptist Seminary, Sioux Falls, South Dakota, U.S.A.